INTRODUCTION TO VC

CW01499809

This Homiliary provides a comprehensive guide to doctrinally based preaching for the entire Church year, presented in the Dominican tradition: a preaching of Scripture which takes doctrine as guide to the clarification of the Bible's main themes. Doctrine is necessary to preachers because in its absence the Scriptural claims and themes do not easily hang together.

The homilies presented here are in the Dominican tradition of doctrinal preaching: a preaching of Scripture which takes doctrine as guide to the clarification of the Bible's main lines. Without doctrine, we should find it more difficult to see the biblical wood for the profusion of the Scriptural trees. Doctrine is necessary to preachers because in its absence the Scriptural claims and themes do not hang together. They do not of their own accord organize themselves into a religion a person can live by: a coherent vision of truth, and a picture of human excellence that is imitable because it makes sense as a whole. Where doctrine is not permitted to serve this purpose, we can be sure that some other scheme of thought will be brought in to do the job instead. That is when theology becomes ideology, rather than a service to the Word of God in the message of the Church.

The grace the Word imparts always has a reference to the Mystical Body which mediates all the grace that is given by Christ as the Head. So, precisely as a fruit of grace, preaching is necessarily related to ecclesial awareness. Doctrine ensures that preaching does not fall short of its true dimensions — expressing the biblical revelation, the faith of the Church. This fourth volume furnishes texts for Weekdays through the Year.

THE FIRST WEEK OF THE YEAR

Monday of the First Week of the Year (Years 1 and 2)

Yesterday, liturgical Christmastide ended, with the arguable exception of Candlemas, the 2nd of February, which is a feast of the Christmas cycle though not within the Christmas season. As a result, we are back in green time, the Sundays and weekdays *per annum*, 'through the year', the year beginning with Advent—though translators have chosen to call it in English 'ordinary time'.

For the Liturgy, there is really no such thing as ordinary time. All time as presented by cult is sacred time, though just *how* it is sacred depends on which religion we are talking about. In our religion, Catholic Christianity, liturgical time is sacred because it is filled with the presence of the God-man Jesus Christ. Each Gospel reading in the Lectionary begins *in illo tempore*, 'in that time', and the *tempus* or 'time' here is the fullness of time occupied by the Saviour. 'In the fullness of time', wrote St Paul, 'God sent his Son, born of a woman', and in today's Gospel we see the mission given to the Son in time beginning to extend itself through the calling of the first disciples.

We are at the intersection, then, of two kinds of time: saving time, which is the time of Scripture and the Church, and profane time, the time of the British Broadcasting Corporation and the Sunday papers. We live our lives in both, but the first is, we can say, a 'realler' time, a time that is more ontologically dense, more packed with meaning, though what is contains and promises is, despite that, less perspicuous. It is Paul again who says, 'You have died and your life is hid with Christ in God'. What we shall be doing for the rest of this year, as every year, is to work out what those riddling words mean.

Monday of the First Week of the Year (Year 2)

At first sight today's readings look like two examples of the same thing: Samuel is called and so are Andrew and his brother Simon. But looking more closely, they could scarcely be more different.

YEAR OF THE LORD'S FAVOUR

YEAR OF THE LORD'S FAVOUR

A Homiliary for the Roman Liturgy

VOLUME 4

The Temporal Cycle:
Weekdays through the Year

Aidan Nichols, OP

GRACEWING

First published in England in 2012
by
Gracewing
2 Southern Avenue
Leominster
Herefordshire HR6 0QF
United Kingdom
www.gracewing.co.uk

ISBN 978 085244 794 9

Typeset by Gracewing

Cover design by Bernardita Peña Hurtado

CONTENTS

For Samuel to hear his call is a matter of interpreting a private experience heard on the inner ear—heard, then, by no one else. Those who investigate the psychology of the mystics have worked out ways of describing such phenomena: sensations, some times visual, sometimes aural, infused into the psyche, at the same time as the mind is provided with a clearer light of judgment which enables the recipient to grasp something of what these sensations signify for his or her life.

It hardly needs saying that not everyone considering their vocation in life has such visitations. And yet really they are not that different in practice from the interior processes the rest of us have to go through: a struggle to make sense out of the movements of our own souls—their aspirations, attractions, repulsions—and a struggle, too, to be faithful to whatever lights we have by which to interpret them. Advising someone about a life-vocation is not an easy thing to do.

In the Gospel, the situation with the call of Andrew is very different indeed. Here Jesus Christ, the God-man, intervenes in the life of these young fishermen and his call is at once as public, as unmistakable, and as simple, as language can make it—and as certain besides! There is no question of interpretation, or, if there is, it plays a very secondary role. The options are either obedient response or outright rejection.

We ourselves also know this kind of call. Through our encounter with the preaching, sacramental life, and pastoral authority of the Church we have heard Jesus Christ speaking in his Mystical Body. Faith, which is the ability to respond with assent to the Word of God is, admittedly, a mysterious gift to each one of us. And yet objectively what we are presented with is the clear-cut call to a definite way of life: the pattern of beliefs and values and behaviour that we call Christian discipleship in the Catholic sense. How ever many difficulties we have about our particular role in the Providence of God, they are made manageable and tolerable through the certainty of this overarching call to be a Catholic Christian, the follower of him who is Lord of History, Alpha and Omega, who gathers the ages into his hand and the Church into his Kingdom.

Tuesday of the First Week of the Year (Years 1 and 2)

The easiest way to think of demonic possession in the Gospels is to see it as a form of psychosis where a part of the personality has become separated from the rest and so a 'Jekyll and Hyde' situation emerges. The disassociated part of the personality then becomes a suitable vehicle for angelic influence—in this case, that of the evil angels. I'm told that in modern psychiatry there is a tendency not to use the word 'psychosis' because it implies that some personality disorders are probably incurable. If our Lord was a healer of psychosis it testifies that his power may indeed have been divine.

But where does that leave the rest of us who, presumably, are not psychotics? Psychosis is the extreme end of a spectrum which runs through schizophrenia to our own experience of not being all together, not being fully integrated, having up to a point a divided self where some sides of us—some aspirations or tendencies—war against other sides. We all provide opportunities for the evil angels owing to our internal disunity, the will or the heart no longer being master in its own house.

So when we read or hear the Gospels of exorcism, we shouldn't think mainly of the films of that name, because examples of true possession are few and far between. We should think, rather, of our own dividedness and the entry it gives to the promptings of evil, and remember the teaching of the ascetic masters that the only lasting antidote to evil thoughts is purity of heart: single-minded concentration on God, something which can go on in, under, and through all the many things we have to do today.

Wednesday of the First Week of the Year (Years 1 and 2)

In today's Gospel, Jesus cures Simon's mother-in-law of a fever, not perhaps 'in order that' but at any rate 'with the result that' she can get on with the cooking. There is something very domestic, familiar, small-town, about the origins of our Lord's ministry and his group of disciples. So many of them came from one small area of the coastline of the Sea of Galilee, a settlement so identified with the fishing trade that its Hebrew name has been translated 'Fishington' or 'Fishborough'. It's amazing to think how the entry of the Godhead into the world could take the form of so ordinary and humble a start to nothing less than the recreation of the world.

But we can go overboard for this ordinariness and humbleness business. If we were told that God had been incarnate in the manager of our local Sainsbury's, leaving no special mark behind him, or, come to that, in a Fellow of a Cambridge College, with similar results or non-results, we wouldn't find that incredibly mind-blowing: we would just find it incredible. This is why those Christians are mistaken who feel a desire to strip away the strange and exotic, or supernatural and miraculous, aspects of the Gospel narrative—the Visit of the Magi, say, or the Walking on the Water. If God really entered his creation, his human creation and his natural creation, we should expect some very unusual stirrings to result: atypical reactions of people, atypical consequences in nature. Those who want to keep the Incarnation but remove from it anything extraordinary on the principle that we must always be asking, 'What will the man-in-the-street or the woman-by-the-telly swallow?', will end up making it more difficult to be a believer, not less.

Today's Gospel ends with two glimpses of Jesus which open onto mystery—Jesus alone in prayer, communing with the Father, and Jesus facing the demons, a concentration of evil. These qualify a too domestic picture of an Incarnation who is always popping upstairs to see how mother-in-law is doing.

Thursday of the First Week of the Year (Years 1 and 2)

People coming to Jesus, thronging, unstoppable—well, until he began to be dangerous to know and the crowd turned against him at Passovertide in the year of his all-sufficient Sacrifice. But notice how, actually, he does not want to be the centre of mass attention, to have what we should now call 'celebrity' status.

Why? It is not, I think, because he rejects the notion of a popular Church, indeed a universal Church. On the night before he suffers he will tell his disciples in instituting the Most Blessed Eucharist that his Sacrifice—of which the Mass is the continuing sign—will be 'for the multitude'. It will be 'blood poured out for many', as the English translation of the consecratory words puts it. The

Church believed herself to be true to the Saviour's intentions when she deplored the suggestions of the seventeenth century Jansenists — the Calvinists of Catholicism — that he did not die for all, and shunned their representations of the Crucified which showed him not flinging out his arms wide on the Cross, but holding them as close together as crucifixion permits, to insinuate that those who will be saved are few.

So why did he avoid publicity in what, after all, we term his 'public ministry'? Surely it was to do with discernment. His movement — his future Church — depended on getting things right: getting him right, getting the plan of salvation right, getting right the message that the Father was embodying in the Son. Only when the original nucleus of the Church was well-formed, in the apostles, in the holy women, and in the other first disciples, could she be launched on the way of the world as what she now is, the teacher of the nations.

Friday of the First Week of the Year (Year 1)

The idea of 'rest', which is central to today's reading from Hebrews, was crucial for the Jewish Christianity of the early centuries, and remained influential in the Byzantine and Western traditions in various ways.

The rest of God is that condition of enjoyment of God and of God's goodness for which the People of God were destined from the beginning. In the Semitic East, it is seen as a kind of cosmic Sabbath when nature and history come to their fulfillment. It is anticipated in the Church, which is the beginning of the Last Day of the world, the world's Eighth Day, and individuals access its energies in the sacrament of Baptism.

In the Greek East and Latin West the emphasis falls on how, as an individual member of the faithful, I can enter this rest of God — in other words, it falls on the spiritual life of individuals. Here what the Greeks called *hesychia* or tranquillity and the Latins called *sacrum otium* or sacred idleness, are key features. It's part of being a Christian to learn how to be really idle in the presence of God, so as to receive great peace and stillness of spirit.

God's rest is God himself as the fullness of life. 'Enter God's rest' means: let God be God; stop pretending that you are God, that anything you do can beatify you, make you fully satisfied and totally happy.

Friday of the First Week of the Year (Year 2)

The early books of the Hebrew Bible are very ambivalent about kings. One tendency is to see them as very definitely a good thing, an instrument of godly government. Another is to regard them with deep-rooted suspicion as an alternative to government by God. The latter attitude eventually worked itself out in the sacred anarchism of the Zealots of our Lord's own time, for whom there was to be in Israel no governor or master save God himself. The reasoning was mostly religious, though an element of secular commonsense also entered in.

Who was right about that kingship business? In the light of the New Testament we can say that both approaches were, in different respects. On the one hand, the Word of God became incarnate as a human king, albeit an unrecognized one, the Son of David who is David's Lord: 'Christ the King', as we call him on the last Sunday before Advent. On the other hand, the true King's worst enemies included the petty potentates of the Holy Land of that time as well as the representative of the Roman emperor: a fulfillment of Psalm 1: 'The kings of the earth rise up and the princes take counsel together, against the Lord and against his Anointed'.

The pro-monarchical Old Testament authors always recognized the instrumental character of kingship: its relative, not absolute, value. They were well aware, too, of the possibility of its abuse. In the subsequent story of Christendom, the sweeping away of kings has been part of a deliberate rejection of Judaeo-Christianity, for the earthly king was seen as a faint reflection of the divine archetype of kingship—the archetype embodied in Jesus Christ.

Saturday of the First Week of the Year (Years 1 and 2)

'I did not come to call the virtuous.' This is one of our Lord's most reassuring statements for those of us who are only too well aware how fragile the tissue of our virtues is—and, therefore, how the thread that ties together such good deeds as we have to our credit does not really merit the name of 'virtue' at all. *Real* virtue is second nature, spontaneous and predictable. We can sometimes do well. That does not mean that we have what educationalists used to call—and have started once again calling—'character'.

But what about those who consider—not without reason—that they do have 'character', and whom others consider so likewise? Are we simply to say that the grace of Christ is not for those golden ones? If so, they would not be fortunate at all—since in every soul there is something that needs healing. 'Character', however admirable, is often won at a very high price.

And in any case, we need to ask, What sort of character are we aiming at in, say, the bringing up of Christian children, or more widely, the 'children' of the Church of whatever age or condition they may be? What is the goal of personality formation? If it is a Christian character we are aiming for, we should always be conscious of the gift-quality of existence. Training the self, training the passions, training our habitual reactions to incident and circumstances (and this is what we mean by 'character' in social life at large), must never be allowed to dim our sense of the most fundamental truth of the human situation.

That truth runs: all is gift, whether of nature or of grace. I must not be a self-made man who, as the joke has it, worships his maker— that is, worships myself. To adapt the words of the apostle, what have I that I have not received?

A Christian character is always one that positions itself receptively towards God.

THE SECOND WEEK OF THE YEAR

Monday of the Second Week of the Year (Years 1 and 2)

Today's Gospel gives us an insight into the ecclesial use of food. Fasting and feasting relate to the absence and presence, respectively, of the Church's Bridegroom. We fast because Christ is not here, though we wait his return in glory. We feast because he is here, though his presence as the Lord here and now—the Jesus exalted in the Spirit—is by way of anticipation of his Parousia, his Second Coming. It's a dialectic—literally, a 'conversation', though not of course one carried out in words—where to get the meaning of the whole you have to attend to all of these aspects taken together. So fasting and feasting, taken together, actually help us to understand how we relate to Jesus Christ.

But this isn't all. Fasting and feasting also make up by their alternation a rhythm of life. Historians who look into how the Catholic community managed to survive in England between the onset of the penal laws and the restoration of the hierarchy in the mid-nineteenth century stress how Catholic identity survived owing partly to a distinctive calendar of feast and fast. Through the recommended use of food, the Church offered a different experience of time. And this helped English Catholics to grasp the wider pattern of their own faith: the total story line from creation to consummation and the End of all things, within which our own stories, the stories of our lives, are set.

Today the pressure of conformity to general *mores* and the pervasiveness of the consumer culture make it hard to keep this sense of identity alive by means of the use of food. The restoration of Friday abstinence is a recognition by the English and Welsh bishops of the importance of this area. In periods when the Church has flourished, both fasting and feasting receive prominence, while in periods of ecclesial decadence their meaning gets lost. Great feasts pass with no more than a dutiful visit to church, sometimes postponed till the nearest Sunday. Their vigils are neglected. The penitential seasons lose their distinctiveness because the practice of fasting dwindles away almost to nothing. It is not right to rely on the initiatives of exceptional individuals in these matters. We can't be Catholic Christians properly as isolated individuals, we need to be sustained by a common culture. Today's Gospel is about the ecclesial—the corporate—use of food.

Tuesday of the Second Week of the Year (Years 1 and 2)

What strikes me above all about today's Gospel is the wonderful juxtaposition it contains of the delightfully normal and the stupendously other-worldly.

What could be more ordinary than a group of young men taking a week-end walk in the countryside? I think we can assume glorious weather or the ears of corn would not have been ripe for picking. When, all too often, male bonding in our own society is in the service of gangs, or of drinking buddies given to end-of-the-week excess, this record of an amble by Jesus and the disciples is a refreshingly idyllic picture. Or let us say, rather, it is just a normal picture of life together once human relations are not distorted by practices that tend to vice rather than virtue.

But look who it is who is in the midst of them! Not just a young rabbi, or a wandering charismatic teacher. Not even the description 'a young prophet' would fit the bill. No, this is the Son of Man who is Lord and Master even of the Sabbath—Master of the all-holy rest incumbent on Israel by the command to imitate God in his contemplation of his own creative work. Even this Sabbath command, which in a sense forms the culmination of the whole revealed law by providing it with its own key—the imitation of God—is subordinate to a young Jew who answers with so high a claim for himself the criticism of the orthodox. Here walks on earth the Vice-gerent of the Father, the Protagonist of the final battle, the One sent from heaven in whom divinity and humanity are joined. This is the sort of staggering contrast with which we are faced at every Mass where it is, once again, bread– but this time the Living Bread of the New Covenant—that is in play. The ministerial priest says over a little circle of unleavened bread, 'This is my Body', and not only does he genuflect, but the heavenly hosts bow low.

Wednesday of the Second Week of the Year (Year 1)

The alliance of the Pharisees and the Herodians in today's Gospel is very rum. We know how the desire for political power can draw together strange bedfellows, but this takes the biscuit. The Pharisees are rigorist Jews opposed to all compromise with pagan culture and its values; the Herodians sit lightly to Judaism, they are supporters of a dynasty originating outside historic Israel which has made its way in the world by subservience to the Roman overlords. Nevertheless, they make common cause against the Saviour.

The Pharisees see that Jesus will not leave the structure of Judaism unchanged. On the contrary, he will change it radically by introducing a new Law, a new worship, a new wisdom. That is bad news for Jewish conservatives. The Herodians see that he will not leave political consciousness unchanged. On the contrary, he will relativise Caesar's concerns by giving undisputed primacy to those of his Father's Kingdom. That is bad news for a pleasure-loving Jewish king. They come together, following the maxim, The enemy of my enemy is my friend.

But as for Jesus himself, he goes his way, unfazed by their opposition, careless of their plotting, totally uninterested in measures of compromise, just as he will in the week of his Passion when that ill-assorted trio, Pilate, Caiaphas and Herod are ranged against him. He knows the path he must tread, and so the new Melchizedek, our Great High Priest—as today's reading from the Letter to the Hebrews presents him—he follows that path with no deviation. 'Why, what hath my Lord done?', asks a well-loved Anglo-Welsh hymn. 'Why now this rage and spite?' But the answer to these questions has already been given in the hymn's opening line. 'My song is love unknown': it is from the humanly unknown, from the abyss of the Father's graciously saving will for the world, that the Son proceeds on earth.

Wednesday of the Second Week of the Year (Year 2)

The most famous person in history to have a withered hand or arm was Kaiser Wilhelm II, the German emperor of the First World

War. Historians with a psychological approach to their discipline often link this to his militarism. He over-compensated for his disability by behaving more aggressively than other people. Whether or not this is a fair comment on the Kaiser (he was hardly a crude Goliath figure), it suggests how a grave disability can affect more than its subject.

In a society where most people worked with their hands, a handicap like a withered arm was indeed grave. It would have put a high level of extra demand on neighbours and kinsfolk of the handicapped person. Perhaps this is why our Lord wanted to end the situation so quickly, even though only a few hours were left till the end of Sabbath.

Today a viewpoint sometimes met with among theological liberals is that such miracles as this supernatural healing of the man with a withered arm are not so much impressive as scandalous: a stumbling-block to rational faith. If divine power intervenes to sort out one messy situation (critics say), then why doesn't it intervene to sort out all messy situations whenever they occur? This is a perfectly good question, but it expects the wrong answer.

The miracles worked by Jesus were actions worth doing for their own sake. Of course they were. Yet they were intended as something more. They were moments of revelation: special privileged moments that tell us truths we need to hear. The miracle in today's Gospel tells us of the nature of God who doesn't cease working to complete the creation he once made. It tells us too of the destiny of man, which is not to remain for ever in this—at best unsatisfactory and at worst tragic—world but to receive the healing, peace and bliss that is the goal of the plan of God.

Thursday of the Second Week of the Year (Years 1 and 2)

In today's Gospel, something theologically strange is recorded—the demons confess that Jesus is the Son of God but, far from congratulating them, he rebukes them.

The doctrines of our Lord's divinity and of his pre-existence—his being God before the world was made—were a settled conviction in the Church within twenty years of the Resurrection, as the letters of St Paul indicate. They are of course vital doctrines for without them the Founder of Christianity is simply one more religious teacher, while with them he is, as the demons said, the Son of God.

If we take the four Gospels as a whole, the most coherent picture we can put together is one of Jesus introducing these themes with the utmost caution—not expounding them to the ordinary Jews who came to hear him nor even to the disciples as such but to the small inner group of Peter, James, and John whom we know to have been his chosen companions at such crucial moments as the Transfiguration and the Agony in the Garden. From the last of these, St John, comes down to us the Fourth Gospel where, doubtless with some re-touching in the light of the Resurrection, Jesus is presented as teaching overtly his own divinity and pre-existence. 'Before Abraham was, I am.'

If we ask why he was so circumspect about the claim that 'I and the Father are one', we can surely find an answer in the difficulty there must have been in communicating these truths in the mentality of the time. Even today, after twenty centuries of Christian theology, it is not always easy to express these claims satisfactorily.

Jews had been brought up to abhor the idolatry and polytheism of the pagan world. An explicit statement of his Godhead, except after a lengthy educative process to the most sensitive of his disciples, would have scandalized, outraged, perplexed. Such outrage is exactly what is reported in St John's Gospel when in argument with the Jewish theological elite, Jesus momentarily abandons his customary discretion.

What, then, was the demons' policy, the policy of minds given over to intellectual evil, when they forced out of people the cry, 'You are the Son of God'? May it not have been in fact sabotage—a deliberate intention of wrecking the mission of the eternal Son, to make him either alienate his listeners or deny his own claims? That would be a subtlety worthy of Lucifer, the erstwhile 'bringer of light'.

Friday of the Second Week of the Year (Years 1 and 2)

In today's Gospel we hear how Jesus 'went up into the hills', and there he 'summoned those he wanted'. In the Old Testament, hills or mountains have a rather ambiguous status. The Old Testament was of course the principal background for our Lord's ministry — not least because it was the witness to God's revelation of himself in history as enacted so far. So it is by no means out of place to take this background into account.

When the Psalmist says, 'I lift up mine eyes to the hills, from whence shall come my help?', we should be mistaken if we interpreted him in terms of English Romanticism's 'Lake Poets' in their more pious moments. The Psalmist is not saying that the hills are a symbol of the sublimity of God from whom help comes. He is thinking of the pagan shrines set on the hill-tops in Canaanite religion, and asking whether in the face of the threat from powers ranged against the Lord's true worship he will find courage in God.

But such hill-tops were by no means all the mountains there were. Mount Sinai was, after all, the 'Mountain of God', the place of the crucial revelation to Moses, and a constant reference point for Mosaic religion subsequently — so much so that other, similar, mountains were, in Israelite religion, the preferred settings of renewals of the Covenant — until with the establishment of the City of David, and the Jerusalem Temple, covenant worship became secured to the mountain of election par excellence, the hill of Zion. There are overtones of Sinai and Zion in the 'mountains' of the Gospel: the Mount of the Beatitudes, the Mountain of the Transfiguration, and of course Mount Calvary. None of these mountains are really more than hills or hilly outcrops. We are not talking about the Alps or the Himalayas.

There are then hills and hills: sinister, possibly diabolic, hills, and divinely utilized hills — for surely, the Romantics were right in principle to think that mountain landscape is an appropriate symbol of the infinite. The calling of the Twelve is an ambivalent affair, as the name of Judas Iscariot reminds us, because the Saviour, being God, allows human freedom its due scope — to choose the kind of hill it wants to make its own. Will the Twelve be with him or against him? This is a question he raises directly with, of all people, St Peter. The struggle for fidelity goes on, inside us, and in the public square. On what hill shall we take our stand?

Saturday of the Second Week of the Year (Years 1 and 2)

Today we have a rather scary Gospel: St Mark's report that many of Jesus's friends were afraid he might be 'beside himself'. That is the traditional English translation of the Greek phrase, which, taken literally, says he was 'outside oneself': meaning, in the brutal words of one modern translation, 'he had gone mad'.

This Gospel draws to our attention how there are limits to the idea that Jesus was 'just like us'. It is true that the Latin Fathers use words that, loosely, could be put into English in that way. The incarnate Son, as, for instance, Pope St Leo puts it, was *totus in nostris*, 'altogether in ours': in other words, he has absolutely everything that we have in the sense of everything that makes us human.

But there are many different ways of being human. So that phrase leaves a lot of latitude, and by golly it needs to if we are to make room among us for One who was personally God.

Each generation is tempted not to let its image of Christ be determined mainly by the biblical witness, interpreted in the light of the Church's teaching, but instead to re-interpret Christ in its own image, the image of the generation concerned. Thus for instance in England in the 1970s Christ could become an enlightened individual of progressive views who, had he lived in that epoch, would have a taken an absorbing interest in the affairs of the Third World.

But his friends thought he was 'beside himself'. And do you know, if we take that English phrase as our yardstick, they were perfectly correct! He *was* beside himself. In his single personhood, the divine nature of the Word and the humanity taken from our stock co-existed side by side with each other in harmony but not in confusion. In his loving kindness towards man, he accepted that these two natures were everlastingly combined in his own person.

Did that necessarily make him very different? Of course it did. He had two natures side by side, with one of them, the divine, constantly affecting the other, the human, which was to be the instrument of the world's salvation, while at the same time that human nature of his was equally constantly drawing on the divine nature to which it was at every moment attracted as to the supreme Good. This is scarcely a usual state of affairs.

The traditional translation will do very well, then, thank you very much. He was beside himself: an incarnation of God as man could never be 'Mr Normal'.

THE THIRD WEEK OF THE YEAR

Monday of the Third Week of the Year (Years 1 and 2)

In the Gospels, it is hard to distinguish the demons from patholo-
gy—hard to distinguish the fallen angels from disease of the mind
or soul or disease of the body brought on by disease of the mind
or soul. And that is what we should expect. The devil and his
angels are present wherever there is disintegration of God's
creative work—wherever what should be orderly, harmonious
unity begins to fall into chaos, into anarchy.

This is why Jesus is so infuriated—so righteously angry—when
his actions get ascribed to demonic infestation. It's also a good clue
to the identity of the 'sin against the Holy Spirit', the one unforgivable sin.

It looks very much from the context as if the blasphemy against
the Holy Spirit consists in identifying the divine with the demonic,
taking God to be the same thing as the devil—ascribing to God (in
other words) a desire to undermine his creation, to subvert it, break
it down: the sort of desire the evil angels have, as their activity
makes manifest.

Ever since the German philosopher Nietzsche argued that you
have to be an atheist if you really want to affirm the world, affirm
unconditionally its greatness and glory, and the French philosopher Sartre added, yes and especially if you really want to affirm
humanity, our freedom and creativity, the temptation to identify
God with Satan, to treat religion as, basically, diabolic, has grown
and grown in the post-Christian West. We see it at work today in
a number of the columnists of the 'quality' press—especially in the
wake of the attack on New York's Twin Towers.

We really mustn't let the fanaticism of a tiny minority of
Muslims tempt us to give room in our minds to this sin. Our God
is the God who has poured out his being to let creation be, and
then lavished on it a supernatural life, a share in his own Trinitar-
ian existence, doing so through the mysteries we celebrate each
year by following the Church's cycle, and each day, indeed, in the
Mass. No one who does not know the God of revelation—the God

of Cross and Resurrection—can possibly understand what the word 'philanthropy' means. Our God is philo-cosmic, the Lover of the cosmos, and philanthropic, the One who loves mankind.

Tuesday of the Third Week of the Year (Years 1 and 2)

Tradition tells us that Jesus had no brothers and sisters by his mother, since she was, as we so regularly say, the *Virgin* Mary. That title—the Virgin—has never been taken to refer simply to the Annunciation, to the miraculous conception of the Saviour in Mary's womb. It refers to his mother's perpetual virginity, her whole life long. She was so taken up with the coming of the Kingdom, so taken up with her Son, that she had no life outside of these realities. The 'brethren' of the Lord are understood by the Church Fathers to be either half-siblings, children by an earlier marriage of Joseph, or, more probably, his cousins. The Greek language allows for this usage.

When our Lord extends to his hearers the names of mother and brothers and sisters he does so, as he himself explains, by way of paying them a high compliment. So eager are they to do the divine will which he is expounding to them that they are spiritually members of his household; they are, morally speaking, members of his family.

The irony is, of course, that this praise of the hearers also redounds to the honour of his natural mother, our Lady. It is because of her thirst for God's will, her single-minded devotion to the covenanted plan of God ('I am the handmaid of the Lord, be it done to me according to thy word') that she became the mother of the Messiah in the first place. She conceived him in her mind, say the Latin Fathers, before she conceived him in her womb. She is his mother biologically and she is also his mother spiritually and morally. That combination is what makes her the Lady she is.

Wednesday of the Third Week of the Year (Years 1 and 2)

What a strange explanation our Lord gives the Twelve of his teaching in parables! He as good as says he has chosen the way of the parable not because it is better pedagogy—more striking, more memorable, more readily grasped by the imagination and the reason working in tandem, but because, on the contrary, teaching by parables is worse pedagogy—more calculated to leave people in the dark, floundering about where they cannot get hold of the saving offer from God.

Surely this cannot be his meaning, and of course it isn't. He is being heavily ironic. Precisely because the parables appeal so effectively and powerfully for the effort of comprehension he asks of his hearers, those who are ill disposed towards the Gospel of the Kingdom will finish up in more clear-cut opposition to the Kingdom message. His teaching will be an occasion for the further hardening of hearts.

And in what sense is that a good thing? It's a good thing because it introduces the clarity that is needed in spiritual warfare. In the dramatic action the Kingdom-bearer initiates in the world we have to know where we ourselves stand. Are we with the protagonist, or are we against him?

Thursday of the Third Week of the Year (Years 1 and 2)

Today's Gospel is short and the sayings that compose it are condensed and riddling. It falls into two parts: the first is about Jesus himself, the second about the disciples.

To begin with, Jesus asks ironically whether people buy lamps in order to cover them up and he predicts that the light in question will just have to become visible eventually. In the Fourth Gospel, our Lord says openly, 'I am the Light of the world'—a statement which would consign anyone else to a psychiatric hospital but which makes perfect sense on the lips of the one man who knows, quite simply and in utter humility, that his humanity has been indissolubly united to the eternal Word of God. In Jesus, time is transparent to eternity so that the radiance of God's own being can shine through to ourselves.

With the words, 'If any man has ears to hear let him hear'—that is, use your intelligence to penetrate what I'm saying—St Mark then moves on to the second group of sayings, those that concern the disciples, the followers of the Light of the world. These sayings tell us something important about the life of grace. The Christian life grows by being shared, by extending itself through mission, friendship, service, and unless we do so extend it our very capacity for living the Christian life ('even that which we have') will wither away.

It is characteristic of the saints to want to pass on the light of God, and for other people to find the saints illuminating for their own lives. Tradition calls St Bede, for instance, *candela Ecclesiae*, 'the candle of the Church', and St Dominic *lumen Ecclesiae*, 'the light of the Church'. We too have to spread a little light as best we can.

Friday of the Third Week of the Year (Years 1 and 2)

The parables in today's Gospel-reading take their illustrations from agriculture and horticulture. The Kingdom of God will come in the risen Lord like grain growing fast and secretly; it will house the Gentiles as a mustard tree could shelter innumerable birds. Elsewhere in the New Testament we hear that the change that will come over our bodies in the Resurrection is like a corm becoming an anemone; the Word of God in the heart is broadcast seed whose yield depends on its soil.

This reminds us that in many cultures, a farm and especially a garden, whether it be a market garden or otherwise, has been a metaphor for the world. We cannot see the cosmos (it's too big), but in a garden or a farm we can see a micro-cosmos, the world on a miniature scale.

Only in the late nineteenth century did it become generally assumed that to be modern you must be urban. The reason—at least in the writings of the influential German thinker Nietzsche—is that to be modern is to recognize man as creator and not as creature, for God is dead. And only in the man-made world of the city can this conviction have its full scope.

If we are city-dwellers, and if we also wish to return to the cosmos its proper mystery as the creation (as Christians must), then soil, plants, animals, need to populate our mental world and give it roots. We must return if not to our beasts then at least to our bestiaries.

Saturday of the Third Week of the Year (Years 1 and 2)

Rather later in St Mark's Gospel the waters of the Sea of Galilee are the setting for the principal theophany of his Gospel-book. It is the moment when the evangelist makes it clear to us that he regards Jesus as somehow personally one with the Lord, the God of Israel. As the disciples cry out in amazement and distress at his walking on the water he addresses them with a version of the divine Name revealed to Moses at the Burning Bush. The 'I Am', the Self-existent One, the God beside whom is no other, is personally present in Jesus, who now calls out to his own, 'Fear not; it is I'.

Looking back from the vantage-point of that affirmation of Jesus' personal unity with the Lord, today's Gospel—not the Walking on the Waters but the Calming of the Waters—takes on a deeper significance. Jesus is asleep in the boat on a cushion. No doubt it was a weather-beaten version of a pretty ordinary cushion, the sort a Cambridge citizen could pick up any day at John Lewis's in St Andrew's Street. But look at it more deeply. The 'cushion' on which the Word incarnate is resting is the love of the eternal Father, the infinite security and comfort of the Son from before all ages. This is the assurance that, in the Gospel according to St Luke, will allow him to pray on the Cross what has been called the typical 'good-night prayer' of a Jewish child, 'Father, into thy hands I commend my spirit'.

The waters he can calm are not only the rough water of the Sea of Galilee in squally weather. They are the waters of the ocean of existence, the chaos waters of a fallen world.

THE FOURTH WEEK OF THE YEAR

Monday of the Fourth Week of the Year (Years 1 and 2)

Today's Gospel is like something from a nightmare. This demoniac, living (if you can call it living) in a cemetery, shrieking, deliberately harming himself, preternaturally strong, terrorizing a neighbourhood. You would need Hieronymus Bosch with his disturbing attraction to the grotesque to paint a picture of it; it would make a suitably sickening scene in a modern horror movie. And what about the pigs? Poor animals. Why did the Redeemer allow this strange transfer of the powers of evil that took them terrified and against all their instincts to a death in the waters of the lake?

These reactions, while pertinent, do not focus on the aspect of the story the evangelist wants to highlight. The focus is the outcome: the demoniac clothed and in his right mind, confessing the Saviour in a way which produces 'marvelling', unlimited admiration. It was the practice of the ancient Church to re-clothe people at Baptism when, having come to faith, they received justifying grace and so had the ability to make their own that mind which was in Christ Jesus—the only 'right mind', right set of the mind, to have once the Word has become human and shown man how to be himself as the image of God.

Our re-making through the gift of salvation is the origin of our proclamation, and an inexhaustible source of marvelling. So this Gospel text does not simply record one of the acts of power which form part and parcel of Christian apologetics about the historical Jesus. It also sets forth an image of salvation which has infiltrated, transformatively, the corporate consciousness of the Church.

That returns us to the pigs. They were *Gadarene* swine, a phrase that has entered the English language. Gadara was one of the pagan cities on the Gentile side of the Sea of Galilee. Only Gentiles would have herded swine. In the minds of the Jews, pigs, which evidently had played some part at some stage in pagan cult, symbolized the idolatrous religion that makes the human situation worse by taking as divine what could never be God. As the New Atheists could tell us, bad religion deepens the human plight. It was not the fault of Middle Eastern pigs to be caught up in this way into our affairs. But it was a fact, and, in the drama today's Gospel records, their contribution to the catharsis gives value to their deaths.

Tuesday of the Fourth Week of the Year (Years 1 and 2)

Who was the woman with a haemorrhage? Probably, it is speculated, a pagan. A statue of her meeting with Jesus was erected in the following century at Caesarea—something only conceivable in a pagan context at that period. If so, she would have been to orthodox Jews doubly unclean—both in her medical condition and because of her religion. This would explain her creeping up behind Jesus to touch the hem of his garment.

Rationalistic interpretation would have it that the supernatural cures and other miraculous events in the ministry of our Lord are literary dramatizations of his personal encounters with others. Here we have the exact opposite—at the moment of cure there was no encounter at all. The miracle testifies to the divine energies coursing through the person of the Saviour and putting him in a different league from the patron saint of the caring professions. And yet this divinity in no way detracts from the humanity—and here especially the human sensitivity and courtesy of Jesus—but rather, we can suppose, refines it.

He turns, aware that power has gone out of him. He asks who touched him. And then he gives the woman a blessing. Why this last? Surely so that she need not go home feeling she had somehow stolen her cure.

God is liberal with his salvation. *C'est son métier.* It's what he's best at.

Wednesday of the Fourth Week of the Year (Years 1 and 2)

'Where did this man get all this?' Where indeed? Today's Gospel raises the question of the human knowledge of the Word incarnate. When we think hard about the person of the Lord in whom the two natures, divinity and humanity, are inseparably joined, we realize that sooner or later the question has to be faced: how did his unique mode of being affect the way that, as a human being, he knew things? His hearers in the Nazareth synagogue came up against the issue sooner rather than later—very early, in fact, in his Galilaean ministry. Of course they couldn't put it in the way I just have. They lacked the key you and I have—the awareness that he is the God-man. That awareness is the fruit of the Church's reflection on his words and deeds, their relation to the promises to Israel as recorded in the Old Testament and their outcome in her experience at Pentecost and beyond. But the Nazarenes were aware of the basic problem, which surfaces time and again in his ministry: he spoke with authority and not as the scribes. 'Where did this man get all this?'

It's not a matter of whether our Lord could, if he wished, access from the divine mind a knowledge of plant genetics or Egyptian hieroglyphics. It's a question of how his mind was filled with treasures of wisdom and knowledge about his Father's saving plan for the world, the saving plan for us. It's no use to us if it's all a matter of his opinions, hunches, guesses, speculations. It's only of use to us if he really *knows*. And this indeed is what we hold. In addition to the humanly acquired understanding he got from studying the ancient Scriptures, observing the operation of the Jewish religion and taking in human reality general, there was in his mind an access of insight which was possible only because the person whose mind his human mind was happens to be the self-same person of the eternal Word whose mind is the divine intellect itself.

Imagine a translation going on, but this particular translation is not from one language to another, it is from the divine mind of the Word to his human faculties. That is where he got 'all this'. On earth, only the Son knows the Father, only the Son knows the Father's plan.

Thursday of the Fourth Week of the Year (Years 1 and 2)

Today's Gospel describes one of what we can call the 'representative tours' in the New Testament—in the Gospels and indeed the Acts of the Apostles and the Letters of St Paul. When in later times we think of missionary activity, we naturally think of what you might call 'blanket coverage'. If there is a parish mission, then missioners or activists would be expected to call at every house which had a name to go with it. And they might well decide to leaflet every house in each street, whether there was a name or not. Again, in a particular piece of mission territory abroad, say in sub-Saharan Africa, you would expect the missionary society or vicar-apostolic or whoever was responsible to divide up the area and share the work out so as to ensure overall coverage.

But this is precisely what is not happening in the New Testament. When St Paul embarks on his missionary journeys his plan is evidently to preach the Gospel in a selection of places scattered throughout what was to him the known world. That was why, had he not been put under house arrest and subsequently executed, he would have travelled on from Rome to Spain. It wasn't because there was nothing left for him to do in the eastern Mediterranean. It is the same with the missioners our Lord himself sends out, whether the seventy disciples or, as in today's Gospel, the Twelve. It is not blanket coverage; it is representative preaching to the House of Israel.

We ourselves can learn something from this. We cannot expect, on present showing, to convert the world, but what we are able to do is to evangelise it representatively. The Catholic Church seeks to establish herself in every country on earth, irrespective of the likelihood or otherwise of gaining significant numbers of adherents—so she is in Nepal and she is in Greenland. It is obedience to the Great Missionary Command on the eve of our Lord's Ascension: go, preach the Gospel to all nations. And it is a matter of changing the dynamics of salvation history: we bring within some sort of reach of everyone, although not actually *to* everyone, the Gospel of the Kingdom.

Friday of the Fourth Week of the Year (Years 1 and 2)

This story is not for children, or indeed for the squeamish of any age—even when read in the comparatively sober language of the Gospels, never mind when re-presented in operatic form by Richard Strauss based on the play by Oscar Wilde, or viewed in various over-the-top paintings of Salome holding St John's head on a platter, or, as in the version by Gustave Moreau, having a vision of the head hanging in the air severed from its body and gazing at her.

John the Baptist's death was a judicial murder instigated by a femme fatale, but underlying it are a cocktail of motives which include anger, pride, envy, lust, and fear. The death of the Forerunner is a warning of what to expect when there steps onto the stage of public society the One whom the Forerunner announced. Why was the Messiah put to death? The motivations of the actors involved were very different. This plurality of vicious motives is appropriate. The Messiah will die to atone for our sins, which are manifold not only in their number but also in their kinds.

Saturday of the Fourth Week of the Year (Years 1 and 2)

If we were asked to ponder all the negative sides of human life—the difficulties, anxieties, predicaments and indeed downright tragedies people face—we might well find ourselves having compassion. I hope we would. What is less likely is that we would expect to express such compassion for people by—as is said of our Lord in today's Gospel—'teaching them many things'.

The ability of teaching—of what we call in the religious context 'doctrine'—to help people is underestimated in our day. To know the truth, to know the truth as the ultimate context of one's life, to know the meaning—at least in broad outline—of what happens, to know the shape of the overall plan of God for us: this can be, and should be, something immensely consoling. It should be in its own way a resolution of our unhappiness, a pacification of our warring thoughts and feelings.

St Thomas remarks there can be no higher task in this world than to pass on to others the fruits of contemplation by teaching sound Christian doctrine, since this is to be helpful to one's neighbour not only for this life but for the life eternal.

And that reference to the connexion between teaching and contemplation also picks up an emphasis in today's Gospel. Jesus' compassion on the crowds and his teaching them follows on his withdrawal with the disciples to a 'lonely place'. Christian tradition has seen this withdrawal—the Greek word is *anachôrêsis*—as the archetype of entry into contemplation in the cell: the life of reflection, meditation, study, prayer, from which we get our word 'anchorite', a hermit. We are not all called to be anchorites or to live in anchorholds. But we must have great spaces for silence in our lives, so that we can enter the cell of the heart. In *The Screwtape Letters* C. S. Lewis suggests that Hell will be noise, because the damned cannot bear silence which would confront them with the heart.

The person who is in touch with the Spirit of God in the heart is the one who can best speak compassionately the doctrine of truth to their neighbour.

THE FIFTH WEEK OF THE YEAR

Monday of the Fifth Week of the Year (Year 1)

We can think of the action of God in creation and redemption as at one and the same time *separation* and *consolidation*.

Genesis shows us creation as separation: separating light from the dark, earth from water, and so on—because there has to be discrimination, sorting out, before there can be things whose identities are stable and worthwhile.

And yet the aim of God, as Scripture tells us, is to bring all things together in Christ: to inter-relate and unify the many realities of creation and bring into one the different aggregations of people that make up the human family.

So separation can't be the whole story. There must also be consolidation. When in today's Gospel Jesus sets foot on the shore, crossing symbolically that great dividing line of sea and land, the people flock to him from every side, not only geographically, we may suppose, but also from those different sociological directions that are represented in a traditional society by country and city. He acts as a point of convergence, then, and it is significant that the activity which flows from that point is one of healing. Divine consolidation doesn't overthrow the differentiation caused by divine separation, but it heals the malfunctioning, the disharmony, that separation can and does bring in its train.

Monday of the Fifth Week of the Year (Year 2)

When the Ark leaves whatever temporary abode it had been given in the city of David during David's own reign and travels up the road to the Temple mount, to the glistening new Temple of Solomon, we might think this was just an architectural makeover. But in Old Testament revelation, going up the road is not just a change of domicile for the Ark. When the Temple is consecrated there is a new descent of the divine Glory, a new manifestation of the divine Being, to mark a new stage in the relations of God with Israel.

From now on—and this was clear if not to Solomon then to the scribes who edited the Books of the Kings where we read about it—all Israelite worship, all sacrifice, all cult, the whole cultic life of the people is going to be centred here. It is going to be centred on the Jerusalem Temple which will become, therefore, the pilgrimage capital of the monarchy and not simply the seat of the king. In the Providence of God, this centralization was necessary if all Israel was to acquire a common mind, and if a common understanding of the Covenant relation with God was to emerge and be the background to the Incarnation.

But at the centre of it all, at the centre of the centre, is a wooden box preserved since the desert wanderings under Moses and inside it are two pieces of inscribed stone. In Ethiopia, where the Orthodox Church believes it still has the original Ark, lost during the wars with the Middle Eastern superpowers at the start of the sixth century B. C., every Orthodox church building has as its holiest possession a small replica of the Ark and its contents. This object, the 'taboth', is considered the most sacred object in any Ethiopian Orthodox church because it has been solemnly consecrated as the sign of the Covenant between God and man. In the Catholic Church in Ethiopia it is something of a disputed point whether Eastern-rite Catholic churches should follow suit.

The taboth is a beautiful reminder of the origins of Christianity in the Old Covenant and therefore of the unity of the Old Testament and the New. But is it more than that? Those who hesitate to say 'Yes' would argue that, with the Incarnation, the God-man Jesus Christ is now the true Ark: he is the divine Word now made flesh, not just words inscribed on a stone. As he walked the streets of Palestine, even to touch the hem of his garment was to be in contact with salvation. The sign of the Covenant now is, therefore, the one he left us: the Holy Eucharist, the gift of his Body and Blood, given for an everlasting Covenant. And so it is the Blessed Sacrament which now should occupy the Tabernacle, the sacramental 'Ark', in the sanctuary at the heart of every church building.

The 'accidents', as the metaphysicians say, of the consecrated Host and the consecrated Wine, are these not for us the hem of his garment as he lets himself be touched by the needy and the sick at heart, as well as the sick in body: lets himself be touched not now in the Galilee of Roman Palestine but in the wider 'Galilee' that is the world?

Tuesday of the Fifth Week of the Year (Years 1 and 2)

When we hear a Gospel like today's, we may be tempted to say, Thank God that we are not like other men—other men, that is, in traditional religious cultures, trapped in ritualism and legalism, unable to sort out the essential from the inessential.

This could be very naïve. Often enough, the essential requires the inessential for its transmission. It needs rite and symbol, code and rule, practice and custom, so as to be handed down in a way fitted to human beings who live in society by way of culture. For the passing on of a revealed religion, as of any religion, or indeed any more or less comprehensive value system, the inessential is—paradoxically enough!—essential.

In this parable, as in other criticisms of the Pharisees, our Lord should be taken as attacking an impure or deviant tradition, and not the principle of tradition itself. Granted human fallibility, tradition as transmission can go wrong. Statistically, therefore, it will go wrong: there will always be some people to get it wrong, and mess up in their relation with God as a result.

That is why Christ did not only provide his Church with accredited traditioners—the apostles and their successors. He also gave her the Holy Spirit whose task it is to keep those office-bearers from error in their guardianship of teaching. The same Holy Spirit is also given to us in Baptism and Confirmation, to help us to use well what we have received, to use it in the service of holiness.

Thanks to the Spirit's mission, tradition can be reformed and renewed. But there can be no break with tradition so as to create a new Christianity from bottom up. A German theologian in the nineteenth century put it wisely: in the Church, Christianity and tradition are virtually synonymous.

Wednesday of the Fifth Week of the Year (Year 1)

Today's reading from Genesis tells us of the garden that was planted in Eden. Many traditional cultures, and not just Christian ones, are haunted by the sense that, at the origin of man, there was if not a garden then at any rate a golden age. We came out of something beautiful, and so the way we are now, which is often quite squalid, morally if not physically, is not how things are meant to be. The Russian philosopher Nicholas Berdyaev once said, 'All beauty in the world is either a memory of Paradise or a prophecy of the transfigured world'.

The Genesis account of the Fall speaks of the loss of the Paradise garden as the result of the desire to have the knowledge of both good and evil — in other words, to experiment with the possibilities of good and evil. And we know the Pandora's box that was opened by that spirit of experimentation. What our first parents did was to cross the limit that defined their humanity. They sought to be like God without having the divine nature. No more disastrous formula can be thought.

All sin consists in replicating the Fall in some way, in some way making it our own. But today too when scientists are looking into the possibility of 'transhumanism' — engineering a version of a human being that, through technology, goes beyond what our species has been hitherto, we are faced with a proposal which mirrors the original Fall in an extraordinarily precise way. Whether it be through keeping human brains alive without their natural bodies, or by transferring the contents of a human brain to a computer, transhumanism is a repudiation of the Garden. It is saying we were not meant to be gardeners of the cosmos but creator-engineers: creator-engineers of a new species of an un-natural kind. This is not to transfigure humanity, it is to disfigure it.

The real transfiguration we are offered is the one that took place in another garden, the Easter Garden of the meeting of the risen Lord with Mary Magdalen. There we were offered a return to the Garden which is also an enhancement of all the Garden represents. For the new Paradise of the Kingdom is not simply the original Paradise restored. It is the fullness of friendship with God when we shall be not only restored and forgiven but raised up and crowned, not through our own efforts but by his amazing grace.

Wednesday of the Fifth Week of the Year (Year 2)

In today's Old Testament reading, the Queen of Sheba's riches are depicted with all the opulence of Rubens or Delacroix. But, it seems, they count for little beside wisdom.

What is wisdom? St Thomas would have called it an understanding of things in their causes, and if that sounds too retrospective we need to add that one of those causes is a 'final' cause. How can you have a final cause? Surely a cause must come before its effect? A final cause is a cause that sets the purpose or goal of something, and thus explains why a thing exists or why an event happens. The final cause of taking a holiday is recreation by a change of scenery. Unfortunately, not everything is as easy to explain as a planned decision such as that. No complete wisdom about why things happen to us in our lives is available even to a Solomon. Nevertheless, we can get some insight into what life is for, according to God's plan.

Today's Gospel shows us the obstacle to such an appropriation of wisdom. The obstacle is not intellectual. Many people are wise who are largely inarticulate, and many people who are highly articulate are not wise. No, the obstacle is moral. It is a deficiency not in brain capacity but in purity of heart. With all those seething passions of envy, hate, ambition, greed, lust, jealousy, going on inside us, we're not well placed to recognise and assimilate wisdom.

The poet Thomas Traherne says of the heart struggling to be pure that there 'are truths it loves without knowing them' — it has an instinct for them so that, when they show themselves, the heart at once recognizes them for what they are. The heart our Lord criticizes, by contrast, is too full of its unpleasant little hidden agendas to let God's great agenda in. So we begin to see perhaps the sense in the sixth Beatitude from the Sermon on the Mount: 'Blessed are the pure in heart, for they shall see God'.

Thursday of the Fifth Week of the Year (Years 1 and 2)

We know that our Lord's mission was first and foremost to the People of the Promise, to Israel. Only via Israel's response to him — which, as it proved, was the response of the Cross — would his mission open out to include the salvation of all the world.

Today's Gospel is one of those Gospels when that wider future comes in view through a seemingly chance encounter, a meeting with a pagan woman from one of the towns on Israel's seaboard.

It has worried people that our Lord appears to refuse assistance to the woman's daughter on the grounds that she is a non-Israelite, and that the refusal is expressed in very derogatory terms.

One of the mediaeval theologians, Peter Abelard, explained Jesus' response as a disinclination which is not in the full sense an act of will: in other words, this was not a refusal in fact. Our Lord's sense of the unique place in the plan of salvation of the Jewish people *disinclines* him to extend his healing ministry to Gentiles but his *act of will*, which coincides with and realizes in human terms the will of God the Word, united with his in his single person, is nevertheless to do what the Syro-Phoenician woman wants. Since it is by the Word that all things are made, the Word incarnate will choose to heal, to help, any needed human creature who approaches him, no matter what their race or position.

I would add that, more simply, we do not know his tone of voice, which could have been gently ironic, mocking not the woman but Jewish linguistic usage in the period.

There is much which the Gospels cannot tell us because they are not the living voice, the living person. This is one reason why they have to be placed in the context of the rest of the New Testament and, beyond that, the Church's own sense of faith, *sensus fidei*—the term we use for her grace-assisted penetration of these texts. The image of our Lord's person as embedded in the Church's deep consciousness: this is our criterion for reading the Gospels, and it allows no shadow of imperfection to fall across the face of Christ.

Friday of the Fifth Week of the Year (Years 1 and 2)

Yesterday, St Mark gave us what you might call a psychological miracle. The casting out of a demon from the daughter of the Syro-Phoenician woman is the cure of a mental disorder, albeit one exacerbated by the influence of the evil angels. Today we are back firmly in the realm of the physical, with the healing of the deaf and dumb man.

Such physical miracles are important to the Gospels because, although Jesus refuses to perform simply to impress, simply to produce signs and wonders, still, when he comes to meet human need in this more than human way he bears witness to his own identity with the God of all creation.

But the Church has seen more in this episode than 'just' the physical cure. When an infant has been baptized, part of the ceremonies which follow involves the celebrant touching the ears and mouth of the baby while saying a prayer based on this Gospel event: 'May the Lord soon open your ears to hear his Word and your lips to proclaim his praise, to the glory of God the Father'.

There is something profound in the connexion thus made. In a real sense we are deaf until we can hear the Word of God. We are sealed off from the true message of existence, locked into the narrowed world of the deaf until our ears are unblocked and we hear that word which tells us of our real origins and final destiny in the love of God.

And similarly, in a real sense we are dumb till that moment. The gift of speech is sterile in us unless we can speak out a response to that message and do so, not just in the words given us by the Scriptures or the Liturgy of the Church (though first and foremost that), but in all the ways we use language in our daily converse to show how we belong to the regime of grace—how we are creatures loved by God and placed in the way of salvation by him, transferred from the kingdom of darkness to the realm of his wonderful light.

Saturday of the Fifth Week of the Year (Years 1 and 2)

Any Gospel which has to do with the Saviour's miraculously meeting some dire need of his contemporaries may seem to raise as many problems as it solves. Those wonderful deeds help to establish his identity: he is the agent in history of the Creator of the world. But they also suggest a question. If it was obvious to the Word incarnate that he should do whatever he could to feed hungry people, including feeding them by supernatural means, then why does he not do the same now? If we think of him simply as the divine Word, he is—is he not?—the omnipotent Logos through whom the Father made all things. And if we are thinking of him specifically as the Word *incarnate*, the Son of Mary, he can hardly be less powerful after his glorious Resurrection and Ascension than he was during his time of humiliation on earth. An international campaign addressing the issue of hunger in the world was entitled, 'End poverty now!' Why does our Saviour not do so, if he can? At the Multiplication of the Loves and Fishes he showed that he could.

We need here to keep hold of two truths. First, if we are really to use our powers as human beings, and be actively responsible for the planet of which we are the stewards, we cannot be God's puppets as distinct from his collaborators. To wish that a divine wand would magic away all the problems of the world is to forget that fact. But secondly, there is a complementary truth: God wanted to show his hand in the process of history. He wanted to reveal his attributes to us there. He did so in the Incarnation of the Word whose public actions, not least his miraculous actions, testify to what God is like. Helen Waddell, in her novel about the mediaeval theologian Peter Abelard, draws a comparison with a tree-trunk. Sawn in half, it will show its rings. When you decide where you want to cut it, only one example of the rings will appear. But that is enough to assure us that the rings run up and down the full length of the tree. The Multiplication of the Loaves and Fishes reveals not just what Jesus felt at that moment, but what God is eternally like.

What, then, about the hungry? We do what we can by all human means to feed them, knowing at the same time from the promises of Scripture how at the End of all things the character of God—his loving mercy towards us—will suffuse the whole world.

THE SIXTH WEEK OF THE YEAR

Monday of the Sixth Week of the Year (Years 1 and 2)

Today's is a rather sad little Gospel. It's almost as though our Lord despaired of his contemporaries, or at least of the Pharisees, and gave up on them. Going away to the opposite side of the Sea of Galilee acts in this text as a symbol of the opposition between them.

We have to remember that his principal converting instrument was not his words—his teaching, his verbal appeal to others (though these certainly had great force)—but rather the power of his Cross, his saving Sacrifice. It was the death of the Messiah and his subsequent vindication in the Resurrection which set flowing the Spirit of God into hardened hearts and touched many of those for whom words, arguments, suasions, were insufficient.

The Acts of the Apostles testifies to the conversion of numerous Pharisees after Pentecost and if we ask what effect that had we need look no further than one name: St Paul.

The Word incarnate will not give a sign of his mission and identity so overwhelming that there is no more need for faith. But as he makes clear on another occasion, he will leave a sign of a different order: the sign of the Cross and its outflow in the Resurrection.

Today as we contemplate the increasing apostasy of our country and our apparent inability to stem the flow and turn the tide, we may feel that he has abandoned our faithless contemporaries too—and sailed to the opposite shore. But he does not give up. Instead he prepares to exhibit his one true sign, the sign of a God who spends himself and a man who is exalted by humility. This, his glorious Cross, is the sign in which, as Constantine saw at the Milvian Bridge, we are to conquer—or, rather, he is to conquer through us. If our age is, as the Swiss theologian Hans Urs von Balthasar called it, the time of the 'Passion of the Church', it is our opportunity to become more fully disciples of the Cross.

Tuesday of the Sixth Week of the Year (Years 1 and 2)

In today's Gospel the disciples are reproved for being somewhat slow on the uptake. It has to be said in their defence that our Lord was also rather riddling in his words.

To understand this conversation, we need to know that the highest destiny of bread on the Jewish table in Roman Palestine was to be served unleavened in the high and holy season of Passover-tide. That is why 'yeast' or 'leaven'—avoided in baking such bread—could be on Jesus' lips a metaphor for undesirable conduct, or what one commentator calls 'a principle of moral corruption'. He is telling them to steer clear of the Pharisees and the Herodians who, if they get a chance, will be negative influences on the disciples' outlook. And that is rather important, for the disciples are going to be entrusted with an amazing mission. Is 'amazing' the right word? Certainly it is, if the Multiplication of the Loves and Fishes is anything to go by! They are going to be taking forward the Greatest Story Ever Told. They will be the apostles of the Lord of history who has stooped to enter his creation as Jesus Christ.

Wednesday of the Sixth Week of the Year (Years 1 and 2)

This is a Gospel about Incarnation if ever there was one. The word 'Incarnation' means literally 'The Enfleshment', and it is an example of Christian Latin rubbing in the *earthiness* of what happened in the life of Jesus Christ. When—on holiday in Corfu, say—we go to church with Greek Catholics we use the original language of the Creed, and say that, at the moment of the Incarnation, the Word was 'made man'—and our modern English translations follow suit. Of course Latin Christians were perfectly aware that the flesh the Word took upon himself in Mary's womb was ensouled flesh: it was flesh animated by a human psyche and a human intellect. He took to himself everything that is ours: all our faculties, all our capacities, sin alone excepted. Nevertheless, the Latin Fathers loved to underline what I called the 'earthiness' of it all by emphasizing that word 'flesh'—for indeed, without our bodies, our souls, our intelligence, cannot be properly human.

And here is a Gospel right up their street. Our Lord gives sight to the blind not by formulating an intention in his mind, nor by expressing in language his desire to heal, but by taking saliva from his mouth and applying it to the eyes of the handicapped man. From flesh to flesh, this is how the curative energy worked, just as his saving energy is also communicated to my body as well as my soul in his redemptive work which aims at my restoration and transfiguration, body and soul, in the Age to Come.

Thursday of the Sixth Week of the Year (Years 1 and 2)

In today's Gospel, our Lord confronts his disciples with the question of his identity. They—or, rather, Peter, acting for the first time as their mouthpiece—give him a very Jewish answer. You are the 'Christ of God', the Messiah, the expected deliverer of the people of Israel. Evidently, this was a correct answer, though, as we shall see, it was by no means the fullest answer that could be given.

Jesus accepts the title. But speaking in his own person he replaces it with another: the 'Son of Man'. With its rather complicated Old Testament background, this title combines one very this-worldly shade of meaning with another distinctly other-worldly one. In the oracles of Ezekiel, 'Son of man' was a phrase which emphasized the prophet's humble, earthly status as a human being. Yet in the Book of Daniel, the 'One like a son of man' was the seer's name for the transcendent Presence who was to be the mighty Vindicator of the elect people. In mythopoeic language this is, as it were, a coded expression for the Lord's two natures as the Word incarnate.

And then in today's Gospel Jesus adds as somehow part and parcel of his self-definition a prediction of his own Passion. As he acts out the logic of his position, the Son of Man is going to be the Crucified. We might indeed think that when the divine in all its blazing purity enters into this world as one of its own creatures it will inevitably be crucified in one way or another. Such is our world, our humanity. By accepting that destiny in our condition and on our behalf, the Son will re-create for himself the glory he had with the Father before the world was made, doing so precisely for all those to whom he will offer a share in that glory.

'He came from his blest throne', so the hymn-writer sums it up. But, as that lyric continues, 'crucify' was 'all their breath'. Yet when we know the outcome of that wondrous death in all its fruitfulness we can go on to say with the hymn, 'Here could I stay and sing'. Yes, contemplation and wonder come first in the Christian life.

Thursday of the Sixth Week of the Year (Year 1)

Today's first reading describes the covenant with Noah, which is the first of the Bible's descriptions of God pledging himself to a future policy with human beings, so as to enter into solidarity with them and they with him.

The content of this Noachic Covenant is a cosmic one. It has to do with the permanence of nature, her processes, her rhythms, her fecundity. Man will never wake up one morning to find (if I can put this in Irish) that the world isn't there. In this Covenant the animals are closely involved, as the story of Noah's Ark shows and mediaeval artists lovingly depicted.

Unfortunately there came a time in Europe when people forgot the significance of the animals for the primal Covenant. Descartes was a very devout Catholic yet he thought of animals as machines: whether scaly machines, feathered machines or furry machines. Today perhaps we are in danger of going to the opposite extreme and forgetting that this primal Covenant is only the backdrop for a more profound and intense sharing of life between God and ourselves as found in the subsequent covenants of redemption.

In today's Gospel, which is St Mark's Passion prediction, we get a hint of the cost of the New and Everlasting Covenant to God made man in blood and tears, the death agony and the descent into Hell.

Friday of the Sixth Week of the Year (Year 1)

The common point in today's readings is power. The Tower of Babel is about power-building on the grandest scale. It's the unification of humanity under a single sovereignty, a sovereignty that is going to organize the scaling of the heavens. Babel towers over the earth; the sky's the limit—in other words, it challenges the true sovereignty in creation, which is the sovereignty of God.

In the Gospel, our Lord speaks of the Kingdom of God coming with power. This shows God has indeed a sovereignty and this sovereignty has power attached to it. It is not, as we often think, power per se that is wrong. It is the quality of power and what it is used for that counts.

So what is the power of Jesus Christ? Pentecost will show us. 'Stay in the city', Jesus tells his disciples after the Resurrection, 'until you are clothed with power from on high'. Pentecost is when the Father's Kingdom comes with power before some of Christ's hearers saw death. It is the breakthrough of what will be God's universal power at the End.

What that power is like no one has ever expressed better than the author of the Pentecost Sequence, the *Veni Sancte Spiritus*. Some phrases from it show the quality of divine power: 'ever bounteous of thy store', 'our hearts' unfailing light'; 'consoler, kindest, best', 'sweet refreshment, sweet repose'. And some show its aims: 'but for thy blest deity nothing pure in man could be, nothing harmless, nothing good'. Yes, it is the quality of power and the ends it is used for that count.

Friday of the Sixth Week of the Year (Year 2)

Today's extract from the Letter of St James has been hugely important in controversy between Catholics and Protestants. It was owing to the passage you have just heard that Martin Luther sought to have the Letter of James thrown out of the Canon of Scripture, famously denouncing it as 'an epistle of straw'. It's all to do with the question, Are we saved by having faith, or through the practice of good works?

There's no question that faith is, for both Catholics and what some call 'magisterial Protestants'—Protestants who hold to the doctrines of the great Protestant divines of the sixteenth century— an indispensable condition for salvation. Faith is the acceptance of God's offer of salvation. It is the self-surrender, in mind and heart, that enables God to act in our lives to redeem, restore, transfigure. We are, as St Paul would put it, 'justified by faith'. But is it correct for that reason to say we are justified by faith *alone*? Magisterial Protestants say, 'Yes'; Catholics say 'No', because for us if faith is living faith it will always be a faith that operates through charity. And, at any rate where the adult person or the responsible person or the person who has reached the age of reason is concerned, charity is unthinkable without charitable actions: actions we put forth as moral agents in the world around us, be that world narrow or large. And indeed, even for children, or the grossly mentally handicapped, or babes in their mother's arms or in hospital incubators for that matter, what regenerates in the sacrament of faith, Baptism, is the seed of such living faith, faith rendered alive by charity, a seed that waits silently for the light of moral consciousness to warm it into action.

So: thank you, holy apostle James, for ensuring by your Letter that we never forget this salient fact about the following of Jesus Christ.

Saturday of the Sixth Week of the Year (Years 1 and 2)

The Transfiguration of the Lord: a Gospel I for one can never hear too often owing to its beauty. Indeed, we might call it the signature-tune Gospel of Christian aesthetics. The Transfiguration is about the beauty of God shining forth from the Face of Jesus Christ, reflected, as the evangelists say, even on his robes. The icon painters, following a hint in some of the Fathers, will take that further still: surely the landscape in which he was standing must also have gleamed with borrowed light.

Jean Corbon, who wrote the marvellous book on prayer which makes up the fourth and last part of the 1992 *Catechism of the Catholic Church*, says that in the Transfiguration of Christ the joy of the Father at the quality of the incarnate Son's self-giving flamed out in Jesus, suffusing him with light. We should not imagine that this was a passing thing. The person of the Son is, as we say in the Creed, Light from Light, for he is God from God, not only proceeding eternally from the Father but everlastingly turned towards him in love. But on Mount Thabor—the traditional site of this event—the disciples were permitted to experience openly the hidden reality which gives the meaning of his entire ministry, from his Baptism to his Cross.

At the Resurrection, the capacity of our Lord's body to be the sacrament of his endless life, oriented to the Father in the Holy Spirit, was freed from its limits, the limits of our fallen mortality. The glory of the Resurrection expresses perfectly the beauty of God, the beauty which in the final analysis is nothing other than the fact that God is love. This is the key to the Christian aesthetic, the aesthetic of the saints.

THE SEVENTH WEEK OF THE YEAR

Monday of the Seventh Week of the Year (Years 1 and 2)

How can prayer and fasting be said to drive out demons, the demons we are generally concerned with, our evil thoughts of lust, pride, anger, and the rest?

There is a psychological level at which this works, as even unbelievers can recognize. Both prayer and fasting involve a displacement of the ego, cutting the 'I' down to size. In prayer, we consciously place the centre of reality outside ourselves. Fasting too is a symbolic refusal to expand the ego. In these senses prayer and fasting help human life in this world. That is why an atheist philosopher like Iris Murdoch can say that the demise of prayer as a common practice has been a disaster for human civilization, or a seemingly atheist theologian like Don Cupitt recommend traditional ascetical practices.

There is also, however, a deeper side unavailable to them and it concerns salvation. Prayer and fasting are both pleas that God will come and save us. Not in so many words, necessarily — fasting not in words at all. But both express emptiness that is ready for God to fill it.

Tuesday of the Seventh Week of the Year (Years 1 and 2)

Something surprising has often been noted about the evangelist Mark. He is far from unwilling to register the slowness of the disciples in taking in the message of their Master — slowness and, perhaps, worse than slowness, for the discussion about who should have the primacy among them suggests they were not just unperceptive, but totally lacked appropriate spiritual dispositions as well. Tradition reports that the Gospel of Mark represents the evangelical catechesis at Rome of the apostle Peter, and this somewhat brutal candour about the holy apostles may well reflect Peter's own rueful reflections on the failures and weaknesses of the band of the disciples before the days of Pentecost.

Can we find any connexion between the two apostolic blind-spots today's Gospel highlights? The Twelve failed to grasp what Jesus was talking about when he spoke to them of the forthcoming Paschal events—that was the first blind-spot. And they didn't understand that for him authority meant service and service in particular of the most vulnerable—that was the second. I think we *can* find such a connexion. It hinges on the image of the *child*.

One of the titles the ancient Church gave our Lord was 'thy holy Child Jesus'. This was not a reference, as it would be in later ages, to the infancy of Christ. It was a way of speaking about the adult Saviour. Jesus is the Father's Child. From all eternity he has been the Son of God, and now as man he makes that eternal Sonship his own through the human experience of so growing up as a man that he knows himself to be first and foremost the Child of the Father. He brings his mission to its climax in his saving Sacrifice with all the simple trust of a child—as Isaac did, in the Book of Genesis, when he accompanied his father up Mount Moriah. Unlike Isaac, Jesus actually did die on Mount Calvary, died in a perfect act of self-oblation, but in his Passion he trusts his Father's goodness with the confidence of a child: a child resting its assurance on a parent's love in a totally unselfconscious way. And his trust was vindicated at Easter.

Those who bear authority in the Church have to emulate this childlike trust, incompatible as it is with ambition or the 'envy of clerics' or indeed with self-preoccupation of any kind. A holy priest or a holy bishop is known at once when he shows signs of this key attitude.

The attitude of spiritual childhood in a Church leader generates an affinity with actual children, or those who are vulnerable as children are. Jesus tells the disciples they must turn and become like little children, and he also tells them they must welcome little children (who here stand, I believe, for all the vulnerable) as their quintessentially special care. That affinity between apostles and these little ones is the sacred bond which abuse of children in Church schools and parishes has so obscenely parodied.

Wednesday of the Seventh Week of the Year (Years 1 and 2)

In mission it is always important to take stock of one's resources. One encouraging consideration is found in today's Gospel, 'He who is not against us is for us'. At first sight, this is a riddling statement. Why should those who are not against you be counted as for you?

It has to do with the way our nature was made. It was made for the supernatural. It didn't have to be, but in fact the way it is made is pointing towards the vision of God—pointing inefficaciously, but pointing all the same. So long as human perversity doesn't grab our poor long-suffering human nature by the collar and haul it off in another direction, this is its bias—though by itself the bias will not take it to the supernatural any more than the bias in the bowling ball will take the ball to its target without an impetus from beyond.

And yet the bias is important. A really valuable book for any present day missionary in our society is Chesterton's *Orthodoxy* where he describes how the faith is (as he puts it) a key that fits the lock of the world. Chesterton picked up this key, tried it in the lock, the lock turned, and he heard a satisfying click. There are so many things that the faith fits that people are longing for, so many impulses of the human heart the faith could satisfy, so many conflicts of value in people's lives it could restore, so many partial glimpses of reality it could unify.

This is what we have to work on. Those who not against us are for us.

Thursday of the Seventh Week of the Year (Years 1 and 2)

Is salvation easy to attain, or is it difficult? Today's Gospel puts this question before us.

The opening saying seems to suggest salvation is very easy—a pushover, or at any rate a door you can easily push open. Giving someone a cup of water because they belong to Christ, that might do it. We know from our doctrine that we lay hold on salvation by faith working through charity. No one could deny that almsgiving fits well in that context. No doubt for some grasping tight-fisted old miser, a Scrooge figure, the discovery that, yes, one is able, as a disciple of Christ, to give way one's money to the needy and to give it light-heartedly, could be how salvation at last takes hold: the key moment when faith begins to be enlivened by charity.

Most people, however, would not regard such behaviour as startlingly heroic—whereas they would be startled by the next sayings, which make up the bulk of the Gospel passage. Here we have a situation where my hold on salvation apparently requires my willingness to be deprived of a faculty or a limb. It is true that the Church strongly disapproved when the great exegete Origen of Alexandria took this saying literally and deprived himself of an especially intimate member. And yet living out salvation does sometimes demand sacrifices many people outside the Church would regard as inhuman. Some vocations are hard, some aspects of the law of Christ and the Church are hard, some situations—like those calling for martyrdom—are hard.

So is salvation easy or is it difficult? The answer is, we don't know whether salvation will be hard or easy for us as individuals until our role in the drama of salvation is complete. We don't know whether the salt of salvation will be for us salt in our dinner to bring out the flavour of life, or whether it will be more like salt rubbed into our wounds till it's almost unbearable. Our task is to follow the Scouts' maxim: Be prepared.

Friday of the Seventh Week of the Year (Years 1 and 2)

We often hear preachers speaking about the Church's doctrine of marriage, not least when we attend weddings. But we rarely hear them speak about the marriage of Christ.

Should we say about our Lord in the words of the broadsheet obituaries: 'he never married'? He himself would not have said so. He considered himself the Bridegroom of Israel come in person to claim his Bride. Various parables and sayings make that clear. He was getting ready for a wedding feast.

The witness of the New Testament is that Christ *did* marry, he married his expected Bride. When was the wedding, then, and where, and did we miss it? It was at Passovertide in the year 30 or thereabouts, on Golgotha (it's amazing the places some people want to get married!), and we were there by proxy, represented by one of the witnesses, our mother, the mother of the Church.

Like all marriages, it was for better, for worse; for richer, for poorer. That was the risk of the redemptive act in a messy world. For this wedding he left his Father and mother. He left his Father in taking on a human nature which cast him adrift in a sea of contingencies. He left his mother, the perfect spiritual security of home life with the Immaculate One. He left them and made himself one flesh with his wife who includes in her corporate persona very great sinners.

For better, for worse; for richer, for poorer. Let us not make it worse and poorer for the Bridegroom. We were washed, we were justified, we were sanctified by the blood of Jesus Christ. Let us never take his marriage lines and throw them in the dust.

Saturday of the Seventh Week of the Year (Years 1 and 2)

The standard baptismal certificate in the Church of England when I was small showed — and possibly they are still in use — an artist's impression of the scene in today's Gospel with underneath the caption, 'A child of God, a member of Christ, an inheritor of the Kingdom of heaven'.

The scene of our Lord's blessing children at Bethany-beyond-the-Jordan can indeed serve as an icon of Christian salvation, and that in three ways. In the first place, notice that the evangelist doesn't present the children themselves as taking any initiative in going up to Jesus. No doubt, under the influence of cultural Romanticism, we could imagine the spontaneously religious child singling out Jesus, as in *The Wind in the Willows* the baby Otter was eventually found nestling at the feet of the god Pan. But in the Gospel it is Jesus who by his mission first makes himself present to the scene and thus can allow children to be brought to him. The practice of infant Baptism in the Church is a testimony to the fact that the primordial initiative in salvation does not belong to the candidate but to God.

But secondly, within the immediacy of the scene created by Jesus' presence, it is not that Jesus himself actually goes to the children. Rather, others, third parties — presumably these are parents but in the social setting not necessarily so—bring the children to him. God's work of salvation generally requires human intermediaries. This is not because God is distant, any more than Jesus was distant to the crowd. It is because God delights to mediate his immediacy through his creatures, through others. That is why we have the communion of saints. It is also why we have an ordained ministry in the Church. We go to salvation together, helped by others.

But thirdly, Jesus does say, 'Let them come to me', as though imperceptibly in the course of the brouhaha the children were ceasing to be passively carried and beginning to signal that they actively wanted to go to him—as it were, holding out podgy arms to that effect. Eventually, the movement of grace is something we have to make our own. No one, at the end of the day, can substitute for me in my acceptance of salvation. As St Augustine put it, he who made us without us will not save us without our co-operation.

THE EIGHTH WEEK OF THE YEAR

Monday of the Eighth Week of the Year (Years 1 and 2)

The Gospel of the Rich Young Man has been an extremely influential one in the Church—especially for monastics. The monastic life is first and foremost a life for Christian virgins: that is, for those who choose to remain unmarried for the honour of the Lord as one of the early apostolic Fathers puts it, seeking the Face of God in a single life where all the energies which would otherwise be expressed in conjugal living are concentrated on God alone. But the virginal life—or the vow of chastity or promise of celibacy, as later ages would call it—is not likely to achieve its end if it is surrounded by all the luxuries that money can buy. That is why monastics are to be poor in this world's goods and not merely emotionally poor, poor in their experience of erotic and companionable living. It's all to do with making space in one's life for almighty God to occupy.

That's fine for monks and nuns, you may say, but what about the rest of us? Before I answer that, I would like to say how—just because it's 'fine' for monks and nuns—we ought to recognize the huge importance of having monastics in the Church. As you may have noticed (if you keep up at all with these things), the number of monasteries and convents in this country is shrinking, and a number that still remain may not be able to go on indefinitely unless new candidates come forward. That is very bad news for our Church. A Church that cannot generate in reasonable numbers members who are happy to live for God alone is not in a healthy state.

So, then, what about everyone else? If you look at the *Catechism of the Catholic Church* you will see that, while not all members of the Church are called to live virginally and poorly, all are called to live in the spirit of the monastics—to have something spare and ascetic about their sensibility and life-style which somewhat reminds people in a faint kind of way of what monastics are like. We do not want a Puritan Church but we want a Church all of whose members are serious.

Tuesday of the Eighth Week of the Year (Years 1 and 2)

The repayment of the Twelve for all they have left in following their Master—from dwelling houses to families to lands—is going to be not only in the Age to Come, so Jesus says, but in this world too. If we didn't know anything more about our Lord, and about the New Testament (especially the Book of the Apocalypse which deals with the Age of the End as well as this age) we might very well grossly misunderstand this passage from St Mark's Gospel.

In a certain segment of Evangelical Protestantism there is just such a misunderstanding—and Evangelicals do not have the excuse of ignorance of the Scriptures to mitigate the offence. The New Testament does not suggest that this-worldly prosperity is a sign of divine favour any more than it holds out the hope of material riches in heaven for God's elect. So what on earth—or what in heaven for that matter—can Jesus be talking about?

The only 'reward' for following Christ that Church tradition knows about in interpreting the Scriptures is the reward of joy in seeing the Face of God in Jesus Christ. That Face is hidden yet not for all that inaccessible to spiritual experience in the Church on earth; it is an open secret, the gladness and delight of all the saints, in heaven. And as the apprehension of the Face is, in its two modes—glimpsed now in a glass darkly, but then face to face—so similarly the *joy which is its sign*, which is also held out to us in two different ways.

What we have now in the Church, as we live the life of faith, ponder the Scriptures, frequent the sacraments, meditate on the dogmas, contemplate the icons, is a *joy that is in part*. It is inevitably limited by its own earthly conditions, of which the possibility of 'persecutions', mentioned by our Lord, is simply the most dramatic case. What we shall have in the assembly of the saints at the End of the Ages is a *joy that is total*, all-encompassing, all-resolving, all-reconciling, because there will be in heaven nothing to finitise it, nothing to confine it in limits. That is the life everlasting, of which we have now, thanks to the Holy Spirit, the first-fruits, another word for which is the 'down-payment'.

Wednesday of the Eighth Week of the Year (Years 1 and 2)

Our Lord had so much difficulty with this kingdom, kingship, Messiahship, business — people thinking he could be talking about a military takeover of the country — one wonders why he bothered with this cluster of ideas in the first place. If people really could suppose that when he taught the disciples to pray, 'Thy Kingdom come', he might mean, 'Restore the Jewish theocracy', would it not have been better to have avoided the word 'Kingdom' in the first place?

What is not always realized is that, unless over long centuries there had been the idea of the kingdom of Israel, no one would have understood that salvation doesn't come to us just as individuals. Salvation comes to us through a corporate society: through what we learn to call 'the Church', which is the first-fruits of the Kingdom, and through the final fulfillment of the Church in the City of God which is the Kingdom in its manifest completeness. Yet today's Gospel is a good example of the misunderstandings that could occur.

In St Mark's Gospel-book our Lord often cautions against making his Messiahship known. It was because he saw his kingship as inseparable from rejection and suffering. It wasn't appropriate to be proclaimed as King in Israel until his Passion had begun. He will be the mocked and rejected King, as described in the Book of Isaiah and some of the Psalms — the King who bears and atones for the sins of his people. St Mark is faithful to this understanding, as we see from today's text.

And so is the Church. Our hymns speak constantly if it. 'He reigns and triumphs from the Tree.' 'O kingly head surrounded, with mocking crown of thorns.' 'Look upon the crown of God, see what he is wearing.' 'His dying crimson, like a robe.' 'When I survey the wondrous Cross where the young Prince of glory died.' What are the implications for Christian kings and queens? What are the implications for all of us who by our Baptism and Confirmation have been given a share in the kingly dignity of the Redeemer?

Thursday of the Eighth Week of the Year (Years 1 and 2)

Bartimaeus ought to be a better known figure from the Gospels than he is. Not only has his cry to the Saviour on the dusty road been incorporated within the Jesus Prayer, perhaps the most popular devotion of the Church in Russia and other places in Eastern Europe. He has also given us a sterling example of discipleship in that, when his sight was restored, he immediately, so we read, 'followed him along the road'. Would that I had the same ready response (perhaps you can echo my reaction here) in thanksgiving for all the blessings my Saviour has given me—given us!

In a way it's just because Bartimaeus' reaction is so archetypal, so much setting the classic pattern for discipleship, that we don't remember his name distinctly. There are some people in the Gospels who figure for their own sake, because they carry out a role for which no one else can substitute. And there are some people in the Gospels who figure for exactly the opposite reason— because they have a profile which any of us can and should resemble. We can and should think of ourselves as stepping into their shoes.

I can see my way around this world through knowing—by sharing the faith of the Church—the plan of God for it. I have not been physically cured of blindness, but I have certainly been intellectually cured of it. What do I need, then, for a lifetime of grateful discipleship? This Gospel gives me a good hint. It comes in the voices from the crowd, 'Courage. Get up. He is calling you'.

Friday of the Eighth Week of the Year (Years 1 and 2)

In today's Gospel, our Lord works a miracle of destruction by withering a fig tree which had failed to produce fruit when it was needed. Of those modern scholars who aren't too embarrassed by the topic of miracle to look further into the matter, some are reserved about St Mark's reporting here. Would Jesus really have carried out a miracle of destruction? Perhaps this is only a parable he told which was later misremembered as an event. Certainly there was a related parable. But was the parable an echo of the event?

We have to beware of being sentimental about God. All the processes of nature are in his hands and these include not only the coming into being of things but also their passing out of being again. All processes—even destructive ones—can serve the purpose of his scheme.

Our Lord saw the fig tree, still flourishing, on his way into the Temple. The Temple authorities rejected his challenge and his claim. The withering of the tree, on his way out of the Temple again, is surely understood by the evangelist as a prophetic judgment, a judgment not on trees but on the Israelite priesthood of the day and its cult.

The cleansing of the Temple was also a destructive act, in the sense of an act that replaced order by chaos—tables were thrown about, seats upturned, bird-cages disturbed, without, we hope, too much damage to the pigeons or indeed to the furniture if it was well-crafted. He was breaking down a false order, an order that contradicted the divine purpose for the Temple: to be a lens that would concentrate the prayer of Israel and a magnet of absolute God-centredness that would draw the nations to itself. Of course it was too late for that on the clock of salvation history. But there remained the honour of God.

Another form sentimentalism can take in Christianity is the suppression, or at least the obfuscation, of conditions that are written into God's Covenant dealings with us. We are not told in the final sayings of this longish extract from the Gospel according to St Mark that all prayer is answered. We are told only that prayer made with a quality of faith that is absolutely pure is answered. We are not told that we shall be forgiven, whatever; we are told that we shall be forgiven if we ourselves forgive from the heart.

Saturday of the Eighth Week of the Year (Years 1 and 2)

We all know the old joke about the man who was asked whether he had stopped beating his wife. And it's true: there are some questions it's difficult to answer without getting yourself into a bind one way or the other. We can see why our Lord hesitated before answering the Pharisees' question, By what authority? Too hurried, too premature an appeal to his divine authority (he was in the Father and the Father was in him) would shock and probably alienate many of his hearers—and so instead he diverts their attention by reminding them that for very different reasons there are questions that *they* don't want to be put on the spot about either. Our Lord could only very gradually reveal his full claim, and the New Testament writings show people still coming to terms with it.

For us too in the later Church, if we are to be good apostles, we don't necessarily tell absolutely everything about the faith to simply everybody straightaway. The *Catechism* doesn't begin with transubstantiation and devotion to the Holy Souls. It begins with the foundations of faith and moves on in such a way that little by little people can build up the whole picture. This isn't Jesuitry. It's just good pedagogy. Blessed John Henry Newman called it the 'principle of reserve' and centuries before Newman St Basil had called it 'the economy of silence'.

Of course we want everyone to share the fullness of the faith, just as our Lord thirsted for them to know that the Father was in him reconciling the world to himself. But there is the wise proverb, *Festina lente*, 'Hurry slowly'.

THE NINTH WEEK OF THE YEAR

Monday of the Ninth Week of the Year (Years 1 and 2)

One of the first things the children of Israel noted when they finally reached the land of Canaan was how amazingly fertile it is. The lowlands at any rate were brimming over with fruit and grain. The Book of Numbers describes how spies were sent ahead to reconnoitre the land and there 'they lopped off a vine branch with a cluster of grapes, which two of them carried away on a pole'. And they tell the community, 'We went into the land to which you sent us. It does indeed flow with milk and honey—this [i. e. the bunch of grapes] is its produce.' Soon enough, 'the vine' or 'the vineyard' became a popular name for Israel. The next step is easy: the God of Israel is the Vinedresser or the Owner of the vineyard. 'Visit this vine and protect it', prays the Psalmist, 'the vine your right hand has planted'.

So far so good. But in the Old Testament, the actual 'visitations' that go on from God to Israel are by no means always enjoyable. Every time a prophet calls, God is visiting, and much of the energy of the prophets was devoted to telling Israel some unpleasant home truths. People like Jeremiah and Isaiah were great religious geniuses, but they were also uncomfortable people to have around, just because they called a spade a spade.

Not infrequently, human beings don't really want to have their sins taken away from them. Either they are too determined on malice, or they find the sins too enjoyable, or sins simply form part of a routine: even our neuroses, through their familiarity, can become a comfort. To be a prophet is, accordingly, to lie on a bed of nails.

The career of our Lord throws the conflictual possibilities of divine visitation into high relief. Though his preaching, in the simple words of the evangelist John, was 'the truth', it aroused sharp opposition. Precisely because it *was* the truth it did so. Men hate the light because their deeds are evil, as (once again) St John comments. Or shall we say at least that we prefer our moral and religious existence to be a bit of a muddle: that way, we don't have to ask ourselves too many hard questions.

In terms of Jesus' parable, it is not so surprising that the tenants, the children of Israel, would want to get rid of these embarrassing servants of the landowner, his servants the prophets. What is more surprising is that they should dare to lay hands on his only Son. But the owner of the vineyard gambles on a last call to reason. He makes himself vulnerable by risking the life of the son and heir. And, as we read, the tenants 'seized him and threw him out of the vineyard and killed him'.

Saying as much would still be possible if our Lord were simply the last and greatest of the prophets—the status Islam claims for Muhammad. It would still be a scandal and an outrage for a man to die because he told the truth. It would come into the category of crimes crying to heaven for vengeance. But for Christian faith Jesus is not simply a prophet, though he is also a prophet. It's not even enough to say he is the Son of God unless you go on to spell it out with the Creed and say, he is consubstantial with the Father, begotten from before all worlds, God from God, Light from Light—just to rub in the fact that we're not dealing here in metaphors.

In the nature which properly belongs to his divine person he is one substance with the Father. One who is God, who has taken human nature to himself in order to come to us: he it is who was seized and killed by men. For this reason a basic Christian attitude is astonishment, wonder, shock, a sense of dizziness and awe. God was so good that he became one of his own creatures to teach and save us, and he submitted to death at our hands as the means (be it noted!) not of our final condemnation but quite the opposite: as the means of atonement for evil and the way to bestow all good.

Monday of the Ninth Week of the Year (Year 1)

Today's reading from the Book of Tobit presents us with one of the reasons for being glad this book is included in the Canon of Scripture, and that is its advocacy of reverence for the bodies of the dead.

As Tobit shows, such reverence was developing in Judaism, partly owing to, and partly making possible, belief in the resurrection of the dead. The human dead are concrete evidence of the unfinished character of God's creation. In the words of the Neo-Marxist philosopher Theodor Adorno who was himself a secularized Jew: 'There is no justice without the resurrection of the dead'. It's no good simply wanting justice for those who happen to be alive now. Reverencing the bodies of the dead is the sign and symptom of an attitude of hope towards the prospect of their resurrection: the 'blessed hope' of an eventually just world.

What was embryonic in Judaism becomes fully mature in the Catholic Church. There are so many ways in which that finds expression: the fraternities for preparing the bodies of the dead for a dignified burial (these survived in Europe until modern times); the chantry chapels in churches great and small up and down the length of pre-Reformation England; the traditional aversion to cremation—a practice which the Church accepted, highly reluctantly, only when the civil authority began to require it on sanitary grounds; the mass visits to cemeteries on the vigil of All Soul's Day, and the lights lit at the graves as dusk falls—all of this is the final outworking of the conviction of the author of Tobit that it is meritorious to honour the remains of the dead.

One might add that it was greatly reinforced by today's Gospel. That the Son and heir, the everlasting Son of God whom the Father made heir to the whole universe, should himself have been a corpse, that the flesh assumed by the almighty Word was itself by human hands taken down from the Cross, anointed and entombed in the hope of the resurrection: this inevitably made a huge difference to the way the human cadavre is considered.

And if today we are faced in our hospitals and morgues with death sanitized, bureaucratized and rendered largely invisible, in this regard we find our society's ethos out of keeping with revelation, and thus out of keeping with the humanity whose destiny revelation is given so as to disclose.

Tuesday of the Ninth Week of the Year (Years 1 and 2)

'A man's rank means nothing to you': this is what representatives of the unholy alliance of Pharisees and Herodians thought it fitting to say to our Lord by way of prefacing their trick-question. No doubt it was a comment chosen to lead in to the crucial question of attitudes to Caesar. And yet it would hardly have been made unless it corresponded to something in Jesus' general demeanour and the impression he made.

Undue deference to people who hold some culturally, socially, politically, or religiously defined special status is not a very pleasing trait (that is a truism, because 'undue' here means 'unduly excessive'). On the other hand, mass democracies like our own are all too familiar with another unattractive quality: the desire to pull down those who have attained some such status, whether by good fortune or their own merits. How should we think of such matters, taking our cue, as always, from Scripture read in tradition?

The sources of revelation are not especially interested in rank, but they are very interested in roles. Our Lord himself, in this exchange with his opponents, recognized the role of the emperor, and the New Testament letters will follow his lead by praying for emperors and kings. One of the most basic assumptions of the entire biblical revelation is that throughout the history of salvation a drama is unfolding where a huge variety of people have parts to play. Indeed, all human beings have to be brought into the plot, given roles of some kind, if they are ever going to reach their final destiny. The roles people play in the human city are relevant to the ongoing drama, because the human city is called to prepare the way for the City of God. The roles people play in the Church community are—in a yet more obvious sense—relevant to the divine drama because the Church herself *is* the City of God—the Kingdom of God—in its initial phase.

A man's (or woman's) rank means nothing to God. But their roles mean a very great deal indeed.

Wednesday of the Ninth Week of the Year (Years 1 and 2)

In today's Gospel we hear from the lips of our Lord who, as God made man, was in a position to know, that the dead who live to God in the life of the Kingdom will be *isangeloi*, the equals of the angels, 'like the angels in heaven'. Both traditional Catholicism and Eastern Orthodoxy have sometimes been reproached for 'angelism': an essentially negative attitude towards this world and the earthier aspects of human society. So it is important to know how tradition has understood this interesting word.

Basically, it has been found to comprise two elements. First, the angelic life to which human beings are divinely called is a life of worship and praise: standing before the Father, redeemed by the Son, exulting in the Holy Spirit. Some people imagine the soul would become bored by such a diet, but this is faulty metaphysics. Our inclusion in the all-creative life which has made the universe and of which the universe is itself only a reflection: how could that possibly be boring?

Secondly, the angelic life is a life of single-minded or single-hearted concentration of energies. This is the rationale which St Paul gives in defence of celibacy: you will be more exclusively devoted to the Lord's service, and it is the root meaning of the word 'monk' in an important early Christian language, Syriac.

If we put together these two elements we get a good idea of why the Church has seen the monastic life as the highest state of life in the sense of being that condition of Christian life which most clearly anticipates the life of the final Kingdom of God. If today in our country many monastic communities, whether of men or of women, struggle to survive, we need to ask what that implies about the local church's consciousness of itself as Church, and how well it understands the relation of the world to that Kingdom.

Thursday of the Ninth Week of the Year (Years 1 and 2)

At first sight, today's Gospel seems characteristically modern. Our Lord meets someone who, though lacking conscious faith in him and his mission as the Only-begotten Son, nevertheless loves God and his neighbour, and Jesus tells him that he is more or less alright as he is. This would be a comforting interpretation for a Church tempted to replace mission by dialogue and to speak only those verities which disturb no one.

Perhaps, though, it is not so simple. First, the anonymous questioner is not said actually to love God with all his powers and his neighbour as himself, but, rather, to believe that these *are* the supreme commandments. That would mean, then, that the truths of Old Testament revelation he had made his own disposed his mind towards receiving the fresh revelation Jesus had to bring.

Secondly, if in fact our Lord's praise of this unknown Jew was based on Christ's own supernatural perception that the man actually lived in the way he spoke, then here we are faced with someone in whom grace has already worked a very unusual transformation. The ground of the will has been fundamentally transformed if someone really does love God with all their powers and their neighbour literally as themselves. To meet one such person in a long lifetime—to meet a living saint—would be unusual.

And lastly, Jesus does not say that his interrogator is *in* the Kingdom but that he is *near* the Kingdom. That might seem unsurprising because even disciples are taught to pray, 'Thy Kingdom come', which seems to imply it isn't here yet. For the New Testament witness as a whole, however, the *Our Father* only implies that the Kingdom is not *fully* here. That Kingdom is, however, already present in the life of the Church where the energies of the Holy Trinity are in act: actualizing the work of Christ for individual persons on the basis of faith and the sacraments of faith.

It is the holiness the saints develop by heroic deeds on the basis of these new resources that alone expands the human heart to the dimensions God wants for us.

Friday of the Ninth Week of the Year (Years 1 and 2)

In today's Gospel the crowds 'heard Jesus gladly'. What were they glad about?

Was it the sheer spiritual beauty of our Lord's teaching, how he showed all the strands of Old Testament expectation coming to a head in his own person—both the idea of a human liberator, the son of David, and also the notion of a direct divine involvement in the affairs of earth: one who, as divine, king David would have had to hail as 'Lord'. If so, the crowds were on to something of profound importance.

Alternatively, were they pleased by listening to someone who excelled in rabbinic modes of dispute, turning the Scriptures to his own purpose? In an age prior to the invention of media entertainment, quite possibly—and frankly that would be an irrelevance to Jesus' claims which have nothing at all to do with being brilliant or a genius. This is the salvation-historical equivalent of a cheap thrill.

So popularity in the New Testament is an ambiguous thing. And the same is true of the later Church. If aspects of the Church's teaching are well received by the general public or their modern tribune, the press, that may be owing to a happy convergence of divine truth and human wisdom. Or it may be for quite inappropriate reasons, as the rejection of other dimensions of the faith would attest.

Vox populi, vox Dei, the proverb runs. But a robust thinker has replied, *Vox populi crucifixit Jesum*: the voice of the people crucified Jesus.

Saturday of the Ninth Week of the Year (Years 1 and 2)

In this Gospel passage our Lord paints a slightly sick-making portrait of the scribes. The combination of strutting around like peacocks and greedily devouring the estates of widows is offputting indeed. Devout Pharisees were not, I take it, avaricious on a personal level, any more than were devout Sadducees when they sought to boost the contents of the Temple treasury. They wanted to augment the resources available to the Pharisee movement, which they saw as the proper means for the rejuvenation of Israel as a people faithful to the Lord. No doubt 'scribes'—lawyers—were involved in supporting both the Pharisee and the Sadducee connexion.

I remember my novice-master saying that the most likely form the leaven of the Scribes and Pharisees would take in a Religious Order is, with the Order's good in view, doing what one would never dream of doing for oneself—and he had in mind avariciousness for legacies. The same applies to monasteries, dioceses, and Church organizations of all kind, and cuts across the distinction of clergy and laity, for the latter may be even more energetic in these matters!

We have to balance two considerations. On the one hand, as was notoriously but not untruly remarked by a Curial archbishop, the Church cannot run on Hail Marys, and almsgiving—recognised since Old Testament times as a meritorious act and confirmed as such by our Lord—includes contributing to the common pot of the People of God. On the other hand, when pounds and pennies mount, those who deal in finance are liable to forget that all money is a condensed form of the life and labour of others, and for that reason requires great circumspection in its manipulation and use.

This is surely why the evangelist places in immediate proximity to Jesus' strictures on the scribes his commendation of the poor widow and her mite. She has dropped into the box the equivalent of her whole living—a moral equivalent to the value she places on her own life. Who would dare to trifle with such benefactors?

THE TENTH WEEK OF THE YEAR

Monday of the Tenth Week of the Year (Years 1 and 2)

Ought our morality to be the same as that of well-intentioned people generally? If morality is essentially reasonable—if to be ethical is to be reasonable in practice, to be rational in your actions, and so something common to all human beings, one might think so. And schools of moral theology have grown up in recent decades for which there is no distinctive Christian morality but only a different religious context in which to place the same basic human ethics shared by everybody. That is criticized by Blessed John Paul II in his great encyclical letter on the foundations of morals, *Veritatis splendor*.

In the Sermon on the Mount, our Lord tells the disciples it is not enough just to follow the example of good pagans. 'If you do no more than the Gentiles do, what profit is that to you?' It is of course possible that since the time of Jesus evangelical morality has worked its way into mainstream morality, so that what the Gentiles do now—in promulgating the United Nations' Declaration of Human Rights, say—is more Christian than what the Gentiles did then. But is that the whole story?

Today's Gospel indicates not. There is a difference in our judgment of what virtues should be paramount as we seek to put into practice our moral beliefs—whether those moral beliefs be entirely the same as other people's or, as seems more likely, significantly different from them.

In the Beatitudes our Lord describes the key qualities he wishes to arouse in disciples as poverty of spirit, humility, docility to the Word of God, a spirit of penitence, hungering and thirsting after justice, mercy, and purity of heart. These dispositions add up to quite a different picture of the moral personality from what we find in Greek ethics, for example, or in those societies where honour is the chief consideration, or where, as in our own society, the main virtues are tolerance and the willingness to criticize the consequences of actions. The qualities listed by Jesus are, as he presents them, the qualities needed for a Kingdom-centred life in the presence of God.

The difference doesn't just lie, therefore, in finding one sort of moral personality more pleasing than another. If we are Christians then we hold that only the pattern of virtues disclosed in the Gospel really prepares our personalities for the vision of God. All the other versions of the moral personality, despite their nobility in certain respects, must submit to Purgatory: they must be humbled and purified before they can be fully redeemed. Are those other versions also in us too? If so, we must work to convert not only our vices but also our virtues as well.

Tuesday of the Tenth Week of the Year (Years 1 and 2)

St Matthew's Gospel is traditionally regarded as the first to be written and if so then perhaps it was written originally in Aramaic, the language of our Lord. Both the priority of Matthew and internal evidence furnished by this Gospel-book suggest the author was writing for Christians who by and large were Jewish by race and sought to retain close connexions with their fellow-Jews outside the Church. When St Matthew transmits the saying, 'Men do not light a lamp and put it under a tub but on a stand and it gives light to all in the house', the 'house' both Matthew and his Master have in mind would be the House of Israel, composed in the time of the first evangelist of both Christian and non-Christian Jews. The first evangelist is keen that those for whom he is writing will give light to their own people.

For us, however, who are overwhelmingly Gentiles, the 'house' will mean the household of faith that is the Catholic Church. This Gospel tells us it is not enough for us simply to seek to be ourselves enlightened, to gain a full understanding, as individuals, of the light we have received in our Baptism. We must also seek to provide a light for other Christians: most immediately, for other Catholics. That involves the way we live as a Church at this particular time in history, with its need to communicate the spiritual sense of doctrine to those at risk from secularization. Now more than ever we must know our doctrine and express it not only in preaching and the Liturgy but also in our spirituality and in the way we relate to others.

But what about those who are outside the Church? The third evangelist, St Luke, has a rather different but complementary picture of the disciple shining with the light of God and he addresses this very question. He wrote his Gospel for Gentile Christians, those who, like the dedicatee of his Gospel-book, Theophilus, were pagans coming to faith from outside Israel. His version of our Lord's saying lends itself to their situation. 'No one after lighting a lamp puts it in a cellar or under a tub but on a stand that those who enter may see the light.' We notice the words. 'Those who enter…'. The lamp here is not placed in the middle of the living room but on a stand in the atrium, the entrance hall, so as to give light to people on their first contact with the household of faith.

This reminds us that it is not enough to keep fellow-Catholics, fellow-Christians, from lapsing. We also have a missionary duty to our non-believing fellow-citizens. We have to engineer some contact of minds with those who may perhaps be on the threshold of the house of Christ. We must be in the atrium, ready to meet them, and ready too to help them look at the world in the light of Christ.

Though our Lord has told us that we are to be the light of the world, fortunately enough he is himself *the* Light of the world, the light par excellence, or as we say in the Lenten acclamations, the King of everlasting Glory.

Wednesday of the Tenth Week of the Year (Year 1)

In today's Epistle St Paul compares the Old and New Covenants to the manifest advantage of the latter. The starting point is a comparison of two faces: the face of Moses, briefly shining with the divine glory from his mystical encounter with the Lord on Mount Sinai, and the Face of Christ, the incarnate Word from whose features we can read off the very character of God.

And from these two 'splendours', one of which far surpasses the other in magnitude, the apostle infers the surpassing nature of the new era of grace which follows on the making of the New and

Everlasting Covenant. For the manner in which the Holy Spirit is present among us now goes way beyond what Israel could have known. The Holy Spirit has always been the Spirit of the Father and the Son, but with the Incarnation and the Atonement he is now something further: he is the Spirit of Christ, who, in the wake of the Ascension and Pentecost, spreads Christlikeness wherever he goes. And that must mean, then, that he is now the Spirit of perfect reconciliation between God and man, the Spirit of forgiveness, the Spirit of justification, the Spirit of regeneration, the Spirit of a new life for us. Looking back from those world-changing events, Paul's fellow apostle John was inclined to say that in comparison with the springtime of the Spirit at Pentecost it was as though the Spirit had not previously existed. That is a piece of rhetorical exaggeration, but it makes an important point: the splendour of the New Covenant is best described not just as very much greater: it is best described as incomparably so.

Wednesday of the Tenth Week of the Year (Year 2)

Today's readings remind us of what we owe to the Old Testament, and therefore in a broad sense to the Jewish religion. The account of Elijah's contest with the prophets of Baal is a dramatic masterpiece. It would require a great Romantic painter like Géricault to do it justice. And its message is of course that the God of Israel is the only God, and is therefore the God of all people, the God of all the world.

To liberate people from false notions of religion and morality, from what the Bible calls 'idols', is true humanism. It is to pay them the compliment of treating them as valuable and important enough to be worth our going to the trouble of re-orienting them to the True and the Good. That is not to say I would necessarily subscribe to all of Elijah's methods!

Then in the Gospel we have our Lord reaffirming the validity of the main principles of Torah, the Ten Commandments, and their reflection in the ethical teaching of the prophets. Possibly he was referring to a much broader array of the Torah's legal commands, including for instance, the elaborate ceremonial requirements, though from what we know of the freedom with which the Messiah treated the ancillary features of the Law such as the food laws it doesn't seem especially likely.

Today, after a century or more when the idea of an objective morality has been increasingly discounted by the intellectually influential, we are well placed to understand why 'whoever relaxes the least of these commandments and teaches men so shall be called least in the Kingdom of heaven'. When people are told that morality is what you feel comfortable with, the hearers are the ones who suffer. On that principle, the wonderful potential our human nature was endowed with when it was made in the image of God will remain forever unused.

Thursday of the Tenth Week of the Year (Year 1)

In today's epistle St Paul pursues his thoughts about the splendour of our religion, the religion of the New Covenant, its marvellousness, which exceeds that of Judaism, the religion of the Old Law.

But do we really practise our religion as people who realize how glorious it is? In the way we think of it, refer to it, express it in worship, and in general live it, do we give the impression of people who, in the words of the hymn, are 'lost in wonder, love and praise'? We shalln't do so unless we let ourselves be fascinated by the beauty of God revealed in Jesus Christ, caught up by it into contemplation, letting it enter our hearts, our minds, our wills.

The Jews expressed their response to the lesser glory of the revelation to Moses by wearing prayer shawls over their heads in synagogue. We have not only Moses but Jesus Christ, the revealer of the Father's Face, the One of whom the Gospel says we 'saw his glory, the glory as of the Only-begotten of the Father, full of grace and truth'. It's a greater glory for us to be brought into living relation with the incarnate Son through his Spirit so as to be ushered into the very presence of the Father.

We are not called on to respond to God's glory by wearing special headgear to show our reverence. We are to respond to this more intimate and complete revelation of who God is by letting ourselves be changed, as Paul says, from one degree of glory to another—letting the beauty of God take hold of us in our very depths and made us by degrees into its images. What are its 'images'? Its 'images' are the saints.

Thursday of the Tenth Week of the Year (Year 2)

I suppose an unsympathetic critic would say today's Old Testament reading is about rainmaking, and so it is—but we have come to associate the word, rightly or wrongly, with shamans and witch-doctors. Possibly because anthropologists tend to have their academic chairs in the countries of Western Europe and North America where the falling of rain is rarely a problem, they have to make a special effort to guard against treating lightly the issue of naturally occurring water. When in the early twenty-first century we are told there is less water available in East Anglia now than there is currently in Ethiopia, we can expect in the future a change in this matter—at any rate in Cambridge. Certainly, litanic prayers for rain, often recited during specially organized processions, have been a feature of many places in traditional Christendom.

But important as rain is, the cloud 'no larger than a man's hand', spotted by Elijah's servant, has been more important still in the spiritual interpretation of this Scripture. A sign of change in the weather that takes keen insight to notice becomes a torrential and ongoing drenching, such that king Ahab has to take to his chariot before the tracks are churned up as mud or washed away. A sign is given that is only just detectible, but it is the harbinger of vast transformations to come. This is how we should understand the greatest of the divine works vis-à-vis creation: the redemption of the world.

The tiny fertilized ovum growing at first unnoticed in Mary's womb; the human figure of Jesus, bypassed by most historians in the Greco-Roman world: that was how it was at the beginning of the era of the Incarnation. And in our own lives, the little symptoms of grace we detect are in no different category. They're like the cloud no bigger than a man's hand: they portend enormous transformations which will change our being forever.

Friday of the Tenth Week of the Year (Years 1 and 2)

Everyone is aware, I suppose, of the attitude of the Catholic Church to divorce: if a genuine marriage-bond has been enacted, there may be separation for husband and wife in matters of bed and board but no further marriage is possible so long as the partners both live. What in St Matthew's Gospel might seem to be an exception to this rule ('except in the case of fornication') is understood by Catholic scholars as a reference to marriage within the forbidden degrees of kinship—broadly speaking, incestuous marriages—and therefore not examples of genuine marriage at all. So much is, as I say, commonly understood, but what is less well appreciated is its rationale.

There is, of course, a practical or, as the moral theologians say, a prudential aspect to this negative attitude to divorce. It is the experience of modern societies than once divorce is allowed as an exception it soon threatens to become the rule. Once one genuine marriage is dissolved, all other genuine marriages are that tiny bit shakier. And when the divorce rate begins to approach fifty per cent of all marriages, the situation becomes dire indeed. As soon as there is a difficulty within marriage the married will naturally begin to think not of its resolution but of escape from it through divorce.

But that is not the heart of the matter. The heart of the matter is given elsewhere in the New Testament, in St Paul's Letter to the Church at Ephesus. I'm almost inclined to say that the words of our Lord on divorce should not be cited liturgically unless they are accompanied by that Epistle, or at any rate by some composition—an introit, perhaps, or, in the Byzantine rite, a troparion—that springs from it. It has to do with the marriage covenant between God and humanity, between Christ and his Bride the Church. Of this covenant every genuine marriage is a sign. Not every monogamous and lifelong marriage is a sacramental sign of it, for not all those so married are baptized and living the sacramental life. But every monogamous, lifelong, marriage, is a sketch of the nuptial mystery which binds God who is the Lover of man to his partner who is humankind.

At the heart of the world is a mystery which combines intimacy with faithfulness. Once we loose the connexion between intimacy and faithfulness to that extent we weaken our hold on the central mystery of the world.

Saturday of the Tenth Week of the Year (Years 1 and 2)

If today in an English court of law we opted not to take the oath, the normal assumption of other participants would be that we were either atheists or agnostics. It was to satisfy atheists and agnostics that the option of affirming rather than swearing was introduced.

It has been usual not just for hundreds but for thousands of years that solemn depositions or agreements should be sealed by oath. The covenant treaties of the Ancient Near East from which the covenant theology of the Hebrew Bible drew its models all involved, for important human transactions, summoning the gods and the cosmic elements—heaven and earth—to witness what was happening. Israel followed their example, putting the name of the one true God in place of the humanly projected deities.

So what is happening in the Gospel? We don't really know the context of our Lord's words but it seems likely he was referring to the very *personal* nature of discipleship. To be a disciple, then as now, I have to take personal responsibility for my decision—my faith and the words and actions that follow from that faith. No one else, no public authority, can do this in my place. I can't take refuge in the common forms, however religious they may be. I have to give a personal Yes or No.

Of course, where discipleship is concerned, it is always to be Yes. St Paul says that Jesus Christ was not Yes and No, he was always Yes, because all the promises of God were fulfilled in him. In other words, he was always saying Yes to the Father. We have to make a personal engagement to let the grace of God scour out in us an ever more generous Yes, letting God take over ever more regions of our life and personality—even though his grace does this in a kind human way that is adapted to us, for in Jesus Christ God is, as the mediaevals liked to say, *humanissimus Salvator*, 'our most human Saviour'.

Saturday of the Tenth Week of the Year (Year 1)

'From now on we regard no one from a human point of view.' Assuming that can be regarded as a fair translation, this is for some people exactly what is wrong with religion. The rich texture of life, the dramatic play of character, is reduced to the one rather thin concept of my immortal soul and its eternal destiny, even if that destiny also involves the resurrection of the body.

How can we respond to this criticism? On the one hand, reality must come first. If there really is an everlasting aspect to my being, and if, in view of it, God has offered man friendship and adoptive sonship on terms he revealed through Christ and his Church, then this must be the most important truth about my life.

On the other hand, we can accept that religion is not the whole of life. To try and live for supernature without nature—to live by grace completely irrespective of creation—is to live as un-really as the Fool in the Psalter who says in his heart there is no God. Revealed religion is not meant to expel feeling for nature or human friendship or the various works of culture, but to place them in a new perspective.

THE ELEVENTH WEEK OF THE YEAR

Monday of the Eleventh Week of the Year (Year 1)

This is our Lord in his most Gandhian moment. Or should we say that it is the moment in which Gandhi most imitated our Lord? Of course it is only the latter that makes chronological sense—not to mention theological! Our Lord needed no pagan sages to instruct him, for he was in his own person the Wisdom of God. But pagan sages have learned from him thereafter.

What are we to make of the content of this Gospel of non-violence? As preached by our Lord, it is addressed to each disciple—that is, to disciples severally, not to a corporate body. Perhaps we can presume that disciples, when considered as parts of the corporate body that is the Church, would expect to hear from his lips the same message. But would that be true when disciples are considered as parts of the body politic that is the civil community?

Did the Saviour think that in a fallen world the order, however imperfect, represented by the emperor may not be defended against what he calls in this Gospel, in frank speech, 'wicked men'? We can of course distinguish between violence and the use of force. Policemen beating aggressive protesters with truncheons are engaged in violence; policemen carrying prone protesters away exemplify the use of force. But not all protesters are so accommodating as to lie down in the streets rather than hurl bricks or Molotov cocktails. Gandhi was fortunate that his opponent was the British Raj, which by and large boxed with gloves on, and not, let us say, the Third Reich.

In a Christian State the ethos of civil government will be set by the Gospel: and such a State will want corporate resistance by citizens to the wicked to take wherever possible the form of that seeming paradox, non-violent force.

Monday of the Eleventh Week of the Year (Year 2)

The story of Ahab and Jezebel the beginning of which is told in today's first reading, and the sayings of the Lord in the Gospel appointed for today: these two texts seem to point in very different directions. The prophet's intervention ends with dogs licking up the blood of corrupt and venal rulers. The words of Jesus in the Gospel end in praise of peacemakers and the meek.

Is this a case of the straight inversion of an Old Testament precept—an eye for an eye, a tooth for a tooth? Yes and no. Clearly there is a discernible change in attitudes to vengeance, a decisive shift towards the primacy of reconciliation. But there is also—and perhaps this is more fundamental—a change of strategy in how to subvert evil. Israel's notion of struggle with evil was largely physical—either her own hosts, supported by the Lord's mighty arm, or, alternatively, other peoples' armies would deal with those in the category of Public Enemy Number One, while as to private enemies, the sacral law of the Hebrew Bible functioned as Israel's criminal code with, ultimately, physical sanctions behind it.

In our Lord's teaching, on the other hand, there is a new awareness of the spiritual character of struggle with evil—of how evil inheres in will, how it is a use of freedom, and hence the great emphasis on the demonic when the New Testament is compared with the Old, and also the more subtle strategies for undermining evil of the sort we heard about in the extract read today.

Ultimately, this has to do not with a development of mentalities, such as social historians might study, but with the dogmatic mysteries of the Incarnation and the Atonement. The paradigm for struggle with evil is not now Israel in combat with Midian, where might could seem to be right. It is the Logos in human flesh sweating drops of blood in the olive garden by night—it is the Temptations, the Agony, the Descent into Hell, when One whose human will was Love almighty's created form confronted evil in its personal source and overcame its power.

Tuesday of the Eleventh Week of the Year (Years 1 and 2)

The paradoxes of the Sermon on the Mount find their best illustrations in the Holy Fools of Christendom, the 'fools for Christ's sake'
(in St Paul's phrase) of the Church.

Consider for example in the sixth century the Byzantine Symeon
Salos: an austere monastic saint who came in from the desert to
begin a life of apparent unbridled lunacy in the great cities of Syria,
not as a reaction against his former life but as its crown and
completion, sharing with the dregs of society in taverns and
brothels the terrible goodness of God he had experienced in silence
and solitude, scandalizing people by dancing with prostitutes.

Or in sixteenth century Rome St Philip Neri, shaving off the
beard from one half of his face, inviting ponderous Polish scholars
to his library only to show them joke-books, devoting himself to
the protection of the gypsies of Rome (generally hated then as now)
who would otherwise have been sent to be galley-slaves.

Exuberance and recklessness are the chief features of these
saints, and they are also the main qualities of the Sermon on the
Mount. And there is a reason for it: the source of all charity is the
mad love of God, the folly of God as Paul (again) calls it, the insane
love of God for us which took the Logos to the Cross and seeks to
remake us in poverty of spirit and simplicity of heart.

Wednesday of the Eleventh Week of the Year (Years 1 and 2)

Today's Gospel consists of our Lord's criticism of his Jewish
contemporaries for parading religion, whether that be by taking
pleasure in its external manifestations, or by using honorific
religious titles.

In Catholic circles in England today to repeat these assaults as
they stand would be to attack a straw man. There is very little of
it around; retreat into anonymity is more the spiritual problem we
face nowadays.

However, if things were different and penitential processions
were as common in Penge as they are in Palermo, we should still
need to ask how over the centuries the Church has actualized these
words of her Founder. Has she taken them as a prohibition on
ceremonies and titles, as she has taken literally his prohibition of

divorce? Or has she regarded them as an exhortation to live in a certain spirit, as with what he had to say about taking oaths?

Evidently, the latter is the case. She has taken the view that rites, ceremonies, and symbols go with human nature where the body manifests the soul, and they fit well with a religion of Incarnation where God took flesh on earth. How she understands our Lord's words is by stressing that our participation in pomp and ceremony does not put us right before God, which is not the task of human devised religious practices, however well-suited they may be to their subject-matter. It is the task of the grace of God in Jesus Christ our Lord.

And as to those titles, the Church has bestowed them liberally on her office-holders, on theologians and on spiritual guides—but always in terms of the relation of these people to God in Christ, the one Father, the one Master.

In these matters we have to trust the intuition expressed in her perennial tradition, that she knows what her Bridegroom was up to.

Thursday of the Eleventh Week of the Year (Years 1 and 2)

Today's Gospel contains the single most important prayer in Christendom. Officially, tradition calls it 'The Lord's Prayer': in Latin, *Oratio dominicalis*, in Greek *Proseuchê kyriakê*. But popularly Catholics know it as the 'Our Father', and apart from the convenience of this name there is a sound instinct behind it.

I suppose most people are aware how crucial the word 'Father' is as the distinctively Christian name for God. What is less recognized is the significance of the word 'our' which proceeds it, and *The Catechism of the Catholic Church* goes out of its way to look into it. One good reason why the Church has always preferred St Matthew's version of the Lord's Prayer to that found in St Luke's Gospel, is that the latter omits the word 'our', while the former keeps it.

The *Catechism* offers various reasons for giving 'our' special weight but two of them seem outstanding.

First, when we say 'our' Father we recognize that not only have we become God's people but that he has become, as the prophets foretold, truly 'our' God: our abiding possession. Through the blood of Christ in which the New and Everlasting Covenant was made, there is a mutually binding relation between us.

Secondly, according (again) to the *Catechism*, I cannot say 'our' Father and then think only of myself. To say 'Our Father' means at least implicitly bringing before God all those for whom he gave his Son. And this should make us want to intercede for others.

Saying 'Our Father' should, then, both reassure us (the first reason) and place a demand on us (the second reason), and this is typical of what the grace of God does.

Friday of the Eleventh Week of the Year (Years 1 and 2)

'The lamp of the body is the eye.' A beautiful metaphor, and we can ask ourselves how many sort of lamps are there and what light do they give.

There are, for instance, fluorescent lamps that shine a harsh even light over all they survey. There are arc-lamps that throw a beam into the far distance. There are electric torches that shine focussed light on particular objects near at hand. There are many other kinds of lamp but these few will serve to give us the idea.

Now our Lord is really thinking of course of our intellectual eye, or our spiritual eye, if you prefer. We are not to suppose that the incurably visually impaired lie outside the range of his counsel. He is talking about the light we must let into our souls, as we evaluate appropriately the world of God. His stress lies on the wholeness or health of our inner eye, without which there can only be distortion or, as he says, darkness. But I think it is permissible to consider the different qualities of such light we need for the interior life of a disciple.

And here the three sorts of lamp I mentioned can all serve our turn. We need the objectivity of neon-lighting. It is always a mistake when people say human beings cannot avoid being hopelessly subjective. We may not be able to be totally objective, but total objectivity should be one of our aims.

Our objectivity will not, however, be that of our unbelieving neighbour, because the light an arc-lamp casts is also needed for spiritual vision. As a result of our faith we can see further than others—as far as the Last Things and the Age to Come. This alters the perspective in which we observe the objective scene.

And lastly, there is the light of the torch, for seeing in a focussed way what is near yet obscure. The Scriptures and sacraments are as near as the nearest bookshop and the nearest church-building where the evangelical faith is celebrated in the apostolic succession. But they are obscured by a combination of prejudice and over-familiarity. We need a bright light to see their beautiful forms and glorious colours in all their radiance.

Saturday of the Eleventh Week of the Year (Years 1 and 2)

'Take no thought for the morrow', a precept it is easy to follow when you haven't got much to take thought about.

The dispossession of personal goods by the vow of religious poverty is one way the Christian tradition has found of inducing the kind of breezy, light-hearted, trust in Providence which this Gospel seems to commend. But even then various office-holders have to take thought for the future of the corporate possessions and take counsel from others in the institution. Fortune smiles or fails to smile on institutions as on individuals, and often what communities or individuals merit has little to do with success.

But this is precisely where our Lord's injunctions come into their own. To be equally ready for the best or the worst because one is content, basically, simply to be, as the flowers of the field simply are: this is a formula for a contentment, a happiness, which can flow at a deeper level than where the slings and arrows of outrageous fortune strike.

That is psychologically possible for us owing to the theological virtue of hope whose object is the promise of God to give us eternal life. As Chesterton saw, the person who believes in eternity can treat life like a child, like a fascinating game. Neither to win nor to lose is fundamentally serious because we are playing at an open door that leads into our home, the home that is another world.

THE TWELFTH WEEK OF THE YEAR

Monday of the Twelfth Week of the Year (Year 1)

So today Abram is told to pack up, move away from home, from his own country, and transfer himself bag and baggage to he knew not where. And this is in the service of a universal vocation, because all human beings are going to be blessed through him.

We are used, I imagine, to the term 'salvation history'. It stands for the whole story-line that runs through the history of the patriarchs, past Moses and Joshua and the history of Israel, after the Exile as well as before it, until it reaches St John the Baptist and our Lady and then Christ himself and the apostolic Church.

It begins here. It begins with the call of Abraham to leave his father's kindred and set out from Ur of the Chaldees on the journey that would end, ultimately, in the Incarnation of God in Jesus Christ. We don't always pause long enough to take note of Abraham's activities on his stage of that journey: how, for example, he creates local cult-centres by erecting altars to the Lord at various places en route.

This important narrative from the Book of Genesis is not just an argument for mobility in the service of God, and a call to humanity as a whole so unlimited that (we might conclude) it no longer has time for anything more local, particular, bounded, rooted in the earth of that or that place.

For as those cult-centres show, there is not only salvation history, there is also what we can call 'salvation geography'. There is a network of places where prayer has been valid by way of special response to divine revelation: places where graces appropriate to these encounters of God with humanity may still be offered at sanctuaries and shrines. Think of the Holy Land, of Jerusalem especially; and think too in the post-apostolic history of the Church of, for example, Rome, Iona, Compostella, Athos, Lourdes. And this is very human, for our history as human beings is bound up with plots of earth. We were never meant just to exemplify universal humanity, not even universal redeemed humanity. We were meant to become familiarized with portions of earth on a human scale, with feet on the ground.

Monday of the Twelfth Week of the Year (Year 2)

Assyria's conquest of the Kingdom of Israel—the Northern Kingdom, after the split-up of the country in the years after Solomon's death—was obviously a disaster of the first magnitude for the theologically minded historian to whom we owe the Second Book of Kings. He was aware that, in the reign of the next Assyrian ruler, a huge swathe of the Israelite population would suffer deportation. At any rate so far as Samaria was concerned, they would largely be replaced by aliens who had no part in the Covenants, no interest in the Promises of God.

He had his explanation: in the colourful expression of the prophets, it was the whoring of Israel after other gods: her tolerance of syncretism, and flagrant disobedience to revealed divine commands. It was not just that the rulers and populace of the Northern Kingdom failed to observe those commands. Rather, they despised them—an important distinction. It used to be said that Catholics who ignored the Church's law of abstinence and ate meat on Fridays committed mortal sin. Not by ignoring the canons could they do that; only by having contempt for what the canons represented—in the case of Friday abstinence, the honouring of the Passion of Christ.

The text of Kings is inspired Scripture, so I do not doubt that the historian's judgment is 'spot-on'. But we would not be wise if we extrapolated from it to similar sounding situations elsewhere. We should not assume that the English Reformation, say, was a punishment for the sins of the late mediaeval Church, or the French Revolution for those of its early modern Gallican successor. And what offences of the Orthodox in Russia could justify Bolshevism as fitting the punishment to the crime? But on the story line of the salvation history that leads up to Christ things are different. It was absolutely necessary—crucial for the world's salvation—that the ancient People of God should play their proper part in the preparation for the Messiah. But the North failed, and the torch was passed, reasonably and rightly, to the Southern Kingdom, to

Judah. In time Judah too would be conquered by pagans, but shortly after it happens the prophetic voice gives reassurance: this exile will be for purification, not the end of the road. 'Be comforted, be comforted, my people, says your God.'

Tuesday of the Twelfth Week of the Year (Years 1 and 2)

The gate of heaven is a narrow door. Only a few can squeeze through it. Only the spiritually slimmed down can manage it. That is one reason why we take the Christian life seriously, try to reform our morals, pray, frequent the sacraments. We are dieting, we are in training—that is the origin of the word 'asceticism'.

But if ascetics are Christian ascetics then they will want to take other people with them. The monastic call, for instance, a classic form of ascetic living in Christianity, has always entailed a task of intercession for other members of the Church, and indeed, for all human beings, great sinners included. The New Testament proclaims grace abounding, divine mercy outstripping all human estimates of how far it can go.

But in that case, what happens to the narrow door? We forget that though a narrow door slows entry it doesn't of itself prevent entry. There may only be few at any one time, but there may be very many times when few get through.

And this is the overall thrust of our tradition: the slimming down process can go on affecting people longer than we might imagine. We have a word for that—Purgatory—when the grace of God beyond all human calculation takes its time.

The call to asceticism is the Gospel call to be perfect. The doctrine of Purgatory is the Gospel reassurance that with God all things are possible—eventually.

Wednesday of the Twelfth Week of the Year (Years 1 and 2)

Here we have a Gospel which compares human living to fruit-bearing trees. It sounds very much like a message of 'live and let live': a Gospel that favours treating the moral personality of the individual as the only thing that really counts. So long as people are morally productive—kind, patient, benevolent, and so on— why worry about what their theoretical doctrine is?

The trouble is that wrong moral doctrine will always tend to undermine the moral personality of the individual just as assuredly it will undermine the moral good of society as a whole. We mustn't overlook that crucial phrase which opens this Gospel, 'Beware of false prophets'. Beware, namely, of teachers who falsify the fullness of truth about the human good in its dependence on the grace of God which Jesus Christ offers.

Through the atoning work of his Son, applied to us by the Holy Spirit, God offers his grace to us in a New and Everlasting Covenant which goes beyond the covenant with Moses—the covenant whose law is the Ten Commandments. At the same time, however, Christ also confirms that law: as he declares in St Matthew's Gospel, 'I have come not to abolish the law but to fulfil it'.

It is true that our religion is not a moralism: it goes beyond morals. It is about deification, union with God in everlasting life. And yet it always includes morals, because to be immoral is not to be more than human (which is what we are aiming at), but to be less than human.

'By their fruits you shall know them.' For the bad tree that means not only the fruits that our secular contemporaries already excoriate: judgmentalism, intolerance, lack of openness to others and the like. It means also the fruits that follow from rejection, distortion or misrepresentation of the fullness of moral truth. And that includes sins that, unlike those just mentioned, are not fashionable today; sins such as self-indulgence (unless it harms the planet), sexual laxity, indifference to religious claims.

By tracing the ill consequences for the life of a community called to be holy, we shall know when false prophets have arisen, whether they be celebrated but mistaken moralists or eminently forgettable pundits of the modern media. That is why we have to summon up all the resources of tradition to counter them, as Blessed John Paul II sought to do in his great encyclical on ethics, *Veritatis Splendor*.

Thursday of the Twelfth Week of the Year (Years 1 and 2)

The house built on a rock: when we hear these words we are inclined as Catholic Christians to think first and foremost of the Church herself, constructed as she is on the rock of Peter. But our Lord makes it plain he is speaking about our personal house, for each of us must have, as Origen of Alexandria expresses it, an 'ecclesiastical soul'. That does not mean that we should want to spend our leisure time (God forbid!) reading the London *Tablet*, or even the *Catholic Herald*. It means that each of us is called to be in his or her own personhood the Church in miniature, the Church in a single biography. There is to be the Church in me, the Church in you.

And as with the Church at large the foundation of our personal church is the virtue of faith. This is the point of our Lord's words here. What do we mean by 'faith'? We mean a firm adhesion of heart and mind to the truth which God has revealed since he is truth itself who can neither deceive nor be deceived. And perhaps we should add, where a foundation for our lives is concerned, that this will of course include a firm adhesion to the promises of God — something our Catechisms generally discuss under the heading of the virtue of hope.

The virtue of hope does not mean just hoping for the best, as likewise the virtue of faith does not mean believing what you'd like to be true. The promises of God are not in fact the future we might have chosen had it been up to us. They do not promise us a rose-garden in this world. But they do promise the share in his own wonderful life that his revelation holds out to us, and they tell us how it can never be lost by anything other than our rejection of him.

Friday of the Twelfth Week of the Year (Years 1 and 2)

About the time St Thomas Aquinas died and the University of Cambridge was getting going, the king of Ethiopia was vexed by the way Moslems were stopping pilgrims from visiting the Holy Places. So he had a replica of Jerusalem carved out of a mountainside at the place now called after him: Lalibela. You could go, as you still can, and see in symbol the river Jordan and the tombs of the patriarchs and the places of the Passion. It seems it has always been a draw for beggars from throughout the country and today is no exception.

The beggars include lepers. The lepers are rather obvious or become so when everyone takes off their shoes to visit the churches. Ordinary Ethiopians do not normally wear socks, so the lepers reveal an absence of toes. To Westerners for whom leprosy is curable this induces no fears. But in ancient times when no cure was known, it is understandable that lepers were made to carry and ring a small bell to warn others away.

The figure of the leper is so powerful that it has become a symbol. Someone is, we say, a moral leper. Usually, this is if he or she has done something of which the tabloid press or a volatile public opinion especially disapproves. But in principle, if you think about it, anyone who is capable of communicating vice could appropriately be made to carry and ring a leper's bell. Moral behaviour is largely learned by imitation and this is true of everything from sexual rapacity to displays of anger, from deviousness in personal relations to sharp business practice. Unfortunately, owing to original sin, no one falls totally outside thus category of a moral menace, which would rather defeat the purpose of the bells.

So it's a sick world, sick in body and soul, and this is why the Logos came in person to begin its healing. The Son and the Spirit, the two hands of the Father as St Irenaeus calls them, will go on at it until man has become, rather than spiritually or physically decaying, fully alive, to the glory of God.

Saturday of the Twelfth Week of the Year (Years 1 and 2)

It seems strange that today's Gospel should refer to Jesus as fulfilling Isaiah's prophecy that the Mediator would 'bear our diseases'. The Gospels don't record in fact that he was ever ill. However, for our sake he accepted what we might call a 'wasting of his being' which is analogous to sickness. His vulnerability, his passibility, his mortality, as indeed those of his mother, the immaculate Virgin: these cut across the strong presumption of Scripture that only those who are under the rule of sin fall under the law of death.

When, in order to raise up our world, the Word of God took a perfect humanity from Mary, there could be no presumption that this particular mother and child would fall like the rest of us under the regime of fear and anxiety, pain and dying, that governs a sick world. But they did. And it was by the special provision of the divine Trinity that this happened. The Son experienced that ultimate invasion of our personal integrity which is death, the disintegration of the human totality into what should never have been sundered, namely: body and soul—so as, by his victory over sin and death to reconstitute a perishing human nature in himself, something whose consequences we see already not only in his own Resurrection but also in the Assumption of Mary in the togetherness of body and soul.

What happened to our Lady is an anticipation of what will happen to the entire people of the redeemed. And so even now dread, sickness, dying, these have changed their meaning. They are no longer signs of man's inescapable fate, but materials for a spiritual warfare through which we reach out to our true destiny in the world of the Resurrection.

THE THIRTEENTH WEEK OF THE YEAR

Monday of the Thirteenth Week of the Year (Years 1 and 2)

The burial of the dead: one of the great pious duties of Judaism. One reason we have in our Canon of Scripture that charming tale, the Book of Tobit, is for its witness to the importance of this work of mercy. Let us notice in passing that it is burial and not the cremation of remains. The Book of Tobit enters the Canon around the time when Jews became more clearly convinced than before that the future of humanity lies in bodily resurrection—the only real consummation of the original creation there can be for human beings who are not just soul-life but embodied existence. Cremation, though the Church tolerates it, on the presumption that those who ask for it have good reasons, does not sit happily with the hope of resurrection. What sits happily is the return to the earth to await the resurrection of the bodies of the beloved—and the not so beloved too.

But in any case our Lord in this Gospel is not counselling the disciple to bury his dead father but to leave the carrying out of that duty to others. And yet the advice throws into high relief the gravity of the pious practice. This saying of Jesus has been recorded so as to show the extreme urgency of the apostolic imperative. It is because the duty of burying the dead is so onerous that our Lord's subordinating it to the needs of the Gospel of the Kingdom is so striking. Suppose the unnamed disciple had said, Could you give me a little longer, please, I need to finish mending my fishing-nets before I come along, there would hardly be any point in recording the conversation. Naturally, the Master would not regard this as a worthy reason for delay. But not to leave him time to bury his father—that only makes sense if the future of the world turns on his coming now. Perhaps it was St Peter he was talking to, or perhaps indeed it was Judas Iscariot. Both in their absolutely contrasting ways were necessary to the *dénouement* of the plot, to the working out of the divine plan.

And what about us? How highly do we rate the urgency of proclamation? We are not, thank goodness, the apostles. But we carry in our generation the task of presenting to the world the apostolic message, the apostolic Church.

Tuesday of the Thirteenth Week of the Year (Years 1 and 2)

What is faith? The English (or 'Penny') Catechism tells us it is a gift that enables us to believe without doubting whatever God has revealed, and to do so because God is truth itself, who can neither deceive nor be deceived. Faith gives real understanding, above all of God himself and his purposes for the world. It is the highest act of the intellect. Faith is something objective, and this is the main way in which, with backing from the Latin Fathers and the mediaeval doctors, Catholic theology in the West has largely presented it.

In something of a contrast, today's Gospel is dealing with faith in a more subjective sense, in terms of personal confidence: trust that one's life is in the hands of God, that one can rely on God's goodness.

The Church has not of course suppressed this Scripture. All Scripture informs the Church's teaching in some way. But for a number of centuries the trusting aspect of faith has usually been dealt with in catechisms under the heading of hope—the hope by which we have a firm trust in the promises of God, God's absolute reliability.

Hope or hoping faith is of obvious importance in our lives. In different ways we can come up against our limits, and seem to be, as we say, at our wit's ends, and then what we need is not usually sharper intelligence but simply more courage: something to happen to our heart and spirit more than to our mind. 'Save us or we perish.'

And yet faith cannot survive reduction to simply hope. That would concede too much to the popular misconception which says, faith is what you feel. One of our congregants said to me, 'Faith is in your heart', but then she added, and here was an important Catholic instinct asserting itself, 'and in your mind, of course'. Revelation is truth as well as goodness.

The two sides are well brought together by St Anselm who stressed that trusting faith operates precisely in the service of the faith that seeks understanding. To have the confidence to carry on exploring the truth of revelation I need a trusting faith in the ultimate coherence and validity of what God has spoken. If I don't see the point just now, I must submit to the authority of the Word of God who is personally Truth itself. But if, seeking in such a spirit, I come to understand, then, says Anselm, I experience a foretaste of the life of the heavenly Jerusalem when I shall know as I am known.

This is important for preachers, theologians and Christ's faithful generally: the goal of the Christian life, beyond the faith that assents and the faith that trusts, is everlasting joy.

Wednesday of the Thirteenth Week of the Year (Years 1 and 2)

There are two ways of responding to a reading like today's Gospel. One would be simply to accept that its thought is archaic, primitive, unusable: an example of how the uncreated Word expressed himself in terms of a culture much simpler and less enlightened than our own, and was content to be sufficiently understood there for his saving work to be recognized and passed on to us.

Here the enduring value of this Gospel would be as an illustration of God's condescension in Jesus Christ, how he stooped down to take on not only material poverty but intellectual poverty as well, even though in his own divine nature he had all the riches of the Father's mind and being.

Alternatively, we could try to make sense of the evangelist's own thought. A crucial concept here would be that of the demonic. The New Testament has no separated demonology: it has no interest in the history or internal relations of the evil angels for their own sake. Its demonology is part and parcel of its account of the world, since it sees the demonic as so implicated in ordinary events as to be almost impossible to disentangle.

Just as the principalities and powers who crucified Jesus are, according to St Paul, both political figures and angelic figures, so in the Gospels what distorts human healthiness is both the pathological and the demonic at the same time. Since we today use the idea of psychogenetic illness—illness that starts in the psyche and transfers itself to the body — we come within hailing distance of the evangelists here.

In St Matthew's version of the story, the demonic and the human are to co-exist, mixed in with each other like the wheat and tares of the parable, until their time. 'Have you come here to trouble us', Jesus is asked, 'before our time?'. At the end of history, the clarification of all causes given with the revelation of that hitherto hidden Person, the Holy Spirit, will involve the identification of the role of the evil angels in the sickness of the human condition. Meanwhile, in the manifestation of the Son in the midst of history, the liberating power of the God who makes man's cause his own is already at work.

Thursday of the Thirteenth Week of the Year (Years 1 and 2)

'This man is blaspheming.' Quite apart from the issue of who the person referred to as 'this man' really is (actually he is God, God made human), how do the scribes understand the idea of blasphemy they invoke against him? Seemingly, for them a blasphemy is when any act whose proper author is God is ascribed to an agent who is other than God even if such an agent might claim to be an intermediary, or a plenipotentiary, or a legate, a divine ambassador. What else, in different ways, in the Old Testament were prophets, priests and kings?

If we turn to the *Catechism of the Catholic Church* we find a more adequate notion of blasphemy than the one the scribes were working with. There we hear that blasphemy consists in 'uttering against God, inwardly or outwardly, words of hatred, reproach or defiance, in speaking ill of God, in failing in respect toward him in one's speech, in misusing God's name'. With reason, the Church considers blasphemy an offence against the second of the Ten Commandments: 'You shall not take the Name of the Lord your God in vain'. And the reason is that not just God's Name but God's very essence, which his Name indicates, is utterly worthy of all praise, since God is Goodness itself. There is something terribly wrong about hating God (even hating God a little bit), because there is something intrinsically awful about despising Goodness itself.

And if we reply that we are not sure that God is Goodness itself, then let us look again: look again at the God who humbled himself to come among us so as to take the weight of our accumulated evil on himself and in the process to give us the credit for our own emancipation since the One who offered this Sacrifice did so in our nature. He let us begin again—as a race and as individuals—with a new clean sheet, and in his loving kindness, whatever our backslidings, he lets us appeal to that credit again and again.

Friday of the Thirteenth Week of the Year (Years 1 and 2)

The Jews were very choosy about whom they ate with. I suppose we still are today. At formal dinners the host gives a certain amount of thought to the question of who will sit next to whom. That of course is largely a matter of who will find whom congenial company, whereas in the Bible the motivation was more strictly religious.

In Judaism all meals were affected by the memory of the sacred meals of the Hebrew Bible, beginning with the meal shared by the three angelic messengers with Abraham under the oak of Mamre, and the meal of Moses with the seventy elders at Sinai when they saw the Lord on a pavement of sapphire and 'did eat and drink'. The aura of those meals extended to all meals and meant you wanted to make sure that only those who observed the Torah and lived out the vocation of the holy nation were your table-companions.

The paradox of the New Testament is that although these boundaries between sacred and profane eating-companions are abolished by Jesus this is not in the name of a secularization of food, as we might be tempted to think nowadays. On the contrary, the boundary between sacred and profane table-companions could be abolished only because the One who in his own person is the embodiment of all holiness is now present. The feeling for holiness which the exclusion of sinners from table-fellowship was meant to develop has at last found its own perfect object, and so the ladder up which the Jews climbed to reach this point can be swept away.

The specifically Christian meal, the sacrificial meal instituted by the Lord Jesus, the Holy Eucharist, is essentially a meal for reconciled sinners, and the virtue that it generates is not, therefore, an habitual sensitivity to categories of clean and unclean persons. Rather, the meal-related common lesson taught by Holy Communion is the virtue of Christian hospitality, which is a readiness to see all human beings as guests of God himself. This super-sacred meal thus casts its shadow—a very benign shadow—over our other eating. When we bless food by saying grace at meal times this is not just to thank God for the gift of food but to remind ourselves of the Banquet of all the redeemed at the End of Ages which the Mass anticipates. *Ad mensam caelestem perducat nos Rex aeternae gloriae*: 'May the King of eternal glory lead us to his heavenly table'.

Saturday of the Thirteenth Week of the Year (Years 1 and 2)

Today's Gospel is in the first place a teaching about the use of fast and feast. Fasting and feasting are practices widespread in human religion. In serious religious practice, people treat religion not just as a set of interesting ideas but as an invitation to bring the body and also the body politic—the social body—into the sphere of the divine. My individual body, which is how I enter the world, and the social body, by which we interact to form the human world: these have be made godly. And what better way to do so than by a rhythm of eating and not eating?

It is by food that the individual body is sustained and it is by taking food together that the human community is sustained as well, whether this is the family around the table or a city or nation celebrating together at some festival time like the American Thanksgiving.

And in the same way, by abstaining from food, religious man gives out a signal that the individual and the society must somehow go beyond the ordinary means of life. The Muslim season of Ramadan and the Orthodox Lent in Ethiopia exemplify this.

In today's Gospel our Lord tells us that, for his disciples, all this is in the future to make sense in a new fashion. Henceforth, fasting and feasting will be in relation to him. It is only in Christ that the body and the body politic will be made godly, as we join our members to him in the Mystical Body of the Church where he is

Head. We feast because he has already in one sense brought us salvation and we have only to enjoy it. He has come as the Bridegroom, the God-man in whom the world and its divine Source and Goal are joined together. But we also fast because in another sense we still await the full manifestation of our Saviour for who he really is, and meanwhile must work out our salvation in fear and trembling, pummelling our bodies, as the apostle says, and offering up our sufferings to make good whatever is lacking in his Body the Church. His glorious Parousia is not yet at hand.

All this is a dizzy novelty that bursts the bounds of human religion as previously known. No wonder the Gospel concludes, new wine, new wineskins.

THE FOURTEENTH WEEK OF THE YEAR

Monday of the Fourteenth Week of the Year (Years 1 and 2)

Today's Gospel contains two of our Lord's most beautiful miracles. Like all the miracles in the Gospels, these accounts are given us not only because they are true, because the events happened, but also because in some way they sum up an aspect of revelation wider than themselves.

Take the miracle of the cure of the woman with a flow of blood, whom we call, by the name of her illness, the *Haemorhissa*. The tradition has been struck by the wider significance of the means of her cure: the *Haemorhissa*'s touching of the hem of Christ's garment. For many writers, this touching stands for our participation in the sacramental life of the Church. Christ clothes himself in the garments of the sacraments so that we too in our turn can touch him. Often our sacramental reception—I think especially here of our Eucharistic reception—is simply that: we touch him as he passes by.

We may be disappointed that we do not have the great graces of experiencing him intimately that some of the saints have been vouchsafed in Communion. But though desirable these are not necessary for the faith contact between him and us that sustains our life-journey. The goal of that journey looks beyond all sacraments. The Byzantine Liturgy prays after Communion that we may experience him more interiorly still in his Kingdom.

The healing of Jairus's daughter is another miracle that opens wide vistas on our faith. The tradition has picked up gratefully our Lord's description of the dead girl as sleeping. In the Roman Canon we pray for the faithful departed as those who 'sleep in the sleep of peace'. Likewise in tradition the Church in Purgatory has been called *Ecclesia dormiens*, the 'sleeping Church'. Despite or because of her belief in the immortality of the soul, the Church can call death a sleep. As psychologists assure us, sleep is not total unconsciousness. Sleep, as dreams show us, is consciousness working in a new way, a nighttime way, but still, nevertheless, working. In the Song of Songs, the Bride says, 'I sleep but my heart wakes'.

In the sleep of death our hearts will still be responsive. We shall be susceptible to the Lord's healing grace while he visits the soul to calm it and strengthen it as it works through its conflicts and exposes whatever is still unredeemed in itself to the sunshine of God's transforming power.

'When I awake', says the Psalmist, 'I shall be filled with the sight of your glory.' May he take us by the hand and raise us up body and soul into the endless life of his new creation.

Tuesday of the Fourteenth Week of the Year (Years 1 and 2)

'Sheep without a shepherd', that is how we seemed to the Word incarnate when he entered our world. His remedy was the sending of labourers, and though he abandoned the simile of sheep and adopted the metaphor of a harvest, he evidently meant, the Father should send shepherds after his own heart.

Whatever our situation in life, we can all do a spot of shepherding from time to time. Shepherding is not restricted to those we call the 'pastors of the Church', the pope supreme among them. But to guide people as good shepherds we have to know the moral law and the programme of human salvation revealed by God. We can't get by just on common sense spiced up with occasional moments of intuition. Much less can we be good shepherds if we have put our money on non-directive counselling.

But though shepherding is not restricted to the Church's pastors, those pastors have a notable responsibility for it—especially if they are parish priests or missionaries entrusted with the foundation and development of new churches.

In the contemporary period, there can be all kinds of seemingly good reasons for not taking the shepherding role too seriously. Surely parish priests must respect the personal consciences of members of the faithful, and recognise the variety of charisms the Holy Spirit has given them? Surely the missionary must respect the existing cultures of the people or peoples to whom he brings the Gospel, and the values already relevant to salvation that those cultures may contain?

And that is quite apart from the perfectly normal human desire not to be thought heavy-handed or a bully, someone who hectors or harangues, but, on the contrary, to be, if at all possible, esteemed and liked by all men (and women). It is always right to seek to avoid being an authoritarian. But to sacrifice, to that end, being authoritative is a different matter altogether—and of no service to sheep who need a shepherd.

At the end of the day the pastors of the Church will not be judged on their universal appeal, but on how they have shepherded the flock.

Wednesday of the Fourteenth Week of the Year (Years 1 and 2)

The names of the apostles are listed in all three Synoptic Gospels. Going through a list of names doesn't normally make for enjoyable reading. So why are they there?

Surely it's for the same reason that, from early on in the Church's history, lists of bishops were drawn up to record who succeeded whom in the major sees—more especially, the apostolically founded sees. It's a way of registering that we have reliable knowledge about Jesus Christ because we know the names of the people who handed down the Jesus tradition.

In modern times, there have been many attempts to separate our Lord from his community on the part of scholars who are hostile to the Church or lukewarm about her or who want to stake out a claim to academic territory that is independent of the Church. They tend to pooh-pooh this idea, the idea that through the apostolic tradition we have reliable access to what Jesus was about. Instead, or so some of them say, we have to go back behind the early Church and underneath the New Testament, to root around among supposed sources for the existing texts until eventually we uncover an allegedly more original version—which could be anything from 'Jesus the Wandering Philosopher' to 'Jesus the Revolutionary' or even 'Jesus the Magician'. That there are so many versions of the 'real Jesus' shows us how hopeless their methods are.

Over against this misplaced ingenuity we have the plain testimony of the ancient record: 'The names of the apostles are these'. The message of these simple sober words is to trust the apostolic Church.

Thursday of the Fourteenth Week of the Year (Years 1 and 2)

The doctrine of Providence would seem to be a consoling one. It tells us that our lives are in God's hands so all shall be well and all manner of thing shall be well. But the version of it in today's Gospel brings us up with a start.

The apostles are to arrive in a given town or household to give people a chance of salvation—a chance in the sense of *one* chance. That chance will be people's providential opportunity, and woe betide them if they fail to rise to it. As they hear the Gospel preached, opportunity knocks, and if they don't open the door, opportunity passes by.

What we sometimes don't realize is: Providence is not only blessing; it is also judgment. Just because everything is in God's hand, God's will is in the course of being presented to us in all the moments, great or small, of life. The chances we are given are circumstantial: each has its time, its season. Each of us is offered salvation through the particularities of our own lives and if God knows how to arrange that infinitely better than we do, we have to seize our opportunities for repentance, for sanctification, for growth in virtue, as they come.

The world is good, we might say, not because everything in it is pleasant (it isn't) but because everything in it is opportune. This is a bracing doctrine, a truth to make us alert, on our toes, a truth to energise us, to inoculate us against boredom and wasting time, and so a truth we can really live by.

Friday of the Fourteenth Week of the Year (Years 1 and 2)

In today's Gospel our Lord tells the disciples at the end of a pretty serious talking-to that 'they will not have gone through all the towns of Israel before the Son of Man comes'. Our Lord uses the title 'Son of Man' to refer to his eschatological coming, his final and definitive advent on the scene of salvation geography. But in that case, surely he was mistaken about the salvation chronology concerned?

Not so. We recall the context. He is addressing the disciples as he sends them out to test public opinion roughly in the middle of his ministry. But he is already looking ahead to their wider apostolic mission after his demise. During the public ministry they were not targeting the Gentiles, nor were they likely to be troublesome enough to bother governors and kings. So you see what he is doing. He is telescoping time. He is saying that the apostolic mission will not be exhausted before his glorious Parousia, but he is fusing that far off perception with one that is to hand.

That shouldn't surprise us if the Church is right about his identity. He is the Word incarnate. His human mind was able to draw on a divine perspective on events when that was appropriate. So he looks ahead, and sees the present mission of the disciples through that lens.

His coming again: this is a wonderful theme for our meditation. Though ultimately it means the Second Coming, it has preparatory modes and phases. The mystery of Pentecost makes possible a certain 'coming again', when he returns to the disciples in the Holy Spirit, more deeply theirs, for deeply *for* them, than ever before. And this continues. He makes his advent in our souls, as we recall in the liturgical seasons we call 'Advent', which teaches us how at all times we should be ready to receive him.

But that spiritual coming is only the first instalment of his new presence to the world. He will come in glory, and that is world-shaking. The hymn says, 'Heaven and earth shall flee again when he comes to reign.' That means: a transformation in the cosmos (heaven) and in society (earth). Our Lord's presence in our souls is not something private to us that we hug to ourselves. It is the beginning of a revolutionary change in all creation. That is why we should nurture it within us and the virtues it calls for and makes possible, so that we shall be fit for the new heavens and the new earth.

Saturday of the Fourteenth Week of the Year (Year 1)

'Fear him who can destroy both body and soul in hell.' Hell-fire sermons, drumming the fear of hell into people: these are supposed to be cast-offs of unreconstructed Catholicism of the worst variety.

But here they are on the lips of our blessed Lord. What is going on?

The first thing that is happening is a reality-check. Is it possible for people, by abuse of their own freedom, to make of their lives a living negation of goodness and so of God? I'm afraid that *is* possible, if one really puts one's mind to it. Life can be made an ego-trip whose maxim is 'To hell with everyone' — and in a far less amusing context than the banner containing these words, held aloft by inhabitants of Olympus about to visit Hades, in a theatre production of Offenbach's *Orpheus in the Underworld*. Can we imagine people who say, not necessarily in so many words, but in their actions, 'Evil, be thou my good'? I'm sorry to say, we can. Are there moods in which 'To hell with everyone' and 'Evil, be thou my good' sum up my own state of mind, heart and emotions? Quite simply: Yes, there are. There is nothing in my psychological make-up that guarantees I shall not, in the right — which is to say, the wrong — circumstances, be hellish myself. Is it conceivable, then, that I could make of myself someone for whom goodness, and therefore God, was absolutely repugnant? Yes, it is.

The further question at once arises from these, How could the Word of God say of himself 'I am the Truth' if he failed to advert to this frightening possibility?

The second thing that is happening in this Gospel-passage is, however, a new look at the fear of God. The God of Jesus is our *Father*, a word which should connote all the tenderness the Son gave it in his own special name for him, *Abba*. He is the 'dear Father' whose Providence comprehends everything about us, whose caring about us requires hyperbole to spell out: those 'hundreds of sparrows'. What Jesus commends, then, is total confidence in the goodness of the Father combined with an acute sense of our own negative possibilities. The Father will do everything for us, but scarcely without us, and certainly not over against us. There can be a radical mismatch between the Father's care and my own response. That is why ultimate disowning remains on the cards.

Saturday of the Fourteenth Week of the Year (Year 2)

'Blessed are the pure in heart', says Jesus in the Beatitudes, 'for they shall see God'. That saying has its most obvious reference to the vision of God for people who, after death, are totally redeemed or, as we say, 'in Heaven'. But today's first reading raises the question, Is there a sense in which someone can see God *now*?

Scripture says, Yes, there is, and the classical theologian of the Western church, St Thomas, seeks to explain how in terms of God infusing—pouring—into the minds of certain believers mental images which give real access to God's own being. 'I saw the Lord', writes the prophet Isaiah, 'sitting upon a throne high and lifted up, and his train [the angels] filled the temple [the temple not only of Zion but of the cosmos].' On the basis of that vision, Isaiah went on to set down verbal images of God as a sovereign Lord, at once dreadful and marvellous, his glory so overwhelming that the whole world—symbolized by the Temple which was designed to have cosmic resonances—is filled with his presence.

One thing Israel and the Church did and do in presenting this text to us as part of the Canon of Scripture is to assure us that Isaiah's experience and the lesson he drew from it remains permanently valid, that his image of God will never become *passé*. The wonderful, terrible God of Isaiah remains the God of Jesus, as we discover in today's Gospel. Jesus' God watches caringly over sparrows and receding hairlines. Yet he is also the One who can cast body and soul into Hell.

This combination of fearfulness and attractiveness is something of a biblical test for all images of God: all claims to have visionary experience of God and in that sense to have 'seen God'. It's essential to the total revealed image of God and it calls for an appropriate response for us. That is the response the Latin Fathers call *timor filialis*, 'filial fear': a deep reverence, hence the word 'fear', but the kind of fear or reverence that is given by those secure in the knowledge of being loved 'filially', as sons and daughters.

THE FIFTEENTH WEEK OF THE YEAR

Monday of the Fifteenth Week of the Year (Years 1 and 2)

One of the titles given the Messiah in Scripture and tradition is 'Prince of Peace'. So it comes as a shock to find Jesus apparently repudiating the notion that peace is part of his programme. 'I have come not to bring peace but a sword.' The first half of today's Gospel is dedicated to the essential divisiveness of his revelation and the conflict it will inevitably stir—focusing on the family, for the family is the most basic social group and can thus stand for society as a whole.

We cannot get away from this. What we carry—as his disciples, as the Church's faithful—is a new revelation of truth, goodness and beauty, and therefore we have through Jesus Christ new criteria for judging human affairs, criteria by which we sometimes find ourselves forced to say that what others take to be truth is error (or at least very one-sided truth), what they regard as good is actually vicious (or at least second-best), what they deem attractive may be spiritually hideous (or at least deformed).

This makes life burdensome. It would be much easier just to be non-committal in all these areas and 'affirm' everyone in their particular preferences and choices. The mission laid on us by Christ does not make for a quiet life. We are out of kilter with our neigbours, and to deny this would only be—in the words of Jeremiah—to cry 'peace, peace' where there is no peace. Our faith is necessarily disturbing, not least to ourselves.

When the definitive truth, goodness, beauty of God appear in this world in Jesus Christ we can't rest easy with anything less. There's no going back now for 'he who does not take up his cross and follow me is not worthy of me'. There is a peace which the Son of Man brings, but it is a peace ahead of us and not behind us.

Monday of the Fifteenth Week of the Year (Year 2)

The oracle of Isaiah we just heard has been subject to rather a lot of abusive interpretation. It is one of the main planks on which is built that contrast between worship on the one hand, social action on the other, so dear to the political activists of modern Christianity.

The supposed conflict between priests and prophets has little basis in the Hebrew Bible. Priests were teachers of the Torah, prophets were involved in the cult. Priests and prophets were mutually enabling elements of the same religion. In that context, we should interpret Isaiah's assault on the cultus as an attack on the substitution of sacrificial worship for ethical effort—a substitution which is aberrant even in the cult's own terms since in large part Israel's worship was a symbolic reparation for sins and offences.

What is the case, however, is that we find in the Old Testament a growing awareness of what we can call the 'inwardness' of sacrifice—an awareness of the sacrifice of the heart, which is a sacrifice expressed in outward worship and to some extent made possible by it.

Under the New Covenant, the Sacrifice of Christ on Calvary is both the perfect visible, outward, homage of man to the Father and the perfect invisible, inward, alignment of human subjectivity with God. The union of the two is summed up in the single word 'charity' which is both outer and inner, social and personal.

The sacrament of the Sacrifice of Christ is the Holy Eucharist. The Eucharist, then, should be the last place where people play off exterior versus interior, social against personal, political against devotional, prophetic against pious. It is the heart of Christ laid open to the world for the world's healing and exaltation in all these dimensions.

Tuesday of the Fifteenth Week of the Year (Years 1 and 2)

All the towns addressed in today's rather terrible Gospel are situated within the 'evangelical triangle'—that's inside the three-sided area, only a few miles across in any direction, where the bulk of our Lord's Galilean ministry was located, on the northern side of the Sea of Galilee.

His words are a pretty damning indictment of their inhabitants, but we don't know the exact circumstances. Presumably it was the sort of thing reported elsewhere in the Gospels where people ask whether Satan could be behind Jesus' actions—the unforgivable sin or sin against the Holy Ghost is to take actions which flow directly from the divine goodness and ascribe them to wickedness.

Our Lord goes on to invoke the wrath of God on these cities, and even allowing for the hyperbole beloved of Semitic peoples it's plain he thinks they would rightly be the object of divine punishment. Some modern Christians will have no truck with this sort of thing. For them the wrath of God—the consequence of the justice of God as it encounters human sin—should be written out of the plot altogether.

But in the New Testament the mercy of God is altogether wonderful precisely because the justice of God is also steadfastly maintained. God will be, we hope, merciful to people because he has freely allowed mercy to become the way he exercises his justice, thanks to the atoning work of his Son. Jesus did not stop at denouncing evil. He took it vicariously on himself in the Crucifixion and in his blood the sins of Chorazin and Bethsaida, and all other places for that matter, can be washed away.

The *Dies Irae*, the Sequence of the old Latin Requiem, gets it right: first the cry of awestruck horror at the purity of the divine righteousness—*Rex tremendae majestatis*, 'King of fearful majesty', and then the plea to the divine mercy—*Salva me, fons pietatis*, 'Fount of love, grant me salvation'. The composer Verdi, by making this text the high point of his setting of the Requiem, may not have been a Christian but he understood what true Christianity was.

Tuesday of the Fifteenth Week of the Year (Year 1)

Today's readings provide three snapshots, two of Moses, one of Jesus.

From the Moses sequence we have two word-pictures: the infancy of Moses and then, following straight from it, the damaging episode when as a grown man he committed manslaughter against an Egyptian. The mercy shown him as a baby by an Egyptian princess did not stay his hand when he saw an Israelite maltreated, and the manslaughter hardly displays him yet as the 'meekest of men' as the Pentateuch will later call him. Evidently, the adult Moses subsequently developed, morally and spiritually.

That is the theme of the fourth century Greek Father St Gregory of Nyssa in his treatise *The Life of Moses*. It centres on the increasing demands made of Israel's champion, notably at Sinai, and suggests how in their course he was purified and sanctified—though not in a way that left no room for further development. Indeed, Gregory makes Moses the model for what he calls 'stretching forward', an attitude of always aspiring to move onward and upward, seeking to know and love God more: an attitude to which God responds by creating in us an ever increasing capacity for knowing and loving him. And so it goes on, right into eternity.

There is a striking contrast here with our Lord. Nowhere in the Gospels is there the slightest hint of this sort of development where someone is gradually purified, made holy, and launched on an adventure of unending spiritual growth. The scene portrayed today is an angry one, it is true. But it is the sort of righteous anger the orthodox tradition has saluted in Jesus, not deplored: the sort that, as at the Cleansing of the Temple, embodies the ardent justice of God.

This difference is no literary accident. For St Matthew, Jesus is the new Moses but that means he is the unheard of super-fulfillment of what Moses represented. 'Unheard of'? Certainly! He is not just another biblical saint, gradually shaped by the divine holiness. The holiness of God doesn't 'shape' our Lord's human personality—his human mind and heart; rather, it constitutes that personality from the first moment of his conception. For the faith of the Church, our Lord possesses his human personality—his mind and heart—only *in* the divine Person of the Word. The divine holiness was always energizing his humanity at full throttle. The mighty works that he did draw attention to the far mightier work that he is. If we have a good chance to glimpse who he really is and reject it, this is shocking: the real scandal of the cities that spurned him.

In the Church, which is the true evangelical triangle, anyone can learn that the heart of Jesus is the heart of God, his involvement with us the more-than-human love that, as Dante says, 'moves the sun and the other stars'.

Wednesday of the Fifteenth Week of the Year (Years 1 and 2)

In today's Gospel, our Lord thanks the Father for revealing the mysteries of the Kingdom not to the wise and understanding but to mere babes. When we think of the theological libraries of the world, the intricacies of modern exegesis, or the metaphysical claims of dogmatic theology, we may well wonder what he meant. Either, it would seem, the revelation *was* made to the wise and understanding, or it was not actually made at all.

But in fact the Church holds that divine revelation can be put into a simple catechism and conveyed via homely analogies to peasants or children, since the human mind was made to receive it, and in receiving it is brought to its own fulfilment—at whatever level of sophistication (or the lack of it) the mind works.

But there is also a deeper sense in which the revelation is to babes. Doctrine is not philosophy. To grasp what God is saying to us demands spiritual experience, ascetic effort, participation in worship. That is what Moses discovered at the Burning Bush, where he needed to uncover his feet and adore before he could receive the revealed Name of God. To put it in more specifically Christian terms: in the life of faith our fallen minds must be nailed to the wood of the Cross and raised from the tomb to new life, restored to the image of God. But for such growth in understanding to be possible, there must be a fundamental childlikeness—childlikeness in receptivity.

That comes across in another saying by Jesus: 'Unless you become as little children, you will not enter the Kingdom of heaven.'

Thursday of the Fifteenth Week of the Year (Years 1 and 2)

In the opening chapter of his Gospel-book St Matthew has already told us what the name 'Jesus' *denotes*. It denotes 'He [God] will save his people from their sins'. But not till now, not till the eleventh chapter of Matthew, do we really hear what the Name of Jesus *connotes*: that is, what its further implications are.

The hymn on the Holy Name of Jesus ascribed to St Bernard, behind which lies the Gospel-reading for today, sums up those connotations for us. 'Jesus!—the very thought is sweet!/ In that dear Name all heart-joys meet.' The yoke of Christ, the New Law, which the Jesus of St Matthew promulgates from the New Sinai in the Sermon on the Mount is, by our Lord's own admission here, repose, ease, rest.

What, we say, can this be the law we hear about in the Church's moral teachings with all their demands on us? These are the teachings that, so the media tell us, are unrealistic, inhuman, even cruel.

As we know from ordinary experience, many things we would otherwise avoid as too arduous or at least bothersome are not only possible but easy and even attractive if they are done for someone we love. As if by magic. Of course in the case in question, it isn't really magic, it's grace. 'Jesu, thou sweetness, pure and blest,/ Truth's fountain, Light of souls distrest,/ Surpassing all that heart requires,/Exceeding all that soul desires!/… /Alone who hath thee in his heart/ Knows, love of Jesus, what thou art.'

Friday of the Fifteenth Week of the Year (Years 1 and 2)

Today's Gospel sounds like our Lord cocking a snook at the Sabbath and, despite the reference to king David, setting out to subvert Jewish tradition in the name of practical convenience. Such an interpretation would be both trivializing and anachronistic. It was not a matter of liberalizing the Sunday (or, as then, Saturday) trading laws to make life a little bit easier if also less interestingly differentiated. The climax of the story, after all, is the proclamation of the Son of Man's lordship over the Sabbath: a claim that, as God's viceroy, Jesus has authority to suspend, modify, or re-apply the Sabbath law in view of the object of that law which was to enjoy creation in union with God's own 'resting', his contemplation of his creative work.

The symbolic resonances of Jesus' action extend a long way. Rather like the water turned into wine at Cana, if on a much smaller scale, the plucked ears of the Sabbath cornfield tell of the new dispensation of grace which the Son is going to bring into the world. The Old Covenant was already a work of grace, but now there is to be grace abounding and super-abounding. The message is not just human liberation, it is divine liberality.

Saturday of the Fifteenth Week of the Year (Years 1 and 2)

Today's Gospel contains a very strong contrast—whether intended or accidental—between the Pharisees who take counsel to destroy Jesus and Jesus himself who heals those who would be helped by him. Healing and destroying are certainly very different activities.

Healing is so much the characteristic activity of the God revealed in Jesus Christ that one of the chief titles we give him is 'The Saviour', One who saves or salves, and the word for the typical effect of his action is *salus*: health for soul and body.

Destroying, on the other hand, does not provide, in either Judaism or Christianity, a divine title—unlike in some versions of Vaishnaivite Hinduism where 'God the Destroyer' is a recognized formulation. It is of course true that the world God keeps in existence is one where things are constantly passing out of existence as well as coming into it. Rhododendrons, fruit-flies, even companionate cats, are subject to this law. But that is not to say that God is a God who exults in the annihilation of beings that otherwise would continue to exist.

Hell is not of course annihilation but we might still want to ask how it is congruent with the work of a healing God. Well, our Lord healed those who would let themselves be healed. The mercies of God surround even those who prefer a negative destiny. God permits them to have their own way since as their Creator he shared out with them his freedom. The possibility of self-damnation is a testimony to the dignity of man, not to the destructiveness of God. Dante put over the entrance to the inferno in his *Divine Comedy* a notice to the effect that not only 'the divine power' and 'the highest wisdom', but also 'the primal Love' made that place or condition.

THE SIXTEENTH WEEK OF THE YEAR

Monday of the Sixteenth Week of the Year (Years 1 and 2)

The modern media find it difficult to work out a line on Jesus Christ. In fairness to them, it must be admitted that the question has been getting more complicated within Christianity itself over the last two hundred years. What is often forgotten is a simple point in basic philosophy. To see something or someone aright you need to bring along an appropriate set of presuppositions, presuppositions that facilitate, or at least don't disable, the interpretation of the data.

In the case of Jesus Christ those presuppositions, as worked out during the first centuries of the Common Era, are that he had received the divine nature from God, the Father, and human nature from his mother, Mary, and humbly accepted that these two natures were intimately and yet without the least confusion conjoined in his own Person. Using those presuppositions as a lens, so to speak, the materials provided in the Gospels arrange themselves into an intelligible pattern. Suppress them, take the resultant framework of interpretation away, and the data become a tangle of conflicting texts from which the observer can draw no clear concept. Insofar as they continue to retain interest they become a quarry for all kinds of weird and wonderful exegetical theses, each contradictory of the others, and none winning anything like a consensus status among the guild of professional scholars. So it's hardly surprising that Jesus has become an elusive, vague and almost unidentifiable figure.

Come, you may say, is it as bad as that? Most people if stopped on the street for a survey would surely tick a box that said, 'Jesus was a very good man'. Not necessarily important, at any rate not important for us, but good: oh yes, undoubtedly.

Interestingly, the holy Gospels take almost exactly the opposite view. They show Jesus describing himself, as in today's passage, by using the Greek construction *pleion* plus the genitive, which means 'greater than'. He is the One who is greater than the prophets, greater than the greatest kings and sages whom Israel venerated from her past. The Gospels also show him rejecting the description 'good' on the grounds that one alone is good, the Father.

This is an instructive contrast. It's characteristic of Jesus to accept the highest titles that any group was willing to accord him—prophet, king, sage, Messiah, and others—and to push these titles in a more exalted or transcendent direction: in, if you like, a *'pleion* plus the genitive' direction. But there is one key exception: 'Why do you ask me about what is good. There is one who is good' (thus St Matthew), or 'Why do you call me good. None is good save God alone' (thus St Mark). No wonder that commentators lacking the right presuppositions are baffled. Without those presuppositions—the presuppositions of the orthodox faith—it's all as clear as mud. With them, however, it's beautifully lucid.

The Father is Goodness itself, the Son has no goodness of his own, but derives his goodness like his being from the Father. Yet the goodness which the Son only has by ceaselessly receiving it is infinite, and so, when joined to the existence of a creature at the Incarnation makes that creature incomparably greater than any other who has lived, is alive now, or could ever live.

The same faith, incidentally, enables to see why the only adequate sign of his identity and mission would be the 'sign of Jonah': the sign that is death and resurrection. The Holy Trinity is itself an eternal productive sacrifice, the Son emptying himself in love towards the Father as the Father empties himself in love towards the Son, so that the life which springs from their love, the Holy Spirit, may be. Jesus' sign had to take the form of *something like that.*

Tuesday of the Sixteenth Week of the Year (Years 1 and 2)

In today's Gospel, Jesus moves from his natural family, those to whom he is related by kinship, to his spiritual family, identified with him since they too do the will of his Father. This was a transition which Christ had to make in his own mind, will and feeling, if he was to enter into solidarity with all mankind as its Redeemer and draw them with him into the sphere of salvation. It carried with it a danger, because if it is divine to love universally, it is human to love particularly. This danger also affects disciples.

It can seem a bit of a 'Hobson's Choice' situation. If we neglect our relatives and friends in the name of the higher brotherhood of Christian charity we dissolve particularities into an abstract universal that may prove comparatively powerless to stimulate the mind, engage the affections, move the will. If on the other hand, we refuse to follow the example of Christ and the apostles in being all things to all men, we abandon the universal thrust of salvation, and our faith ethos may degenerate into something reminiscent of paganism, which found the holy in local places and natural bonds.

Somehow, then, we must make our solidarity universal while still remaining concrete. Our Lord died for the nameless multitude, but his encounters with them in the Gospels are extremely specific. He did not in fact repudiate his mother and his brethren, but opened them out to a wider fellowship of being.

The icon of this is our Lady: in receiving the motherhood of the whole Church she did so through the act of making her home with the exemplar disciple St John. And though the exegetes cannot verify (or falsify!) this speculation, perhaps it was there that St John learned to deepen his concept of *agapê* — the love of charity — which is neither general benevolence nor the recognition of already existing particular ties. Instead, as the continuation of the love of Christ, it is as concrete as it is universal.

Wednesday of the Sixteenth Week of the Year (Years 1 and 2)

'Jesus left the house and sat by the lakeside.' Does it matter, we can ask ourselves, where, topographically speaking, the Incarnation took place? Could it have been set exclusively in the midst of the Sahara desert, so that the Incarnate One never in his life saw fields, or in some vast inland conurbation so that he never saw stretches of water? I think we must assume that all the main conditions which held when the Creator underwent Incarnation in his own creation have a reason, or at least a suitability about them.

The Word came to his own: he came to his own world, the natural world made through him and made (as Genesis tells us) 'very well', very beautifully. And he came to the human world, the world 'sub-created' (as J. R. R. Tolkien would say) by human beings who themselves had been made in his image. He came into both the natural setting of human life, and into the heart of that human life itself. He was going to re-orient human living, but he was also going to set a new direction for the cosmos. The Resurrection, after all, is not just a question of what happened to a person, how a spiritual destiny was opened up; it changed a body, and therefore biology as well. So both the natural world and the world made by humankind were involved.

That tells us one thing straightaway. It was right that the incarnate Word knew from within his creation the city, and the town, and the village. But it was also right that he should know— again from within the creation—all the main dimensions of the natural world. It was entirely appropriate that he experienced the wilderness and the fertile lands, the sea (at any rate an inland sea) and the mountains (notably the snow-capped Mount Hermon, which probably has a better claim to be the site of the Transfiguration than does the better known, but much lower, Mount Thabor). It was appropriate that he could make use in his parables not only of human trades and customs but also of his acquaintance with natural things. This is what we should expect of the Logos when he took flesh: that all these varied intelligibilities should come together in him. Yes, it comes as no surprise that 'Jesus left the house and sat by the lakeside.'

Thursday of the Sixteenth Week of the Year (Year 1)

Today's first reading describes the preparation for the encounter of the Lord with Moses on Mount Sinai—a high-point, in both the physical and the theological sense, of Old Testament revelation. If we ask, What is revelation?, the answer is it is God's disclosure of himself and his plan for us, and if we go on to ask, And how does it happen?, we can answer, in tune with the Dogmatic Constitution on Revelation of the Second Vatican Council, it happens through a combination of events and words. Something happens, and in the midst of that something happening, words are found which interpret the events and enable their meaning to be passed on to others.

The author of Exodus doesn't leave us in much doubt about what that something that happened was. It was the father and mother of all thunder storms combined with a volcanic eruption—a pretty dramatic way of getting your attention especially if you'd spent all your life as immigrant labour in the Nile Valley where such things are unknown. But how were the words found that interpreted this 'theophany', this manifestation of the divine power via cosmic nature? Moses understood himself to be called up the mountain to enter into the divine darkness at its summit. There he heard words on his inner ear, words that he knew did not issue from himself, words that did not express him so much as confront him—confront him with divine demands.

First and foremost among those demands, so tomorrow's continuation of Exodus will tell us, come the Ten Commandments which the Church has understood as divine confirmation of the moral law in its most basic form. It is the beginning of the gift of the Torah, of God's disclosure of his will for his people, for their covenant life together with each other, together with their God.

Thursday of the Sixteenth Week of the Year (Year 2)

Today's readings contrast two theophanies—two manifestations of God. The Old Testament one, we might think, is only too obvious: thunder rumbling, lightning flashing, a sound like trumpets blaring: this is the stuff of which Hollywood was made. Perhaps anyone who saw Cecil B. de Mille's *The Ten Commandments* at an impressionable age will take away the lesson that a meeting with God is going to be world-shaking, ultra-dramatic, unmistakable, as plain as a pikestaff, or rather as plain as an earthquake and a volcanic eruption rolled into one.

In which case the theophany in today's Gospel will prove rather a disappointment, for theophany it is. 'Blessed are the eyes that see what you see', Jesus tells the disciples, 'and the ears that hear what you hear'. These organs are 'blessed' because in seeing and hearing Jesus they see and hear that for which, in the last analysis, they were made. Our sight and hearing were given us to equip us not only for moving around intelligently in this world but also for our supernatural destiny when we shall see God as he is and hear the voice of the One who sits upon the throne say, 'I am the Alpha and the Omega, the Beginning and the End'. And all this is already happening, says Jesus, as you the disciples watch a young Jewish prophet outlining his teaching—something which can only be the case, of course, if, as Church teaching has it, this prophet and this prophet alone is personally united to the Godhead.

So it is a real theophany with which we have to do when we gaze on images of Christ drawn from the Gospels and read his words there. The discretion of the theophany makes us overlook the fact that contained within it lies human salvation. The German poet Stefan George wrote:

> I know of lofts about each house,
> Full of running wheat, ever newly heaped—
> And no one takes it.
> I know of cellars under every yard
> Where the noble wine languishes and seeps away into the sand—
> And no one drinks it.
> I know of tons of pure gold, scattered in the dust:
> people brush it with their ragged hems—
> And no one sees it.

Friday of the Sixteenth Week of the Year (Year 1)

The Ten Commandments. Everyone ought to know them, I realise. Ever since modern catechisms were invented, at the time of the Reformation, they have been included. But for some reason I have difficulty in memorizing them. I recall my embarrassment in a café in Belgrade when, in conversation with a Serbian Evangelical who challenged me to recite them, I failed egregiously, thus proving to his satisfaction that Catholics no more knew the Bible than did the Orthodox.

But how do we use them? How have Catholics made use of the Ten Commandments in their catechisms and other typical works? I think the answer is that the Commandments as listed in Exodus (and Deuteronomy) have functioned as pegs on which to hang a lot of stuff about the moral life. The Commandments sum up areas of moral concern and they give us a direction—and the direction they give us can take us a long way, into a large moral universe where many virtues and vices are at play (or perhaps we should say 'at war'), and where all kinds of further precepts, both positive and negative, come within our ken.

As Catholic Christians we need to be well-instructed about doctrine, and doctrine concerns not only matters of faith, it also entails matters of morals, for as the saying has it, 'Morals maketh man'. To be in the image of God we have to be living a life where the virtues are flourishing and the precepts that belong with those virtues are faithfully kept. That is where the Commandments come in, by introducing us to key areas of morality. And unless we are trying to be, with God's help, 'in his image', it's rather presumptuous to seek to go further and become 'in his likeness'—to seek to share in his own intimate life through deification, through being lifted up with the mystics and saints into the transforming union. Let us be human, and then let us be divine.

Friday of the Sixteenth Week of the Year (Year 2)

The Ark of the Covenant was incomparably the holiest thing in Israel. No one knows what happened to it. Did the Babylonians deliberately destroy it when they captured Jerusalem? Was it accidentally lost in the *mêlée*? Was it taken somewhere for safekeeping by faithful Jews whose secret died with them? There is a legend that the prophet Jeremiah himself escaped with it to Egypt. Is it the object which the Ethiopian Orthodox church guards so jealously from prying eyes at Axum? If it were, it would be the greatest archeological find of all times, far exceeding the treasure of Troy. No wonder Mussolini's armies in invading Abyssinia sought (in vain) to take possession of it.

Yet the oracle of Jeremiah we heard today tells us not to get over-excited about the Ark since something greater will enfold before human eyes: the conversion of the Gentiles.

We who belong to the universal Church, the existence of which fulfils that prophecy, could easily misunderstand this. We could mistake the prophecy as really about how the revelation to Israel is to be transcended and even to become *passé*, so that there is no need now to pay it serious attention. All its fears about idolatry and purity of worship, its anxious striving after obedience to ethical absolutes, its concern to demarcate the People of the

Covenant from the world around them—this can now be abandoned as impossibly narrow and confining when compared with the Church of the Holy Spirit, the Spirit who fills the whole world.

Or can it? When the prophet adds that on that day, the day of the conversion of the Gentiles, 'Jerusalem shall be called the Throne of the Lord', tradition has taken his words as confirming the universal Church's continuing commitment to the revelation to Israel. The revelation to Israel is the permanently valid foundation on which all else is built. When Augustine goes to Ambrose for instruction in the faith, Ambrose gives him to read not the Gospels but the book of the prophet Isaiah. Ambrose pointed Augustine, and all would-be converts, to the rock from which the Church is hewn.

Saturday of the Sixteenth Week of the Year (Years 1 and 2)

'An enemy has done this.' In the Gospel tradition this enemy is identified quite straightforwardly with the Devil. Yet if human evil were simply the work of the fallen angels, there would be no moral responsibility for us. So far from being threatened with everlasting death, we should all be automatically exonerated, quite as much as we are for the social or the psychological determinists.

But no, it is man who is the true subject of human evil: the Church's moral teaching, her doctrine of salvation, and her penitential practice all make this plain.

And yet, to return to today's Gospel, if man is the subject of evil he is not necessarily its initiator. In the overall witness of Scripture, evil as we know it is begun in the angelic realm. That sound like a metaphysical speculation, but it has highly practical aspects. For human beings, evil is essentially something we appropriate, something we pick up or take in from our environment in the widest sense of that word. Awareness of this should make us more vigilant towards our milieu at all its levels.

It should also make us more reliant on the help of the Shining Ones, the good Angels, whose help even the incarnate Word gratefully accepted—in becoming man he entered the world not only of our bodies but also of our spirits, which are open to their realm.

THE SEVENTEENTH WEEK OF THE YEAR

Monday of the Seventeenth Week of the Year (Years 1 and 2)

'Things hidden since the foundation of the world.' That sounds interesting — and it *is* interesting! Everyone likes a 'mystery' in the sense of a detective story and a story of detection always concerns a currently hidden explanation of a crime. Everyone likes the idea of cracking a code or breaking open a secret, though not all secrets are appropriately divulged, as much avoidable unhappiness, the result of indiscretion, bears witness. And where things hidden since the foundation of the world are at stake, everyone likes the idea of getting at the secrets of the universe, writing a history of time, or producing a theory of everything that will show how everything came from not quite nothing but almost nothing, 'in the beginning', at the moment of that original 'singularity' which the physicists talk about.

How did Jesus speaks about things hidden since the foundation of the world, and what did he say? Surely it can't have been the parables, these modest little comparisons based on observing plants and cooking ingredients? Well, it was and it wasn't. The mystery hidden since the foundation of the world was the Father's will to deify his creation, to join it to himself in the New Adam, Jesus Christ, who is the Word made flesh and the Lamb of sacrifice, slain, as the Book of the Apocalypse tells us, from (precisely!) the foundation of the world. The Kingdom of God is the new being we are to inherit, the condition of existence to which the history of the cosmos and the evolutionary process have been pointing even though astrophysicists do not know it, any more than do evolutionary biologists.

Why do they not know it? Because it's a secret, of course, and only revealed to those who know the Father through the Son. Yes, the greatest code of all is cracked if we know the *Catechism of the Catholic Church*.

Tuesday of the Seventeenth Week of the Year (Years 1 and 2)

Today's Gospel presents the holy angels in an unaccustomed context—the punishment of the wicked. This is not how we usually think of our angel-guardian, or indeed of those sublime figures whose ranks are named in the Prefaces of the Roman Missal: Virtues, Powers, Dominions, Cherubim and Seraphim. We think of them, rather, lost in wonder at the attributes of the divine Trinity—when they are not, that is, coming to the aid of the human race.

But on the other hand, we associate the archangel Michael with the war against evil spirits, and wars—at any rate legitimate wars—have no purpose unless to overthrow the unjust. We must not be squeamish, and start to feel sentimental about Satan. And likewise we should not in a gush of misplaced benevolence regret that penalties fall on those humans who have purposed, consistently and with a superabundance of malice aforethought, the ruination of their neighbour's good.

Compacts between thoroughly wicked men and the evil angels do not need to be explicit—after the manner of the novels of Denis Wheatley. Strip away the paraphernalia of the horror movie and find the spiritual truth laid bare.

Wednesday of the Seventeenth Week of the Year (Year 1)

Today's readings are about concealed glory, buried treasure.

The reading from Exodus speaks of the overwhelmingness of God's glory: Moses had been bathed in it only briefly but he was —so to speak—positively contaminated by it. Instead of radiation sickness, this was radiation health, but for other people even this side-effect of the glory was too much to bear. Hence the veil which Moses thoughtfully draped across his features.

To overwhelming glory in the Book of Exodus there corresponds in the Gospels incomparable value. The Gospel of the Kingdom is the treasure hidden in the field, lying presumably side by side with gee-gaws in a Middle Eastern bazaar and so unrecognized. Here too it is the breathtakingness of what is involved, the tremendousness of it, that is at the forefront. But there is also a difference. In the Gospel it is not that what was once disclosed must now be concealed for safety's sake, as with Moses. Instead, what has hitherto been concealed is now going to be forever disclosed, for the sake of the true 'health' we call salvation.

Wednesday of the Seventeenth Week of the Year (Year 2)

We do not, I think, in the Roman liturgy, make enough of the holy prophets. Though they figure in the Roman Martyrology, hardly anyone ever hears it read, not perhaps even in monasteries. And they make no appearance in the Calendar for the Mass and the Liturgy of the Hours. We lose a lot by not being invited by the prayers of our rite directly to consider them, these saints of the Old Covenant. Members of the Oriental Catholic churches are more fortunate in this regard.

But at least we have the Scriptures read to us, and there we can meet them, and think on their lives, words, and deeds. And because, when we read the Old Testament, we always read the New as well, we shall not completely overlook the ways that the prophets, like the patriarchs, prefigured in various ways the Messiah himself.

Take Jeremiah, for instance, because today's reading from his book is among its most autobiographical passages. Here we have the heart of this prophet laid bare for us. We hear of his delight at receiving the Word of God, the suffering brought him by the negative reaction of his contemporaries (his message that, without repentance, the withdrawal of God's protection from Judah was inevitable did not exactly go down well among them), and the promise of God that he would 'fortify' Jeremiah, so that the wave of angry criticism will not bear him utterly away. This is a prophet whose joy in God is mingled with anguish at the thought of what human beings have made of their calling. In all these respects Jeremiah is a type—an anticipation—of our Lord.

And the thing about a type is: not only does the antitype, the corresponding fulfillment, throw light on the type; the type throws light on the antitype as well. We can understand Jesus Christ better because of knowing Jeremiah.

As I said, it is a pity we are not invited more often to show devotion to the prophets.

Thursday of the Seventeenth Week of the Year (Years 1 and 2)

In today's Gospel our Lord tells us (by implication) to bring out of the treasure-house of the Church things both old and new.

There is a rebuke here (implicitly) both to Modernists and to those whom we can call 'Antiquarianists'. The rebuke to Modernists comes first, because what the scribe brings forth from the treasury is described first as what is 'old'. Modernists, by contrast, are always trying to accommodate the Church to the latest fashion in scholarship, or to re-define her in terms of political correctness. But there is also a rebuke to Antiquarianists who are not willing to include the 'new' in the treasury. Antiquarianists are people who only value the Church for what is ancient in her: for formulae and rites received from the distant past and therefore quite untainted by the modern age.

The first set of people refuse to credit that anything really old can be valuable—and more valuable often than what we find in the culture around us. The second set can't believe that tradition is a living reality which the Holy Spirit illuminates from different angles according to the interests and questions of each successive period, so that the Church's treasury actually expands, grows richer, in terms of what we can take out of it, from age to age.

A plague on both your houses, we cry!

Friday of the Seventeenth Week of the Year (Years 1 and 2)

'This is the carpenter's son, surely?' Among the evangelists it is St John, not St Matthew, who is famous for his irony. Yet there is, for those who are familiar with the Christology of the Church, a sort of irony in these words.

The carpenter or joiner (the word can also mean the *builder*) was, at one level, St Joseph, the foster-father of Jesus, whom, outside the brotherhood, common account took to be his natural parent.

But at another level, the carpenter—or, better, perhaps, the builder—was the Maker of the House of God: the Power through whom all constructive movement takes place in the universe. Recognised by the Hebrews as the Lord, he had built the House of Israel, and now he was to build it anew on the foundation of his humanized Word, his Son made man.

Saturday of the Seventeenth Week of the Year (Years 1 and 2)

Herod's reaction to reports about our Lord is a sudden rush of fevered speculation in which he asks himself, Could John the Baptist have come back from the dead? It seems to have been a reaction born of a generally superstitious attitude fuelled in this particular case by guilt feelings—feelings of an entirely justified kind as the sordid story of how Herod came to order the beheading of St John makes plain.

But if 'guilt feelings' is surely a correct description of Herod's state of mind, how are we to rate his 'superstitious' attitude—or indeed superstition at large come to that? When we look into it, we find that superstition is a more complicated subject than meets the eye. Literally, it means 'what is over and above' something, rather in the way that, physically, an attic is above a house. In some houses, attics are not conceived, really, as organic parts of one's dwelling. It may be they are only accessible through a rather inconvenient trapdoor reached by a ladder. So likewise, if you entertain some belief that is not organically connected to the rest of your belief-system, not integrated with the rest of the way you look at the world and everyday happenings within it, we call such disconnected add-on belief a 'superstition'.

But then we ask ourselves, Should Herod's belief that John may have been raised from the dead really count as an example of superstition? For acceptance of the idea that the human creation will only come to its consummation in a general resurrection when all the injustices of history can be made good, is perfectly integral to orthodox Judaism, a perfectly good organic aspect of its way of seeing the world—or so many commentators in Herod's time and later would argue. And the further question whether that final condition could be anticipated in the case of some utterly special servant of God, such that with the resurrection of this or that individual the general resurrection actually begins, is answered by orthodox Christianity, Judaism's daughter religion, with the simple reply, 'Yes, it can, and it did, and this is what the events of that first Easter in a garden near Jerusalem mean'.

Herod's surmise was factually incorrect. It was not John the Baptist who would be the First-born from the dead, and the

First-fruits of a new humanity for the world. But if pathological guilt made him misidentify the candidate, he was, actually, on the right lines in the way he looked at human history under God. This reminds us of a truism that is often attested in the writings of St Thomas Aquinas: truth is truth, no matter how unpalatable its spokesman.

Saturday of the Seventeenth Week of the Year (Year 1)

In the Hebrew Bible, each of the five Books of Moses is called by its first few words, just like a papal encyclical, or a conciliar decree. That may or may not be illuminating about its subject matter. When the Bible was put into Greek the translators wanted to make it user-friendly for Gentiles, and so came up with such titles as *Levitikon* for which the most attractive English translation or, rather, paraphrase is perhaps, as has been suggested, 'The Book of the Service of the Sanctuary'.

Leviticus lovingly describes the cultic set-up prescribed for Israel's worship, down to the least detail—and the Christian tradition, not least in St Thomas, will be highly imaginative in thinking up ways in which all the accoutrements of worship under the Law of Moses can be given a wider—and often a Christ-centred—significance.

But as today's reading from Leviticus shows, the Book of the Service of the Sanctuary was not exclusively focussed on worship, though that is its central concern. Worship was why the Israelites had been freed from slavery in the first place—to offer sacrifice in the desert where, precisely as a worshipping community, they would receive the Torah. The laws of Leviticus range widely over a host of topics, including, as we heard today, agriculture. Agriculture was necessarily going to be important to them because the divine promise was, among other things, the promise of a land,

The law of jubilee includes provision for giving rest to the land and not just to the people who live on the land. Through Israel the land itself was to share in the Sabbath rest of God. To say as much is obviously to regard Israel and the land—or, more widely, man and nature—as bound up with each other. It is to see them as bound up with each other, more specifically, in relation to God, and that in a very strong sense. God's blessing on Israel, God's demands on Israel (which are not something altogether different from his blessings, for to know the Law is already to be blessed): these have a desirable spin-off for the land as well.

Modern agriculture—agribusiness—would have a hard time understanding this unless it could be cashed pragmatically. But it is not mainly pragmatic. If one word were wanted for it, the word would be 'mystagogic'. In a living cosmos there is a mysterious bond between soil and humans, and to get right what that bond entails, we need to enter into a sense of the mystery of creation. That mystery it was Israel's destiny to represent, and also to take further, toward the new heaven and the new earth.

THE EIGHTEENTH WEEK OF THE YEAR

Monday of the Eighteenth Week of the Year (Years 1 and 2)

Twice in this Gospel we hear how the setting is a 'lonely place'.
The disciples use the phrase when they come over in the evening-
time to where Jesus is. They notice the light failing, perhaps a chill
coming on with the onset of darkness, and realize the logistic
problem that will be facing them soon enough unless the crowd is
dispersed in a homeward direction. Here the 'loneliness' of the
spot is distinctively negative. The place is inhospitable, and
inconvenient.

But that is not the impression we get the first time we hear of
this unfrequented locality. Jesus selects it so that he can be 'in a
lonely place apart'. The Jerusalem Bible presumes he will have the
disciples with him, though away from other folk, 'by themselves'.
But from what we know of our Lord's practice from other, similar,
contexts in the Gospels it is surely more likely that he wished to
be alone with the Father.

Either way, the attraction of the lonely place has to do with
seeking out solitary places for intense prayer, whether alone or
with others. And the word used for a lonely spot is the word which,
when we come across it in the ancient monastic sources, we
translate 'desert'. There is a 'withdrawal' going on—the Greek verb
enters into our word 'anchorhold', meaning a hermitage—a
withdrawal into the desert to which, not so many years into the
future, hundreds of Jesus' disciples will flock so as seek the Face
of God, in scattered dwellings so numerous, according to contemporaries, that they made the desert a city.

That is a permanent impulse in the Church. The Church does
not only imitate Christ when she sends medical missionaries
among the poor of the Third World. She also imitates him in the
way of life chosen by her hermits and other contemplatives. If we
understand what communion with the Father means for the Son
made man, we shall have no problem in understanding—and
explaining to others—why this is so.

Tuesday of the Eighteenth Week of the Year (Year 1)

Like me, you were probably told as a child to wash your hands before eating. It's good hygienic practice so why did it alarm our Lord? It alarmed him *in the context*.

In the period immediately preceding the Incarnation, orthodox Jews laid an unprecedented weight on the importance of their separateness from Gentiles. Ancient Israelites were called to be separated from paganism, but that was so as to be separated *for* the Lord. But by way of reaction against Gentile rulers, the introduction of Gentile customs and marriage with Gentiles, the strict party felt obliged to emphasise the importance of separateness *for its own sake*.

Using to eat with hands that had been in contact with Gentile neighbours—shopkeepers, officials and the like—transmitted ritual uncleanness to what you were eating (this was the Pharisee view) and made you yourself unclean: unfit for entering the presence of God in prayer, in the Temple, in synagogue worship.

Our Lord denies that this development has any real rooting in the Father's will. And we can see why. It undermines the whole point of the original Israelite stress on separation for the Lord as found in the revealed Torah. Only a people set apart for the Lord could really appreciate their vocation to witness to the Lord before all the nations, to be a light to the nations as the subsequent prophets had understood it.

By being separated for the Lord, Israel was in the last analysis *for* the nations and not *against* them. She was for them so that they too should be brought into the divine community, that the holiness of the Lord might encompass all the earth.

That is what the mission of the Son, taken forward by the mission of the Spirit at Pentecost, would establish once and for all.

Tuesday of the Eighteenth Week of the Year (Year 2)

In today's reading from the Old Testament the prophet Jeremiah describes the incurable guilt of God's people and yet records the divine intention nonetheless to 'restore the tents of Jacob'. So this prophecy of woe suddenly turns into one of weal, a prophecy of blessing. Crucial to the turn-about is the promise of a 'prince' who will be 'one of their own', one of the people, and yet be someone who will 'come freely into my presence', even though that presence — the presence of the divine holiness — is deadly dangerous to sinful men. 'Who else would risk his life by coming close to me?' I think it's not going too far to say this is a prophecy of the means of our redemption.

How could the restorative intent of God for his people be reconciled with God's just repugnance at our iniquities? In the endless wisdom of God a multitude of strategies might have been found for satisfying at once the plans of love and the demands of justice. But the strategy actually chosen — the Incarnation of the Word for a mission of redemptive suffering — was the one most fitting not only to the abundant generosity of God but also to the compromised dignity of man. Our Redeemer was to be in our nature: 'Their prince will be one of their own', but there will be nothing patronizing about the manner of our Redemption. The horror of the death he will endure is a suitable sign of our profound alienation from the holiness of God: 'who else indeed, would risk his life by coming close to me?'.

The way in which our Redemption — the turn-about — was carried through went way beyond the demands of justice, and that was how it testified to the sheer excess of the divine love.

Wednesday of the Eighteenth Week of the Year (Years 1 and 2)

The question of the relation between Jews and Gentiles in our Lord's time was evidently as much of a mine-field as that between Christians and Jews is today. In the prophecies which prepare the mission of the Messiah, the universal salvation he is to achieve takes place in and through the salvation of Israel. The Messiah could not abandon his focus on his people in the name of simple human equality. We see, though, from the Cure of the Daughter of the Syro-Phoenician Woman that his mercy did not, however, leave a needy Gentile in the cold.

Today, if we were to follow where some voices lead, we would turn this situation completely upside down. We would say that the Church of the Messiah is for the Gentiles, and Israel, the Jewish people who have their own Covenant in Abraham, must shift for themselves. In that case, it would only be by way of exception that we should permit Jews to be baptized and enter the Church.

This is not how the apostles thought, nor how they acted. Catholics in later ages have no right so flagrantly to defy the example of the apostolic generation. We too, the continuing apostolic Church, are sent 'to the lost sheep of the House of Israel'—not only to them, of course, but also to them, most certainly. There is neither charity nor truth in making Hebrew Catholics feel they are anomalies in the Church of the Jewish Messiah.

Thursday of the Eighteenth Week of the Year (Years 1 and 2)

Poor Peter, he had a lot to learn about the ways of God's Messiah. But he was to be the first pope, so he had to start as soon as possible on a swift learning curve. Hence, I take it, the sharpness—the 'over-the-top' quality—of our Lord's rebuke. Being morally equated with the personal principle of evil cannot have been an enjoyable experience. But it had to be endured if the chosen leader of the apostolic Church was not to set himself against the divine plan, rather than follow its grain.

We can generally take it for granted that following the grain of the divine plan will equate with the negation of common sense views of human living. Of course there are basic decencies, fundamental moral virtues, that are in play at the natural level— but the natural level is not necessarily the common sense level, which considers not what human nature may most deeply require for its flourishing but how a fallen world actually works. And in any case, the plan of God is not just for the consolidation of human nature. It is for our deification, our entry through a dedicated, sacrificial way of living, into the sphere of the all-holy Trinity itself.

How can popes expect to be popular if that is what they represent? Peter might let down his Lord and Master through embarrassment and fear, but at least he would not make this mistake again.

Friday of the Eighteenth Week of the Year (Years 1 and 2)

How could our Lord possibly have said that some of his hearers would not see death before the Kingdom of God came in power? Surely, people say, the Kingdom didn't come! On the contrary, the world continued very much as before. So how is this saying compatible with the faith of the Church about Christ as the divine, and therefore all-knowing, Word of the Father and the Scriptures as the unerring testimony to his message?

Well, in the first place we can say, the Kingdom that he preached *did* come, actually. It came with his Death, Resurrection and Ascension, and the Sending of the Holy Spirit. Those events changed the relation between the world and God. They set in the midst of the world a first instalment of the life of the Kingdom. The Second Vatican Council calls the Church the sacrament of the Kingdom because in her the life of the Kingdom is already accessible. People may report that they do not find it accessible. They wouldn't, unless they developed their spirituality using the resources she brings.

That is where Christian contemplation comes in. Without the saving events you can still have contemplation of some sort. Platonic contemplation, for example: contemplating the eternal realities of which this world is the shadow cast. But you can't have *Christian* contemplation, which is a savouring of the first-fruits of salvation.

But then secondly, we can refine that answer a little and say, yes, it's true that the Kingdom hasn't come yet in power, in glory, in a manifest rather than hidden way. And then we can think of our Lord as telescoping present and future in the Gospel saying. Owing to the inter-communication between his human mind and the mind of the divine Word, which was also his, it is obvious that his attitude to everything would be somewhat different. He could never be ordinary. This will be true of his experience of time also.

As the One destined to be the Lord of history, Christ sees the redeemed future as already bursting forth from the womb of the present where his redemptive action was there and then being brought to bear. So he can speak of the hidden inauguration of the Kingdom on Calvary as though it were the gift of the full reality.

In fact, insofar as it makes that gift a certainty, it is just that. As his own dying words put it, 'It is finished'.

Finished for him, but not finished for us, and this difference locates for us the place of Christian mission. You could have mission in some sense before these saving events. You could have Jewish mission, for instance, which consisted in witnessing to the God of Israel before the Gentiles. But you couldn't have Christian mission, which consists in hastening the full coming of the Kingdom by closing the gap between where people are now and where Jesus is at the Father's right.

Saturday of the Eighteenth Week of the Year (Year 1)

Today's first reading contains the single most important text of Judaism, our parent religion. 'Hear, O Israel, the Lord your God is one.' It's a bare statement, but it's far from being a threadbare one. It's an affirmation not only of monotheism—there is but one God—but also of God's uniqueness, which entails that nothing else is fit to be compared with him. It also asserts (or so it can be argued) what later generations would call God's 'simplicity'—everything he has he is, for his 'God-ness' penetrates totally everything about him.

And this truth is so wonderful that the faithful Israelite has to remember it constantly. In a little box on a headband this text should be bound to one's forehead which stands for our highest powers of understanding and love, and by an armband to the hands which are the instruments of our action. And it is to be placed on the gates and doors of the home so that one can see it when going out or coming in.

All this, we can say, is meant to bring about a condition of transparent relationship between God and man. And that is what prayer is. Prayer is the openness of man to the God who is always opening himself to us,

In the Gospel, that same openness is expressed in terms of the disciples' being a channel for the power of God, his healing power for souls who are sick and lost. We must not be put off by our Lord's hyperbole. 'Command the mountain to move to yonder place and it will do so.' Of course he would not have wanted the disciples to say to Mount Kilimanjaro, 'Be thou re-situated in the South China Sea'. The point is that the disciples had failed to carry out the mission they had been given by the incarnate Word: to heal and exorcise as a sign of the imminent coming of the Kingdom. God was ready to energize them, but had they been ready to be energized by God?

It is for us to find the parallels in our own lives.

Saturday of the Eighteenth Week of the Year (Year 2)

The reading from the Book of Deuteronomy today introduces us to the *Shema*, which is the nearest thing Jews have to a Creed. 'Hear, O Israel: the Lord our God is one Lord'. It tells not just of how there is only one God, which is a position all kinds of people have embraced, for reasons more to do with philosophy than with religion. It also speaks of how this God is identical with the One who addressed Israel, and called her to be his own: 'The Lord *our* God'.

Moses' speech looks back to the ancient patriarchs, and it looks forward to the next generation, and, by implication, every generation after that in its turn. And so, we can say, it also looks forward to us who are, in the words of Pope Pius XI, 'spiritual Semites'. We too are children of Abraham because we are children of the promise, the promise that Abraham's descendants shall be as many as the stars of heaven, or the grains of sand on the shore of the sea.

When did we become children of the promise, spiritual descendants of Abraham? It was when we were baptised into Christ Jesus in whom, as St Paul says, all the promises of God were Yes. All the promises made to Israel came to their culmination in him, found in him their divine fulfillment. We now know, in and through Christ, that the one God of Israel is so rich in his interior life that he is not only the Lord, but is Father, Son and Holy Spirit. Yet what that means is: his unity is even more wonderful than Israel guessed. The *Shema* joins us to Israel, it does not divide.

THE NINETEENTH WEEK OF THE YEAR

Monday of the Nineteenth Week of the Year (Years 1 and 2)

Here we have a Passion prediction followed by a rather curious little exchange between Jesus and St Peter. For once the disciples do not greet the Passion prediction with stark incomprehension. Instead, we hear, 'a great sadness came over them'. By this point in the ministry they evidently had a foreboding that the mission of the Messiah would end in tears. This is a new note of realism, for their Master will indeed be a crucified King.

That gives the cue for the exchange that follows. Throughout his ministry, our Lord tended to produce alliances of his enemies—he challenged people on so many fronts this was itself predictable. He could hardly expect the pagan Roman power to be on his side, and aware of the penchant of his Jewish opponents for improbable coalitions, he could have expected some collusion between the Romans and at least one of the Jewish parties. It was in fact the threat of Jewish leaders to delate Pilate to the emperor as 'not Caesar's friend' that, humanly speaking, sealed Jesus' fate.

The Messiah can be discreet but not mendacious. The Romans in Palestine, he says, are in the position of foreign kings who take tribute. They make God's people no longer at home in their own land.

But then there follows an extraordinary exercise of preternatural knowledge. No doubt the kind of fish that scavenge on sea-beds do occasionally grub up such things as small coins. Jesus tells Peter exactly how he can find a half-shekel that will not mean either of them is supporting the Romans from his own pocket.

Some commentators think this a wonder that is not at all in his authentic style. But he was the Word through whom all things were made. Not only, if he wished, could he draw on his divine knowledge to underline his teachings. In his sovereign freedom he was one with the utter freedom of God. Let us in turn, then, give him the liberty to bring together his divine and human understanding as he pleases.

Tuesday of the Nineteenth Week of the Year (Years 1 and 2)

By a judicious selection of verses from the eighteenth chapter of St Matthew's Gospel, the compilers of the Roman Lectionary have created for today a continuous Gospel reading where sheep, Angels, and children are just about equally essential.

Any connexion between sheep, Angels and children is not at first sight apparent. Little angels are what we know children not to be like, and if we hope that our children will follow us like sheep we shall be disappointed. So perhaps the Fathers of the Church—well-known for helping preachers over difficult Scriptures—can help us.

The Fathers interpret the one sheep which the Good Shepherd went in search of and brought home as the human race itself. Our race went astray whereas the myriad choirs of Angels kept faithful. The rejoicing in heaven takes place at the Ascension when our Lord takes back our human nature to where it belongs, with the Angels in the divine presence. As Jesus tells the Sadducees elsewhere in St Matthew's Gospel, those who are accounted worthy to get there will be 'equal to the Angels and be sons of God, being sons of the Resurrection'.

But how can we be accounted worthy to get to Heaven? This is where childhood comes in, but, as St Thérèse saw so clearly, it is spiritual childhood that is in question. That means all the directness and spontaneity of children, but separated off—painfully if need be—from the selfishness and limitation of outlook of a child. In spiritual childhood, the child's capacity to receive becomes as large as the gift of grace. It becomes as wide as the vocation of a disciple. This is how we enter on the glorious liberty of the sons and daughters of God.

Wednesday of the Nineteenth Week of the Year (Years 1 and 2)

In today's Gospel, the evangelist Matthew brings together some sharply contrasted sayings of our Lord about the Church. The contrast is between hard sayings and soft, between cold and warm.

The hard, cold sayings concern the Church's power of the keys, her not just right but duty to excommunicate, to cut off from her body diseased limbs. Historically that has meant those whose life-style was in flagrant contradiction with the law of Christ and those whose thinking was in flagrant contradiction with the mind-set of Christ.

The warm, soft sayings, by contrast, speak of the presence of Christ in any gathering of his brethren, no matter how small and unpretentious.

To some these two sets of sayings may conjure up two different churches: one authoritarian and legalistic, the other fraternal and caring. Yet it is obvious that the Christ of St Matthew is describing one Church and that, furthermore, there is not the slightest sign of hesitation to mark the transition from cold and hard sayings to warm and soft ones.

The inference must be that you can't have the one set without the other. A Church which lets fall its disciplinary and doctrinal authority will soon lose hold of the identity of the One who mysteriously indwells it and is present to the least of his brethren. The Church is *mater*, a 'mother'—a real mother, not an auntie, because she is *magistra*, a 'teacher'. And she is a teacher—an effective teacher and not a mere pedagogue—because she is a mother to those to whom she has given birth in the baptismal waters.

Thursday of the Nineteenth Week of the Year (Year 1)

In today's readings we are meant to be following two journeys from the margins to the centre.

In the Old Testament reading, the children of Israel under Joshua's leadership come up out of the desert and, carrying the Ark, prepare to enter the Holy Land by crossing the river Jordan. In today's Gospel, St Matthew has our Lord finish his preaching in Galilee before crossing over into Judah to his goal—Jerusalem where he will perform the Sacrifice that saves the world. So the true divine Presence, Jesus, the Word made flesh, prefigured in the Ark of the Covenant, comes to a crucial boundary. He crosses a threshold on his own journey, leaving behind the familiar territory of Galilee which has been his home and that of his disciples.

Because this is such a significant stage in the development of our Lord's ministry, the choice of the parable of the Wicked

Steward with which to mark it must surely be significant as well. This parable seemed an appropriate climax of Jesus' preaching to his original hearers on their home ground.

Its message is the duty to show mercy to others, based on the fact that the Father's will for us has been mercy first and last. Our Father is not, however, a sugar-daddy who will be indulgent to us whatever we do. Such a teaching would be puerile, and turn us into spoiled brats. We are called to bear the burden he makes light. If we refuse to do so, refuse to show mercy to others, we cannot expect to continue receiving mercy ourselves.

Thursday of the Nineteenth Week of the Year (Year 2)

Today's reading from the Book of Ezekiel provides us with an excellent example of a prophetic sign. The prophet is instructed to behave like an exile would, clearing out of Jerusalem with a bundle, and to make sure everyone notices by making a hole for that purpose in the city wall. The prophet acts out what the entire population will have to do when the prophecies come true and Judah falls to a religiously alien power and begins its long exile 'by the waters of Babylon' where they 'wept, remembering Zion'.

Such prophetic signs are crucial background not only to our Lord's ministry but to the Catholic sacraments as well. They accustom us to the notion that gestures can be, in a divinely intended sense, revelatory of far-reaching meanings. So it was when our Lord healed paralytics or multiplied bread for the hungry. So it was when he entered Jerusalem on a donkey on Palm Sunday. So it is when the seven sacraments of the Church are celebrated in just such signs.

We must be careful not to minimize these signs on the grounds that they are simple actions. They are divinely intended gestures with, potentially, a vast significance. And, in the era of the Incarnation when the power of God is conjoined with human realities, they have the capacity to trigger the transformations of which they speak.

Friday of the Nineteenth Week of the Year (Year 1)

Today's first reading describes the marriage between God and Israel. It is one of those marriages where the husband appears considerably older than the wife. God is the Ancient of Days, Israel at this date a mere millennium and a half old. Of course we cannot speak literally of God as old. His eternal life is a perpetual 'now'. It is also the source of all fresh being, all freshness of being, all rejuvenation, in the creation. So we might just as well call God younger than Israel.

In point of fact the prophet presents God in this text as an older man who marries a ward whom he first adopted as a foundling infant. And this is one of the great structuring metaphors of the Hebrew Bible—the marriage between Israel and her Lord. The same way of speaking, thinking, experiencing, is preserved in the New Testament and serves there as a foundation for understanding the Covenant relation between Christ, the consubstantial Word of the Father, and the New Israel, the Church.

Now in Catholic Christianity calling the Church 'the Bride of Christ' is not just a piece of language. The language refers to a reality really present in the world of today. Thanks to the unique grace bestowed on the Church, God is indissolubly united to her and she is totally, abidingly committed to him.

Two ways in which to see this clearly expressed are the two states of life Jesus speaks of in today's Gospel—the marriage of disciples and, as an alternative to marriage, their taking on the celibate life for God's sake. The indissolubility of sacramental marriage and the permanence of the vows made by a Religious at solemn profession are icons of the bridal relation between God and his people.

It is noteworthy that in the Church of the contemporary period, both of these icons are under attack: the first in favour of the remarriage of divorcees, the second in favour of periodically renewed temporary vows. The modern world finds commitment hard and change natural. But the modern Church does not necessarily have to yield to this. It may be that what the modern world needs is the biblical revelation of God's everlasting faithful-

ness and its manifestation in the abiding self-gift of the Christian
married couple and of Christian monastics.

Friday of the Nineteenth Week of the Year (Year 2)

Probably few people realize that the Sacred Scriptures contains
texts as powerful as this one from Ezekiel—simply considered as
a piece of language used to make an effect. It is an amazing oracle,
addressed ostensibly to Jerusalem, standing in here for the Hebrew
people as a whole, and giving a God's eye view of their birth and
development.

As you heard, it compares Israel to a baby with rather disrepu-
table parents. Unloved, it has been abandoned, and is found
struggling in blood, presumably from the afterbirth, by the Lord
who passes the field where it has been dropped off. In words as
rich as they are shocking, God describes how he took pity on this
(female) infant and prepared to make it, once it had grown to
womanhood, his own bride; how he lavished every possible
blessing on her and made her a queen by the marriage covenant
with himself, only to find that she then re-invented herself as a
prostitute.

It is, as I said, language powerfully used to make an effect—but
what effect does it aim at producing? It is intended to induce the
sort of guilt that uniquely belongs only to the elect of God, such as
Israel is, and such as we are, considered as his holy Church. Only
those who have been as richly favoured as we have been, can fall
so spectacularly from grace. 'So remember and be covered with
shame, and in your confusion be reduced to silence, when I have
pardoned you for all that you have done—it is the Lord who speaks.'

Saturday of the Nineteenth Week of the Year (Years 1 and 2)

Today's Gospel is one of the main texts by which the Church has
defended the practice of baptizing children and infants over
against a variety of critics, ancient, sixteenth century, and modern.

At first sight, this looks like a clear case of manipulating things.
The situation described so briefly in the Gospels is obviously not
a case of administering Baptism. So from the viewpoint of secular
or more-or-less secular readers, looking at texts by the methods of

historical criticism, this Gospel tells us nothing about the problem concerned.

The Church, however, doesn't normally use her Scriptures according to such methods. Instead, she plunges each text into the global totality of her tradition and draws it out again looking rather different from its bath. So what shall we say about this Gospel in the light of tradition?

Jesus' gesture towards the children betokens a certain attitude. It testifies to his conviction that even those who do not understand can still benefit from a blessing by the Saviour. And it fits with this that we believe Baptism does children good.

People say, But wasn't Hitler baptized? Wasn't Stalin baptized? They were. Many children start out with a fine patrimony and throw it away. They can have good and loving parents, a cheerful and confident personality, be born and brought up in an environment where real truths are affirmed and genuine virtues praised. It is a matter of daily experience that all of this, as they grow up, can go for nothing.

Likewise with the supernatural life. The grace of Baptism works within the will, but it doesn't work without the will's co-operation. There is a dialectic here by which, throughout the Christian life, we are first of all recipients of the gift of salvation but then on the basis of that gift, together with our own freedom, we have to start being agents—to move from recipients to agents, and indeed to donors: to those who help pass the gift on. Otherwise it turns to dust and ashes in our hands.

THE TWENTIETH WEEK OF THE YEAR

Monday of the Twentieth Week of the Year (Years 1 and 2)

Our Lord's advice to the Rich Young Man is pretty uncompromising, but should it be turned into a general rule for all Christians? This Gospel could certainly be read in that sense. After all, the situation to which this counsel is the response is defined in very broad terms. Jesus is asked a very open question: How one can start living the blessed life, life as God himself envisages it? And the answer he gives is in suitably general terms. You begin by living the moral life as defined by the Ten Commandments (we can think here of each of the commandments as defining an important area of moral living, so it need not be just a negative matter of avoiding wrong-doing). Then you round off your effort by embracing voluntary poverty, giving away all your goods to the poor. It does read like a general programme that in principle all disciples should adopt.

We know, however — that is, as Catholic Christians we know — that this is not how the Church has interpreted this Scripture. She has taken her Lord to be discerning the vocation of a particular young man, not laying down a maxim to be observed by all his followers, rich or not, young or not, male or not. Though praising almsgiving, especially when such almsgiving is structurally significant for someone's budget and creates life-style change, she has not sought to make it a condition of being a faithful Catholic that everyone has to beggar himself before seeking Baptism. You might say cynically that to do so would ensure the drying-up of candidates for Christian initiation. Yet there are plenty of hard sayings of the Lord that the Church *does* treat as non-negotiable by all her members — which is precisely why in ancient times, and even later, as among the Vikings, some people postponed Baptism till what they imagined was their death-beds.

It boils down to the question, Do we trust the Church to know the mind of her Lord? Do we trust the Bride to know the mind of her Bridegroom? If we do, then we should be orthodox Catholics.

If we do not, it is hard to see why, except for reasons of cultural nostalgia, we remain in the Church at all.

Tuesday of the Twentieth Week of the Year (Years 1 and 2)

Today's Gospel is important in shaping what we can call an apostolic ideal of Christian discipleship. The apostles, it seems, have left everything to follow Jesus on his missionary journeys: notably, home family and landed property—though presumably the latter was on a very small scale.

From time to time in history, the Christian ministry goes sedentary. It stays at home, rears a family, and even holds lands like the hereditary glebes of clerical families in the early Middle Ages. Perhaps this is something that will come again in the West, just as it has never died out in the churches of the East.

But then there is always a renewal of evangelical fervour. The ideas of the apostolate and the ascetic life come together again, and the profile today's Gospel gives us is re-assembled.

Wednesday of the Twentieth Week of the Year (Years 1 and 2)

Today's Gospel gives us the embryo of the Church's later doctrine of grace and election—how in different ways yet all together we are called to share God's life, either effectively or not as the case may be.

Three points suggest themselves. First, although the workers in the vineyard contribute unequally, everything takes place within the owner's original offer: his contract, or what the Bible terms his 'Covenant'. Reward and rest are only given to individuals within this overarching plan—made, actually, in Jesus Christ, as we recall at each Mass when the celebrant refers to his 'New and Everlasting Covenant'.

Secondly, the Covenant is made with workers—that is, with people who contribute in some fashion. All Catholic theologians, however fearful they may be of ascribing the fruits of the Covenant to our own independent efforts, agree that we must in some way collaborate, co-operate, let our freedom be called into play so as to share in Covenant activity: building the kingdom of God through charity.

Thirdly, within this Covenant and the need to make a contribution to it, God is supremely free as to how he rewards and gives his rest to the redeemed. The saints differ in glory, and no one in Heaven resents this because they see it as 'to the praise of his glorious grace'. It may be the humble sloggers who persist in unspectacular virtue who are the stars. Or it may be great sinners who have suddenly exploded into light like fireworks. It will be one of the great surprises of eternity. God may dispose as he wishes of what belongs to him—his divine life and love.

Thursday of the Twentieth Week of the Year (Years 1 and 2)

The identification of the Christian life with morality is still fairly common. To be a good Christian is regarded as the same thing as to be virtuous, with a narrow focus on one or two uncontroversial virtues like benevolence or an attitude of concern for others. The Gospel is certainly concerned with morality and its transfiguration by grace, but this is never outside a wider context of belief and practice, a wider whole.

We see this in the Gospel passage set for today. The ways in which the invitation of the king are ignored or rejected include morally reprehensible ways like the committing of assault and murder. But these take their place on an unbroken spectrum with morally legitimate actions like being concerned for the condition of one's farm or one's business. Moral ways of ignoring the invitation and immoral ways of rejecting it are not separated by a jump in the scale so much as joined by a glissando (to continue the musical metaphor). There are, evidently, more ways in which to close oneself off from grace than immoral ways, just as moral reform is not in and of itself an entitlement to grace and glory.

In speaking of grace and glory as respectively the means and the goal of the Christian life we show we are dealing here with a new order of relationship between God and man: a new creation, St Paul will call it. Understandably, then, the Fathers of the Church interpret the guest without a wedding garment not as a morally reprobate man, but as someone who has refused to stoop down beneath the waters of Baptism—someone who has refused to be regenerated into the living hope which comes from the Incarnation, Death and Resurrection of the Son of God.

Friday of the Twentieth Week of the Year (Years 1 and 2)

Today's Gospel consists of our Lord's two great love-commands: love God, love your neighbour. This might seem difficult in practice but simple in theory. In fact, however, there are various ways of inter-relating these two commands and how we do so tells us a lot about our attitude to our religion and so, if we are consistent, about our attitude to life.

One could for instance adopt what they call a 'horizontalist' interpretation of the two commands, and say that the command to love our neighbour re-expresses, or states the moral content of, the command to love God. As St John, for example, points out, we cannot see God, or, one might add, do anything for him in any obvious sense of those words. So instead we express or love for him by loving our neighbour whom we can see and help.

Unfortunately, as experience shows, this attitude can easily become indistinguishable from simple humanitarianism or humanism with a religious overtone. That fate befell a number of those working for Catholic Action in France in the years after the Second World War and it is an obvious temptation for supporters of Liberation Theology in Latin America.

Then there is, at the opposite pole, the 'verticalist' interpretation of the relation between these two commands. Here we treat the second commandment as simply a logical consequence of the first. Our primary task is to love God and this must include loving and wanting to do his will. But his will turns out to be that we should love our neighbour. Here our neighbour is in danger of being reduced to so much material on which we are to practice our love for God. If God's will had been that we should love something else altogether—the natural environment, say—then that would have served equally well. On this view, our neighbour seems to have no intrinsic value of the kind which would justify their being mentioned as the subject of the second command. Of course, if we believe in a Creator then no one else and nothing else has any independent value anyway. But to say my neighbour has no independent value is different from saying he or she has no intrinsic value—not of the quality required, anyway. This is the mistake the verticalist interpretation makes—and perhaps it leads people by reaction to have recourse to the horizontalist view.

Now neither view is correct—which is not to say that they possess no element of truth whatsoever. St Thomas Aquinas, in his theological method, often proceeds by distinguishing out the nugget of truth in even incorrect views, and we can take a leaf out of his book here.

The verticalist view is correct in treating the love of God as something which should be practised in its own right—and not treated as, in effect, a religious rhetoric for commending love of our neighbour. The horizontalist view is correct in treating the neighbour as more than just a human space in which to practice the love of God. The neighbour is divinely valuable in his or her own right, and is not merely an opportunity for obeying God.

The truly integrated love of God and neighbour is not, however, found in either of these views: verticalism, horizontalism. Where then shall we look for it? We shall find it displayed not in a theory at all but in the distinctively Christian virtue of charity.

Through the theological virtue of charity, our love for God urges us to love the neighbour whom God also loves, and it does so precisely because the neighbour—and he or she alone—is in God's image and likeness. Loving the neighbour with the same love by which we love God—the love of charity—we hope to bring him or her to love God likewise. The typical manifestation of charity is to love our neighbour to the end that he or she may be in God, their archetype and goal.

Saturday of the Twentieth Week of the Year (Years 1 and 2)

So when the Son of Man sits on his throne of glory, the twelve apostles will also sit on thrones likewise. In an age such as our own when people in the Church want to de-emphasise the power and the glory, this is a rather uncomfortable message. Christ the Servant, the poor Christ, Christ the brother: these are all attractive images for many of our contemporaries, and they sit rather uneasily with the mosaics and frescoes of our historic churches in

East and West, where Christ stares out in majesty from apse or cupola, or presides in lordly fashion over scenes of the Last Judgment.

But it is true. The Son of Man will sit on his throne of glory. It is useless to identify with the pathos of a Jesus swept along by the force of history, just another victim, like the many victims we read of in our newspapers, distinguished only by the fact that God was in him. A Christ who is, essentially, in the same boat as the rest of us is ultimately no use to us. If history is going to be more than the celebration of the de facto victors, we need to know that the Lamb is the Lion, the Lamb of God the Lion of Judah who reigns. Unless he is the Pantokrator, the One who already in principle rules all and in practice will do so at the end, then nothing has really altered since his Crucifixion. But in fact everything has altered, and it is because we know he reigns that we can find his humiliation and suffering so huge a source of comfort and strength.

THE TWENTY-FIRST WEEK OF THE YEAR

Monday of the Twenty-first Week of the Year (Years 1 and 2)

It's hard to see that our Lord's criticism of the Pharisees for their teachings on the extreme importance of the way oaths are formulated is pertinent to modern Western societies, where an elaborate culture of sacral oath-taking is simply not found. What we do experience, however, is what he calls the 'shutting up of heaven in men's faces'.

The most obvious example comes from those influential pundits of the English-speaking West, the 'New Atheists'. Their whole *raison d'être* consists in seeking to suppress the sense of transcendence in human life, the haunting feeling that we are called to something beyond. That feeling is both a reflection in ordinary experience of a true metaphysics (we are from the first moment of our existence in a relation to our Creator) and a buried memory of the supernatural vocation we received before the Fall. The New Atheists, believing—in all honesty, no doubt—that the sense of transcendence, or the dim intuition of the supernatural, is hocus-pocus, want to obliterate the practices, monuments, and artifacts that tend to trigger it in daily life. We should be less likely to have these irrational sensations if we never heard a prayer offered in public, or saw a church door wide open, or glimpsed the habit of a nun as she crossed the street.

But now we come to the other way of shutting heaven in men's faces. When did you last see, actually, a nun in her habit crossing the street? In addition to militant secularism outside the Church there has also been in the twentieth century a hardly less damaging internal secularism within the Church—the 'secularisation of Christianity', one prominent Anglo-Catholic theologian, in a effort to alert the faithful, chose to call it. It may present itself as the friend of the Church—making our thought-forms closer to those of our non-believing contemporaries so as to make evangelization easier, getting rid of 'archaic' customs that erect unnecessary barriers between Christianity and everyday life. But the upshot is that, eventually, people find it hard to say what makes the difference between a decent person living a reasonably upright life, on the one hand, and the priestly people of God on the other. The distinctive language and customs and, yes, even dress that calls people toward heaven evaporates, and lo and behold, the gates of heaven seem to swing shut.

Tuesday of the Twenty-first Week of the Year (Years 1 and 2)

'These you ought to have done, without neglecting the others.' In the original context that means justice and mercy, the great divine attributes revealed as a model for us to follow in the Jewish Law. Let us take this maxim in relation to the Catholic Church today. What we ought to have done in the Church is to keep in view at all times the wider landscape of the Christian life.

We should have done this, however, says our Lord in the Gospel, 'without neglecting the others': which signifies, in his address to the Pharisees, the tithing of mint, rue and cumin, as gifts for the kitchens of the Temple clergy, also legally prescribed.

What, then, are the herbs of the Church? I would like to suggest that three good candidates are: the canons, the liturgical rubrics, and the minutiae of theological orthodoxy. None of these ought to be neglected.

First, then, the canons: the canon law which sets out our duties as well as our rights as members of the holy people of God. We respect the civil law because, naturally, we have to or else. We should respect the sacral law because supernaturally we ought to. Since this law sets out the relations which should hold in the Mystical Body of Christ, its provisions are, as the Eastern Orthodox say, the 'holy canons'.

Secondly, the rubrics of the Liturgy. The public worship of God in the Church is crafted. It is designed as a tapestry of words and gestures. Are we sloppy about it? Have we noticed that, for instance, the Liturgy asks us to beat our breasts at the *Confiteor*, to bow at the *incarnatus est* in the Creed, to incline our heads at the names of Jesus, Mary and the saint of the day? These gestures have been carefully devised; they are appropriate, worthy, and conducive to devotion.

Lastly, there are the minutiae of theological orthodoxy. It was the historian Edmund Gibbon who pointed out that the Church nearly fell apart over an iota, the Greek letter 'i': one letter which made the difference, in the various credal formulae doing the rounds in the fourth century, between saying the Son was of like substance with the Father and saying he was of the same substance as the Father. Had that iota not been removed, banished, deleted for evermore, we should now be worshipping a demi-god, and one who, because he was not fully divine, could not save and complete his own creation. We should never assume that the doctrinal controversies of the past are not important now.

So let us keep hold of the big picture, the great outlines of divine revelation and the way of life it holds out to us. But let us do so without neglecting these others.

Wednesday of the Twenty-first Week of the Year (Years 1 and 2)

Today's Gospel, I imagine, played its part in making the case that the Jewish people are, corporately, a deicidal people—a people responsible for the death of One who was God. If we have an orthodox Christology, if we share the faith of the Church about Jesus' identity, we shall hold that One who was God was executed. The human being we call 'Jesus' had, as the personal subject of his humanity, the uncreated divine Word. As Chesterton said of Good Friday: 'dead is the King who was never born'.

Against this background it is hard not to hear this Gospel as a prophecy of deicide. 'Fill up then the measure of your fathers', or, in the Jerusalem Bible's more vigorous translation, 'Very well, then, finish off the work that your fathers began'. Your fathers persecuted the prophets and were responsible for the deaths of some of them—go on then, take your ancestral practice to its logical conclusion: slay the prophet who is not only the greatest of the prophets, the prophet 'like unto Moses' of the last times, but is personally the Word who spoke in all the prophets and has now come as Emmanuel, God with us, to realize all the promises his servants the prophets spoke.

Looking at it historically, while the Romans were the actual executors of the deed, in his Passion and Death Jews certainly played their part: not only individuals like the high priest and Herod Antipas but also the Jerusalem populace who turned against Jesus at the end and in a famous and dreadful cry claimed in this to commit the people and their descendants: 'His blood be upon us and our children'.

But there is a prayer mandated by Pope Leo XIII which found its way into many pre-Conciliar Catholic manuals of devotion. In the course of an act of dedication to Jesus' Sacred Heart it calls to mind without flinching that dreadful cry. But then it adds, 'Yes, let his blood be upon them now, as a laver of mercy and forgiveness'.

Thursday of the Twenty-first Week of the Year (Years 1 and 2)

Today's Gospel exhorts us to be ready to receive the Son of Man who will come in judgment at an hour we do not know and cast into outer darkness those who have maltreated others — especially those with authority who have abused their position is so doing while all the time indulging themselves.

The element of social radicalism, or at least social concern, is thoroughly familiar to modern Christians. Less heard perhaps in many of the historic churches in the West is the note of divine judgment and, especially, divine punishment.

We can note that a good doctor always warns people when their life-style is damaging their health and leading, if uncorrected, to premature demise. With those who are inured in their excesses, a good doctor will 'scare the living daylights out of them' as the saying has it. When our Lord speaks as Judge or even, as here, as prosecuting counsel, he is not switching personas like Jekyll and Hyde. He is still our loving Physician. But we need to know, indeed we have a *right* to know (something which is highly early twenty-first century!). Do the behaviours we persist in mean spiritual death for us? Ultimately, unrighteousness will not be able to co-exist with the holiness of God.

Friday of the Twenty-first Week of the Year (Years 1 and 2)

Today's parable concerns the attendants of a bridegroom. They are girls whom the Jerusalem Bible calls, more functionally, 'brides-maids' and the older translations, more hopefully, 'virgins'. But one obvious character is missing from the scenario. Not the bridegroom, who is very decisively present at the end, but the bride. Who is she, and why is she not mentioned?

If we bear in mind that in all traditional exegesis of this passage the Bridegroom is Christ, and the wedding the celebration of his saving work, then the Bride can only be one person, and that is the Church. If we think about what is involved in the covenant of salvation between Christ and the Church, the 'New and Everlasting Covenant' as we call it each time the Church's mysteries are celebrated, each time the Mass is sung or said, then we shall see at once that whatever happens to the bridesmaids—to individual Christians—the Bride at least can never be absent from the wedding-feast.

The reason why the Covenant we live under in Jesus Christ *is* a definitive—'New and Eternal'—Covenant is precisely that, by raising up in his Church-Bride an indefectible Covenant partner— one who, whatever the apostasies of her individual members can never fall away from her Bridegroom, the Lord has ensured that humanity, in her, is bonded to him for evermore. This could never be said of the world until the Church was born from the side of her crucified Saviour on Calvary.

Of course we need to worry whether, in the terms set by the parable, we are more like the wise or the foolish bridesmaids. But we also need, and need even more, to have the confidence of faith to affirm the indissolubility of the marriage between the Bridegroom and the Bride.

Saturday of the Twenty-first Week of the Year (Years 1 and 2)

Today's parable includes a fierce message from our Lord. The eternal Word of God, when he stooped down to assume our nature, took on all of our essential passions, which include what Plato called 'spiritedness', and so the capacity for righteous anger.

Here Jesus speaks harshly against those who do not use creatively—in God's service and that of others—those talents God has given them, but hide them away in a napkin: a fitting symbol of what happens when we clutch our gifts to ourselves and keep them to a little private domestic world we have made for ourselves.

St Thérèse of Lisieux says somewhere that God's love is more terrible than his anger; we might say, alternatively, that anger is the heat of God's love—it is the demandingness of God in our regard, seeing that he loves us enough to care that we make of our gifts what we have it in us to be, and don't fold ourselves up like a napkin, to be tucked away in a drawer.

In St Luke's version, this gospel ends by referring to Jesus' going up to Jerusalem, which for St Luke is not just a geographical reference but an allusion to the Crucifixion and hence to the Ascension, the glorification of Christ. Our Lord earned the right to speak strongly to us by his Sacrifice for us. Those whose love for us led them to do difficult and demanding things for our sake have a right to ask us to pull up our socks in return.

THE TWENTY-SECOND WEEK OF THE YEAR

Monday of the Twenty-second Week of the Year (Year 1)

The epistle of today's Mass is drawn from St Paul's First Letter to the Thessalonians and it reads rather strangely to our ears.

What is strange about it? Well, firstly there is Paul's evident assumption that Christ will return in glory soon: in Paul's lifetime, most probably. And secondly, the actual scenario the apostle presents us with for this event doesn't sound especially persuasive.

At one time, the critical exegetes were of the opinion that the delay in the Parousia was a traumatic crisis of epic proportions for the early Church. Now they are more likely to say that if it *was* such a crisis it has left remarkably little trace in the New Testament and elsewhere. They would be well advised to look to what the dogmatic theologians have to say on this matter, and especially at the way the God-man might see the course of time and the end of time bi-focally, in their essential unity. The apostles coped quite easily with the notion that while the Kingdom of God came initially with Christ's Resurrection, a truly final end was still awaited, on the timing of which people might have different views. Only experience would tell.

But how should that truly final End be conceived or imagined? Better than imagining it might be conceiving it through the idea of a final event which is more than just the last event in a series but is what has been called a 'meta-event', an event of a different order since it makes sense of all the events within the series that precedes it.

Or, if we are going to try and imagine it, then better present an imaginative picture allusively, with discretion, as R. H. Benson does in *The Lord of the World* where the Parousia happens as the bombers dive low to target the chapel of the last pope, a refugee in Palestine at Armageddon, while the faithful gathered for Benediction sing the *Tantum ergo*, and the shuddering sounds of the aircraft, along with the singing and incense smoke, open onto an End which is itself never portrayed.

It was something Paul got better at as he got older, and we can sympathise because even to begin to portray the Parousia by an exercise of literary imagination is to strain the resources of language to the uttermost. 'God is a New Language' was the title of a book in the 1960s. We already reflect that in our distinctively Christian language which comes from the Incarnation, Resurrection and Pentecost. But we shall find our tongues behaving differently again in the Kingdom.

Monday of the Twenty-second Sunday of the Year (Year 2)

In his Second Letter to the Church to Corinth from which we read a rather famous extract in the Liturgy of the Word today, St Paul disclaims any gifts as an orator, and ascribes the effectiveness of his proclamation to the Corinthians to the power of the Spirit. The apostle was such a wonderful writer that we might have expected him to be an impressive speaker, but the two do not always go hand in hand. He himself thought it was just as well, because he didn't want there to be any mistake: the acts of faith of the Corinthian Christians are the fruit of divine grace not of human gifts. And raising an issue which has caused gallons of ink to flow in the later Church, he contrasts with each other 'human philosophy', on which their faith does *not* depend, and 'the power of God', on which it does.

St Paul is perfectly right to say that philosophy cannot of itself generate the act of faith. The act of faith comes about when the grace of God illumines our mind and attracts our will so that in the word that is preached to us about his Son we apprehend God himself drawing us to him. This is how 'the power of God' works in our lives.

That said, the tradition of the Church does not reject the help of philosophy, not to generate faith but to clear away objections to faith and to help us grasp the implications of faith. The apostle objects not to philosophy as such but to philosophy in the wrong role, the wrong place. 'Don't attack reason', advised Chesterton's fictional detective Father Brown, 'it's bad theology'.

Tuesday of the Twenty-second Week of the Year (Years 1 and 2)

How often do we hear in homilies about the 'depths of God'? Not simply the fundamental assertions about God as One and Three, Creator and Redeemer, that are found in the Creed and echoed in the basic preaching and catechesis of the Church, but the mystery which leads into the cloud of unknowing, the abyss of the divine Essence? 'The depths of God': if the apostle feels obliged to mention it in a piece of inspired Scripture the Church has taken into her Canon, then perhaps we should from time to time, 'in fear and trembling' as Paul himself would say, advert to them.

The reason we have mystics in the Church, particular Christians who are in receipt of special charisms of the Holy Spirit for the more intimate experiencing of God, is so that the whole Church can recast her doctrine as a 'mystical theology': not just a set of truths about God but an invitation to taste the sweetness of the Lord. It isn't important to know about the individual life-experiences of the mystical saints, and their transitions to this or that state of contemplative prayer. But it *is* important to know the upshot of this process, to have a glimpse of what the revealed teaching looks like when it has been not simply believed, credited, accepted, but has come alive in conscious encounter with the realities of which it speaks. This is how the 'Spirit that comes from God' teaches us to 'understand the gifts that he has given us'.

The mystical saints have entered the darkness of God, which is dark because the mystery of God is an excess of light at which they blink as bats do at sunlight. But in the darkness, where God offers himself to be experienced not so much by knowledge as by love, there is the transforming union. For the love concerned aims at just that, not simply for the mystics but for us all: to enter into union with God and there to become like him. And how could that be unless the union transforms?

Tuesday of the Twenty-second Week of the Year (Year 1)

In today's epistle we're told that the Day of the Lord, the end of history, will come 'like a thief in the night'. The simile St Paul chooses—a criminal break-in—is at one level hardly reassuring, but in another way it *is* reassuring in fact. One thing a criminal break-in is not is chance, haphazard, or unintentional. Whatever the ending that is the end of the world will be like it will not be pointless, futile, as so many human endings within history can seem to be.

A lot of the things that go on in the world around us are what theologians call 'permitted' by God rather than intended by him. They fall within his will inasmuch as he allows them to happen rather than chooses that they shall. And if we ask what the end of the world—this supremely intended event or meta-event—is *for*, one answer must be that it is to align the consequences of what God has permitted with what God really purposes for his creation.

For the individual—who, long before the world as a whole, reaches the end of time in his or her way—we call that 'Purgatory'. Purgatory is the Day of the Lord for the individual—which is why we apply to it the imagery of purging, fire, the purifying of dross, the very same imagery Scripture uses for the end of the world as a whole. In Purgatory, everything that was dross about ourselves: the imperfections that God permitted and the damage done to us by events he allowed—all this can be removed and God's real, intended will for us stand out in all its final beauty. That is what all prayer for the dead takes as its aim.

Wednesday of the Twenty-second Week of the Year (Years 1 and 2)

In today's Gospel we see in a nutshell what you might call the three main occupations of our Lord's public ministry: healing, exorcism, enlightenment.

All three continue in the Church: *healing*, in the care given to diseased bodies and minds by Christian doctors, nurses, counsellors, and, in its own way, in the sacrament of the Anointing of the Sick; *exorcism*, sometimes in actual ritual exorcisms but more often by the Church confronting men and movements that are opposed to the good, whether the saving good or the ordinary human good; *enlightenment*, by teaching which can range from a catechist instructing a pagan in the rudiments of the faith to a pope defining doctrine.

These three things both look and are remarkable different and perhaps in that way they can stand for a problem we face as preachers of the faith today. It is the problem of getting a firm hold on *the aims of Christ*.

We may find that hold slipping amid the thickets of New Testament studies and the investigation of Church history. There are the varying theologies which, we are told, can be detected in the Gospels and the way the evangelists used their sources. Behind that lie the different uses to which memories of Jesus were put before they were ever committed to record. And after that come all the Christologies of later writers, and the different images of our Lord presented over the centuries in literature and art.

But if this alarms us, today's Gospel reminds us that his story was never without its complexity. It always called for an effort of Christian intelligence under grace to see the total picture in which everything falls into place and makes sense.

The apostolic preaching, the Creeds, the catechisms and the dogmatic theologies approved by the Church, are there to give us the framework we need in order to see the figure of Christ in its correct proportions.

Healing, exorcism, enlightenment: these are as different as chalk and cheese. But with the framework in place we can see their convergent aim, which was God's enabling our human nature to reach its goal. This is the Saviour's work: to make us whole and raise us up to share the life of God.

Thursday of the Twenty-second Week of the Year (Years 1 and 2)

Today we get a glimpse of the kind of experience which started off the Church in the first place—the miraculous draught of fish, followed by St Peter's confession.

As a professional, Peter presumably knew the difference between a catch that was statistically improbable and one that was in principle impossible—normally speaking, that is. The miraculous draught of fish triggers in Peter a rush of conviction. The divine attribute of Lordship over creation is shared with the Man from Nazareth, his fellow human being—and if God's sovereignty then surely also his holiness, for these are all one in Israel's Lord. That would explain what he had felt about the Master for so long. Hence his cry: 'Depart from me, for I am a sinful man'. Such an experience shows how the faith of the Church in the Incarnation got underway.

But had things stayed there, with a simple affirmation of God's sharing of his being with his Son, we should have known, so to speak, Christ the Lord but not Jesus the Saviour. Every Gospel-book ends, however, with a narrative of the Passion. That reminds us that faith in the Incarnation is incomplete until it has grasped the Incarnation's purpose, which is seen only in the Cross.

Our faith is not only in a God who in his Son made himself gloriously present within his creation. It is also in a God who in his Son made himself vulnerable to that creation, so as to know our experience of frailty from inside. And so the Gospel is always of the crucified Christ from whose open side flow forth the marvels of salvation — the miraculous draught not of fish but of grace, and in whom God's holiness becomes mercy and pity for a sinful world.

Friday of the Twenty-second Week of the Year (Years 1 and 2)

The idea of Jesus as divine Bridegroom is one that Catholics have long associated in a special way with the consecration of nuns. The nun, or the Religious sister, is a bride of Christ. That is shown by the ring on her finger, a sign of her spiritual marriage with Christ. Sometimes the headgear that goes with the traditional religious habit for women is regarded as a form of wedding crown: brides are crowned on their wedding days in places like Greece and Western Norway. Some monastic communities even prescribe a ritual bath before a nun is veiled and consecrated, as was the case for a bride in the ancient world.

Today some Religious women find all this embarrassing or out of place, but that may be a symptom of how Religious life can itself be interpreted in a rather ordinary and even banal way.

Anyhow, the symbolism of the divine Bridegroom is wider than this. It has its roots in the Old Testament. It is a way of countering the claims of Baal, the fertility god Israel was tempted to follow her Canaanite neighbours in worshipping. Not Baal but the Lord is the one to whom Israel is betrothed, and their marriage covenant is a lot more demanding than just being thankful for fertility. When in the Gospels Jesus Christ is identified as the divine Bridegroom the same claims are transferred to him.

What, then, does it mean to say that Jesus the incarnate God is Bridegroom? Two things, above all. First, that God in Christ is united with us in an intimate fashion that should create joy and celebration. Secondly, that he comes to make us fruitful in the life we live in the Holy Spirit. To acclaim Christ as Bridegroom of the Church and to make the nun the icon of the Church as Virgin and Mother this is to say that, first, we should enjoy his presence, and, second, that we should let that presence bear fruit in the Christian virtues, in evangelical living. That is the new wine old skins cannot contain.

Saturday of the Twenty-second Week of the Year (Year 1)

In the Epistle of today's Mass, St Paul tells the Colossian Christians they are able to stand before the Lord 'holy, pure, and blameless'. That is certainly a desirable state of affairs, but how can the apostle be so sure? He can be so sure owing to the mysteries of baptismal rebirth when the Colossians were justified and sanctified in the blood of the Lamb, the virtue of which flowed out through the life-giving waters.

How often do we think of our Baptism and the spiritual and moral beauty that was ours in that moment, with all the resources within us to keep that beauty intact until we reach Heaven? If we gave more thought to the nobility into which we have been re-born we should have a powerful incentive to abhor vice, love virtue, and in the old phrase put on the lips of those making a sacramental Confession, in the future 'avoid the occasions of sin'.

It is true that we do not always know what occasions of sin will be. The night of the world has long fingers, stretching out and probing our weak spots. But the baptismal covenant always holds good; our baptismal 'character' is never lost. It is for us to remember the beauty that was ours, and which, at one level, can never be lost by us, and to let its radiance dispel the shadows in which we live.

Saturday of the Twenty-second Week of the Year (Year 2)

The apostle tells the Corinthians that, like his co-workers in the apostolic ministry, he has become a 'fool for Christ's sake'. And he spells out in detail what this 'folly' has involved in terms of putting up with hardships and insults that no normal person would endure without speedily forming the intention of getting out of it as soon as possible. The Gospel of Christ crucified is always going to lay itself open to claims that those who embrace it are fools indeed. So it has been from late antiquity onwards: one of the earliest known representations of Calvary is the graffito of a crucified donkey. It is certainly the case today when to the difficult and paradoxical message of orthodox Christianity there is added to ancient rationalism the militant secularism which wants no civic religion at all.

One of my teachers at Blackfriars Oxford used to remark that there is a difference between 'being a fool for Christ's sake and being a bloody fool' (pardon my French). I am sure I have neglected that distinction myself. But let us not suppose it is an easy distinction to draw. There is a sense in which to be a fool for Christ's sake is to throw one's life away, and if that is not being a bloody fool in the eyes of the world it is difficult to know what would be.

We must not underestimate the force of these apostolic words.

THE TWENTY-THIRD WEEK OF THE YEAR

Monday of the Twenty-third Week of the Year (Year 1)

The opening of today's epistle has seemed to some commentators to stick out like a sore thumb. How could St Paul, who declares Christ to be on the Cross the propitiation put forward by God himself for human sin and thus the only Mediator of sinners with God, seriously propose to supplement the atoning suffering of Christ by his own efforts?

The text raises large questions about the nature of Christ's vicarious suffering and whether that suffering leaves room for what in Catholic piety is called 'reparation': a contribution by us to the re-making of a spiritual order damaged by the sins of others. The lives of a number of the saints make little sense if such reparation is baseless, so we do have a stake in all this.

Reparation is certainly not baseless: it is based on the idea that Christ's mediation, though it was exclusive of any other *independent* source of atonement between God and man, is inclusive of *dependent* sources.

We can draw a comparison with what happens at Mass. In the Mass our offering of bread and wine is in itself incapable of bringing the blessings we expect from God. But that offering is transformed by the consecration when it is united with the sacrificial self-offering of Christ and in that way achieves the goal of blessing at which all sacrificial systems aim. Likewise here too Christ allows the saints to share in his vicarious suffering in a way that makes them distinct but not independent sources of grace.

The French philosopher Henri Bergson said of human beings, God has created creators. We can say of saints, Christ has saved saviours.

Monday of the Twenty-third Week of the Year (Year 2)

In today's epistle, St Paul comes down very heavily indeed on an example of illicit sexual relationships. A man had begun an intimate relationship with his father's wife — meaning presumably a second wife, rather than his own mother, and after the death of her husband. This is not as bad as incest gets, no doubt, but it's pretty bad if you think through all the implications—indeed, the apostle says he has never come across it even among pagans. But unusual though this kind of case may be, I don't think we should interpret Paul's response as exceptional.

There are plenty of other passages in Paul's letters to make it clear he did not believe in what is now called lifestyle liberalism. He thought there was such a thing as the order of creation, an order which surpasses in value the satisfactions of particular individuals and presents them with the framework in which sexual life is to be lived. Its maxim is, as the recent debate in Western countries about 'gay marriage' reminds us, complementarity and fertility— and it seeks to preserve those wider relations that are already established in the family setting by avoiding situations like the one Paul describes here.

The Catholic Church is often described as obsessed by sex. Sexuality is certainly a power that can wreak havoc in families, and human lives more widely—a sign that it does indeed belong within an order that needs respecting and is not simply a question of pleasurable diversion.

Notice, however, that the apostle—like, one hopes, the later preachers of the Church—having made his point, and made it with great severity, moves serenely on to the good news. Christ our Paschal Lamb has been sacrificed for us, and this Easter message about the regeneration of the human world gives us all grounds for hope.

Tuesday of the Twenty-third Week of the Year (Year 1)

In today's epistle St Paul chides the members of the church at Colossae—a little city up country in the south-west of what is now Turkey—for their 'worship of cosmic powers': he means, the adoration of Angels.

Today Angels are said to be making a come-back, but they are not in any danger of displacing God. The revived interest in the angelic is a healthy sign because these mighty spirits have been too neglected. If in our case anything corresponds to the situation at Colossae it is more likely to be the cosmic religiosity we call 'New Age': a worship of cosmic potency, the power and glory of the universe as a whole. Paul's positive comments on how Christians should actually be living fits with this.

The apostle's deepest objection to what was happening at Colossae was that—as with New Age now—people were simply seeking to enhance, enrich and empower their lives, whereas after the Incarnation we know that salvation comes not through self-aggrandisement but through self-dispossession.

The share in the fullness of God in Christ which Paul promises the Colossians is only available if we are willing to let go of our own fallen personality, what Paul calls the 'carnal body' with its assertiveness and pride, and enter on the way of self-sacrifice and self-surrender which is for the sinful self a real death and so, as the apostle says, a burial with the crucified Christ.

It was on the Cross, Paul concludes, that God showed up that archetypal self-assertiveness which is the sin of the fallen angels for what it is—a complete misreading of the nature of divine power. Divine power is essentially the power of love since God is love. Thus on the Cross God revealed the apparent power and glory of the fallen angels for what it really was—mere parody of himself. That is how God on Golgotha made of those misguided spirits (in Paul's final words) 'a public show' and, leading them off captive, himself triumphed in the person of Christ.

Tuesday of the Twenty-third Week of the Year (Year 2)

Today St Paul inveighs against the habit of taking issues disputed between Church members before the secular tribunals. It's part of the dream of fraternity—of brotherhood and sisterhood—in the Church that we hope not to delate the fellow members of our spiritual family to those who are not of the household of the faith. But clearly, Paul was not envisaging a situation where civil society had itself become formally Christian: magistrates, judges, law-courts, and all.

So what are we to make of his advice—or, rather, instructions? Obviously enough, what he has in mind is civil lawsuits not criminal cases. It is when 'a brother', not the established authority, brings some legal action that Paul expects things to be dealt with out of court, in the family (as it were). A great deal here turns, or so it seems to me, on the shape and spirit of the law as civilly practised. If a legal system has been thoroughly Christianised, so that the virtues, organized in an appropriate order, permeate it through and through, then even if the magistrate himself is an unbeliever there is no obvious incongruity in seeking the adjudication of a civil tribunal. The judge, after all, speaks not for himself but as the voice that articulates the law. Where some particular law is not straightforward to apply, and the presiding officer has to be more 'creative' in his verdict, then (if he is good at his job) his will be the voice that gives expression to the sense of justice animating the law as a whole.

But what if we are not living under such a regime of law? What if the law under which we are living has become distorted by populism or utilitarianism or a false concept of human rights? There may come a point when we would want to take the apostle at his word: the Church which, with Christ, will judge the evil angels on the Last Day can surely manage to decide what is equitable in the squabbles of everyday life.

Wednesday of the Twenty-third Week of the Year (Years 1 and 2)

The Kingdom, our Lord tells us in this Gospel, is for the poor. But is that Kingdom a sheer gift to the poor, in such a way that in order to be one of its intended recipients, to be poor suffices? Or is it for those who are poor but are also meek, hungering for justice, merciful, pure in heart, peacemakers, and persecuted for righteousness' sake?

Just as the Catholic Church in her self-reform in the sixteenth century rejected, over against the Protestant Reformers, the notion of an automatic salvation through a total corruption of the human will and a consequent sharing in God's righteousness that is not inherent, interior, and intimate but only imputed and external, so today she cannot rest content with a proclamation of the Kingdom which identifies as its predestined members those who are involuntarily poor—without any reference to the spiritual poverty that is found in faith, repentance, and freely chosen loving behaviour.

That is not to say we can ignore the voices of the poor and their claims as found in this Gospel. For us who, often enough, are neither materially poor nor spiritually poor, the Beatitudes must be a question mark and an act of judgment on our lives.

Wednesday of the Twenty-third Week of the Year (Year 1)

'Your life is hid with Christ in God.' Those words of St Paul are directed to the whole Church but they have a special pertinence to those who are cloistered.

The cloistered represent in a public and official way something all Christians are called to do in their lives—namely, to locate themselves not so much in the world as in God, to be more fundamentally with Christ in God than in the world. It sounds paradoxical, but it's true to say that the cloistered are the visible expression of the essential invisibleness of the Christian life. They are the manifest expression of its intrinsic hiddenness.

Without the cloistered, without monastics, the rest of the Church would not be able—or would be markedly less able—to get hold of an essential dimension of all Christian existence.

And that is the way the centre of our life does not lie in this world but in the new world of the Kingdom inaugurated by the Ascension of Christ for, as Paul says elsewhere in the Letter to the Colossians, 'our citizenship is in heaven'. The city to which we belong is more fundamentally the City of God, the eternally radiant City which, so we read in the Apocalypse, needs no lamp for the Lamb is its light.

We all know of the objections that are levelled at such an eschatological or heaven-centred approach to life—escapism, lack of responsibility for the earthly city, carelessness about the creation, refusal to engage with history. But in the end all these objections must yield to two overwhelming facts: first, that the Word incarnate chose to save the world by taking our nature through death to the Father, and second, that it is from beyond this world, from the Father's side, that he continues to redeem the world by drawing it to himself.

Thursday of the Twenty-third Week of the Year (Years 1 and 2)

'Give and there will be gifts for you.' This is a saying of our Lord
with huge ramifications. Notice, however, that it is not an example
of the old Latin maxim, *Do ut des*, 'I give *in order that* you may give
back'. That maxim vitiates gift-giving more than it commends it.

'Give and there will be gifts for you' is a statement about the
Providence of God which spans our lives from our creation to our
final end. Just in what way there will be gifts for us, if we give
ourselves in the service of God and our neighbour, we do not in
detail know. Some unexpected blessings may come our way
already. Others belong to the future of God, many of them beyond
the deaths of Christians. But the truth of the statement is not in
doubt, and the reason for saying so lies in its rooting in the Paschal
Mystery of Jesus Christ.

The self-giving of the incarnate Son in the humiliation that
climaxed in the Passion and the Cross was the way to his glorification as man. And that self-giving, and its outcome, were also the
way to the outpouring of the plenitude of gifts that we call the
descent of our Lord the Spirit at Pentecost.

Friday of the Twenty-third Week of the Year (Years 1 and 2)

We live in an age of psychology where people are very concerned
with—even obsessed by—the individual 'self'. So it's natural for
us to read the Scriptures, or the ascetic tradition of the Church, in
a more psychologizing way than was intended.

People like the Desert Fathers were shrewd observers of human
nature and one can learn a lot at the purely natural level from the
wisdom of their sayings and anecdotes. But they themselves
wouldn't have thought they were what we call 'practising psychology'. Rather, they were helping people to be purified in heart and
detached from the world. These are preconditions for growth in
holiness. If you want to use the word 'psychology', theirs was a
psychology that was Kingdom-oriented, and only there for supernatural reasons.

Today's Gospel—do not criticize the speck in your brother's eye
before removing the log in your own—has been called the charter
of Christian psychology. But we need to be a mite canny about that

description. When St Catherine of Siena tells us to enter into the cell of self-knowledge she *may* be expecting us to ponder this sort of text (how often the things we dislike about other people are versions of things we can know to be true of ourselves; our own vices may be more striking or more subtle than those that bother us in others). But she is chiefly alerting us to the mystery of the self in its relation to God—which is why virtues like humility and charity are the most important ones for the spiritual writers.

If we take our Lord's words to mean that we must wait until we've got ourselves completely sorted out before we begin to do anything for his Kingdom, then we shall perhaps still be waiting at Doomsday—and then the doom, the judgment, may not be very kind to us. Our Lord was attacking conscious hypocrisy, not recommending a scrupulous analysis of the authenticity of our personal experience—something for which most people have neither the aptitude, nor the opportunity, nor even the time. And meanwhile the time left in which to preach the Kingdom is short, if not in itself then for each of us.

Saturday of the Twenty-third Week of the Year (Years 1 and 2)

In today's Gospel, we have two of our Lord's most important metaphors, the heart and the house.

Our emotions, our passions, are so crucial for how we live that they are like the *heart*, which is the indispensable centre of our physical system. What comes out from the heart is not always easy to fathom. As St Augustine says, 'a great depth is the heart of man'. But the Gospels and the Liturgy are there to feed us with images which will purify the heart: above all, the image of the Crucified, the voluntary abasement of the God-man which is the antidote to our pride.

The *house* points to something else: our need for a dwelling, a base, a foundation, a protection against both the anonymity and the evils of society—the world outside rather than inside. Our house is to be built on hearing the word of God and keeping it: receiving by faith the truths taught by the Church, and acting on them in hope and charity. Hope is to be emphasised because God is faithful to his promises which reach beyond our deaths into the

Age to Come. Charity is to be emphasised because even here and now we can show something of the everlasting love of God, and give our home a little of the solidity of the eternal home he gives his saints in heaven.

THE TWENTY-FOURTH WEEK OF THE YEAR

Monday of the Twenty-fourth Week of the Year (Year 1)

In today's epistle St Paul asks everyone to pray for everyone else—a pretty safe proceeding which could hardly be called controversial. But he then steps on to thinner ice, singling out for special mention those in authority, especially kings.

One might respond that no one needs prayer more than those in authority. But in a modern context that could have a slightly sardonic ring to it which is quite absent in Paul. His letters show he had a reverential feeling about rulers which stems from the belief that the authority they wield—though not necessarily the way in which they wield it—comes from God.

Especially kings. That might seem natural. Though the early Roman empire was not in any obvious sense monarchical, monarchy was the principal form of political organization Paul knew. Ancient Christianity was realistic in taking kings seriously. But there was more to it than that. The Church found kingship an institution that was susceptible to Christianisation. Kingship in Israel was biblically sanctioned. Christ himself was Christ the King. Around the king or queen the Church could focus its images of what godly government consists in, and the virtues it demands for its exercise such as justice and mercy. The good king could be regarded as a mediator of Christ as Christ was the Mediator of God. Some theologians in the late Middle Ages wanted to regard the sacring of kings as a sacrament of the Church.

But then what about the rest of Paul's epistle, his insistence that there is only one Mediator between God and man, Jesus Christ? Surely that should have ruled out this development in advance?

Not necessarily. On the Catholic view of Christ's Mediatorship, the uniqueness of his mediation shows itself in the way it is generative—it sponsors further mediations of itself. We see that in today's Gospel. Christ heals the sick boy via the faith of the centurion which he makes a mediation of his own saving action.

That is our task in the Church in culture today: to build up institutions, of whatever kind, that can be vehicles for the grace of Christ.

Monday of the Twenty-fourth Week of the Year (Year 2)

The Epistle of this Mass is St Paul's account of the institution of the Holy Eucharist, and though we may have been told that the Mass is first and foremost a meal (the apostle calls it indeed the 'Supper of the Lord')—and certainly it *is* a meal, albeit of a most extraordinary kind, the whole point of Paul's account is to distinguish the Eucharist from any normal meal his correspondents have experienced.

A good text for us to meditate on in this context is St Thomas's antiphon in honour of the Blessed Sacrament, where he hails the feasting on the Eucharistic Species as a 'sacred banquet in which Christ is received, the memory of his Passion is renewed, the mind is filled with grace and a pledge of future glory is given to us'. These formulae are not just consecutive, they are cumulative. They build up a rationale for why we should wish to receive Holy Communion.

Each little phrase repays careful attention. We consume this sacred meal so that the *memoria* of Christ's Passion—Thomas's Latin word is stronger than our English word 'memory', and already suggests the idea of presence—be renewed in us. We come here to meet the Christ of the Atonement in such a way that our minds (once again, English can mislead, *mens* is something between heart and mind) can be filled with grace. In that way we shall anticipate the beatific vision when, please God, we will see God with our mind's eye. This is why Thomas says that in the Mass a pledge of future glory is given to us.

Tuesday of the Twenty-fourth Week of the Year (Years 1 and 2)

The God of Scripture is the living God: that is, the God who is the Source of life. He is the Creator, the Preserver, the Restorer. Human death confronts us in an especially powerful way with the contrast between the God who is life and everything that is not God. This makes the miracles of raising the dead particularly effective as testimonies to the divine origin of Jesus' mission—and ultimately to his own divine origin, because in his work, the man and the message, or the person and the mission, are one and the same.

He is what the Byzantine icons often proclaim him to be: 'The Lifegiver'. And that is a name we also use in the Creed for the Holy Spirit. Not an accidental coincidence, of course: the Holy Spirit is the Spirit of Christ, the Spirit who proceeds from the Father through the Son, and hence is marked by the Son's role in his spiration.

Today's Gospel also shows the tender mercy of God and not just his livingness. It was on a widow's son that Jesus carried out this act of power. All the divine attributes are inter-connected, and here we see how a revelation of strength was a revelation of goodness too.

Wednesday of the Twenty-fourth Week of the Year (Year 1)

The Church, so Paul tells Timothy in today's epistle, is the 'pillar and bulwark of the truth'. Truth is not perhaps the first thing we would associate with the Church today. When today the Church is evaluated positively it will probably be on humanitarian grounds, for the works done under her aegis for suffering man-kind. And so far so good. No one opening the Gospels could suppose the Church's Founder to be a stranger to that.

But the miracles of healing the sick and feeding the hungry in the Gospels function as parables of a mission with a wider scope: healing the wounds of sin, and feeding humanity with the life of God. Jesus has come to bring the truth of God—a truth that heals and nourishes because it is the Truth God himself is. If the Church, then, really is, as Paul says, 'the Church of the living God', her primary characteristic will have to be that she enables us to grasp that truth of God in a way otherwise impossible.

One way the Church today shows herself to be the Church of the Word incarnate, the Church of him who said 'I am the truth' and promised the Spirit of truth as his first gift to his followers, is the way she attracted the same crossfire of contradictory criticism Jesus notes in today's Gospel when speaking of his own mission in relation to John the Baptist's.

John's prophetic severity attracted opposition. Wasn't this a negative Puritanism, rather than true religion? Jesus' anticipation of the joys of the Father's Kingdom aroused animosity. Wasn't this a careless hedonism, rather than true religion? Likewise today the Church is accused of both rigorism and laxism: having a moral code that is too demanding to practice, and yet irresponsibly encouraging people to enjoy spirituality when the real tasks of meeting the world's needs are still waiting.

And this contradictory criticism suggests the Church is grounded in truth — the Truth of the Crucified and Ascended Lord in whom sacrifice and joy are united. So too in our own lives discipline and delight go hand in hand. Not for nothing did Chesterton describe orthodoxy as a wild adventure where we career down the high road of truth leaving the heresies — including moral heresies — falling to left and right on either side.

Wednesday of the Twenty-fourth Week of the Year (Year 2)

St Paul's Hymn to Charity is read on more occasions than today. Made available by the Roman Lectionary for couples getting married in church, many there are who avail themselves of it. We hope they are able to distinguish between romantic love, or indeed erotic love, and the love of charity, because the time will come for them when romantic love will cool and erotic love will fade, and then — my goodness! — they will need the love of charity.

It is the beauty of the love of charity that it can enter into all other loves — and even all other virtues — and warm them, enlighten them, and finally transfigure them from within. This is the supreme virtue, the key disposition in all our acting. It is the sign that we have (or do not have!) that mind in us which was in Christ Jesus. Not for nothing has it been suggested that the apostle, who, coming to his mission as one untimely born, did not know the Christ of the public ministry has given us here, in a subtle way that suits his genius, a pen-portrait of our Saviour.

Thursday of the Twenty-fourth Week of the Year (Years 1 and 2)

Today's Gospel shows what can go wrong at even the best-prepared dinner party. In the ancient world where the distinction between public and private as we have it today was unknown, anyone could step in from the street, through some kind of awning, and take a look at what was going on. That did not mean, however, that no conventions were to be observed. The appearance of a woman of easy virtue at the house of a strict Jew meant a crisis of social management. So much so that the host missed the point of the scene that was unfolding.

It wasn't just catharsis in the grand manner—repentance for an ill-spent life flowing out in floods of tears. It was also an event of the highest theological significance. Jewish prophets and priests—and kings, indeed—were anointed on the head, considered for obvious reasons the noblest part of the anatomy. But now Jesus is anointed on the feet, which were considered the least noble. Unencumbered by socks and shoes, feet were in daily contact with the dust of the earth and only slaves washed it off. The message of the anointing of the feet was the all-holiness of our Lord, and it took repentance like the fallen woman's to see it, to have the appropriate insight.

The two things—conversion and insight—go hand in hand. The more fully we are converted and begin to live for God's glory, the more we shall see the glory of Christ for ourselves.

Friday of the Twenty-fourth Week of the Year (Years 1 and 2)

It was said, 'The Church does not run on Hail Marys'. Someone has always to pick up the bill. Today's Gospel gives a good idea of who that someone was in the public ministry of our Lord and his companions. It was devout women—women devoted to God.

This Gospel text is very short but it should not be overlooked. The evangelist Luke has three crucially placed passages that attest the role of women disciples during the ministry: here, at the Cross, and at the tomb. The love lavished in financial generosity as the ministry unfolds becomes at the Crucifixion a love that accompanies—helplessly, but not perhaps hopelessly. Finally, at the tomb, it turns into a love that is rewarded when the Myrrh-bearing Women are greeted with the news of the Resurrection.

It wouldn't be difficult to put together from out of those three episodes a little theology of growth in holiness. To begin with, there is the active or practical life, the life of growing in the virtues summed up here as munificence or financial generosity. Then afterwards there is the contemplative life, taking place in two moments or phases, the first of which is a phase of passive purification (the Cross) and the other a phase of union (the Resurrection).

And this reminds us that the Church has two hierarchies not just, as is sometimes alleged, one. There is not only the hierarchy of the apostolic office. There is also the hierarchy of evangelical holiness. The first—the hierarchy of office—represents our Lord's significance for the world through official words and signs, duly authorized preaching and sacraments. The second—the hierarchy of holiness—embodies what the world's response should be in conversion of life and perfect charity.

No woman can fully represent Jesus in an official manner in the specifics of his humanity because he was the Bridegroom, not the Bride. But no man can fully embody the hierarchy of holiness, because its apex is already predetermined: it is the model of all holy women, the Mother of the Lord.

Saturday of the Twenty-fourth Week of the Year (Years 1 and 2)

The parable of the Seed and the Sower seems to crop up a great deal—no pun intended!—in the modern Lectionary. But actually this is nothing new. In the old Roman Missal the selection from Scripture is far smaller than in its mid-twentieth century rival, but this same parable, by occurring in early spring among the Sundays after Epiphany, was also available for use in autumn, in years when the dating of Easter transferred the texts of those Sundays to the fall of the year. Pope Benedict in his book on the Liturgy has made the nice point that sowing belongs indeed both to spring and to autumn since in many places farmers plant in both seasons. But in any case since the parable concerns the dissemination of the Word, and our reception of it in the most basic sense, it is a Gospel for all seasons, really.

The parable concerns how the seed of the Church, sown by the Word, will flourish, or otherwise, in the field of the world. Is it optimistic or pessimistic? It is neither, or, if you prefer, it is both. The scary part of the parable has to do, I think, with those who, as the Lord says, 'have no root'; they 'have no depth of soil'. We can all heed the lesson about not letting extraneous distractions spoil our life of faith. That's to say, we can all do something about that if we choose to. But what can we do if we are simply shallow, without depth of soil? Perhaps the sorrows of life will deepen us. It often happens so. Or perhaps we shall somehow catch the virus of prayer, and find ourselves digging deeper, to where the water-table is from which roots can be fed. Let us hope it is so.

THE TWENTY-FIFTH WEEK OF THE YEAR

Monday of the Twenty-fifth Week of the Year (Year 1)

The re-building of the Jerusalem Temple was in a real sense the re-construction of the People of Israel as a God-centred people, the People of God. We sometimes hear nowadays that to build beautiful churches is a comparative waste of money. The real churches are people, communities, not the buildings of stone, mortar, stained glass and painted wood. This is a false dichotomy. In its sacred beauty the church building is there to enable the people, the community, to become aware of itself as what it is called to be—a people, a community, filled with the mystery of God and intended to share his glory. Our houses are a night-shelter while we are on the journey, our churches speak of the eternal home which is journey's end.

But it is of course true that the Church, with a capital 'C', is first of all the people—the people constituted by faith and the sacraments of faith. The light the Church gives off is not, therefore, primarily the material light of a church building filled with beauty and radiance. It is to be, first and foremost, a light that comes from—or at any rate through—ourselves. We are to be illuminators, a light to the world.

And however we discharge that responsibility, whether by teaching and preaching, or by practical assistance, or by presence to others through contemplation and intercession, our Lord has a warning for us. If we 'have not'—if we have nothing to show in our lives despite what we have received—then even the 'little we have' will be taken away from us. The Christian tree that produces no fruit is good for nothing.

Monday of the Twenty-fifth Week of the Year (Year 2)

Today's readings are both exhortations to virtue; they want us to be good. But the kind of goodness involved and the level on which we're encouraged to pursue it, is not the same in Proverbs and in the Gospel.

In Proverbs, the focus could hardly be simpler, it is basic practical goodness. Be kind, be neighbourly, be peaceful, be honest. These are all important virtues—tendencies that become second nature in us and make us truly moral agents.

In the Gospel, however, our Lord implies a deeper grasp of what might be involved in our conformation to a goodness that is ultimately God himself. We sometimes do what is good from motives that are not. We don't always want to acquire virtues for good reasons, and sometimes we don't know what the real causes of our behaviour are. In other words: the heart is a wilderness, with secrets dark even to ourselves. The Saviour tells us there is a light which will one day show up our follies, so we are warned not to be content with going through the motions of decent, 'respectable', human behaviour. Instead, we have as best as we can to purify our hearts.

This light Jesus is speaking about: is it a cruel light or a kindly light? Is it a light that warms the heart as well as enlightens the conscience? We who accept his claim to be the Light of the world hold that the light in question comes from the fire of love. In Newman's 'The Dream of Gerontius', this is what the Angel of judgment says about the matter, 'Know that the fire of the ever-lasting Love doth burn 'ere it transform'.

Tuesday of the Twenty-fifth Week of the Year (Years 1 and 2)

Our Lord's relations to his own family are an issue still capable of dividing his followers. It has been characteristic of Protestantism to see in his words in today's Gospel a deliberate distancing from his natural mother and his 'brethren'—half-brothers or cousins. As he says elsewhere in the Gospel record, his real mother and brothers are 'those who hear the word of God and put it into practice'.

We need not deny that the family had themselves to undergo a conversion to his message, the Word of God, as embodied in his person. The simple fact of kinship did not suffice to give them insight into the paradox of a crucified Messiah, a God who freely made himself powerless and vulnerable, so as to draw the world by bonds of love. In the case of our Lady, such a conversion was surely a gentle, organic, imperceptible affair: with the grace of her

Immaculate Conception she would have been already pre-attuned to the way of her Son. In the case of the brethren, on the other hand, conscious in all likelihood of their Davidic descent, it must have been quite a wrench to tear themselves away from a standard kind of Judaism into the new world of the Gospel. One at least made it, James, the brother of the Lord, head of the Jerusalem church at the time of his martyrdom.

Given these facts—Mary's holiness, James's martyrdom— Church tradition has not found these Gospel texts the embarrassment critics of Catholicism suppose it should. The mother and one at least of the brethren of Jesus pre-eminently heard the Word of God and put it into practice; they are mother and brothers by grace as well as by nature.

Still, the preservation of this saying reminds us of something of great importance—the centrality of the Word of God, God's self utterance: the Word Mary conceived both in her mind and in her womb, the Word found in Scripture and tradition, served with the intellect by theologians, with language by preachers, with feeling and imagination by artists and poets, and by the martyrs with their blood.

Wednesday of the Twenty-fifth Week of the Year (Years 1 and 2)

What sort of healing was it, do we suppose, that the Twelve went in for on this mission? The presumption is it covered the same range as the healing ministry of Jesus himself: a combination of physical healing, psychosomatic healing, and exorcism. But while the various ailments, of body, psyche, and spirit respectively, were in need of healing, and, should the power to heal be available, thoroughly worth addressing in their own right, we need to bear in mind that our Lord is not a supernatural physician. Rather, he is the Saviour of the world. It happens, however, that the language of salvation and the language of health are intimately related. For example, in my home town, Lytham St Anne's, the motto of the borough was 'Salus populi suprema lex': 'The salvation [or is it the health?] of the people is the supreme law'. One ideal way in which Jesus could picture for people his role as Saviour was in miniature, so to speak, since restoration to health is as it were an icon of being granted salvation. In salvation we become whole and happy. Salvation is healing writ large.

So the question about the Twelve becomes, then: What icons of salvation did they select in order to present the healing power of the Kingdom? Their role as heralds of the Kingdom continues in the later Church, so it is a question for us too. How shall we show the salvific health the Lord makes available to us and through us? Will it be, perhaps, in the healing of our culture—to which we can all contribute (as parents, and as spouses, for example) in a huge variety of ways.

Thursday of the Twenty-fifth Week of the Year (Year 1)

Today's Old Testament lection promises the return of God's glory to Jerusalem if only the ruined Temple is re-built—it's a scandal that people are living in their panelled houses while the House of the Lord is a shambles. And the prophet plays the tune of preachers down the ages: getting more and more things to own is ultimately unsatisfactory, dissatisfying, a money-bag with holes in it through which what you thought you supremely valued drops out of the bottom.

And though the prophet doesn't say so, we with hindsight, and with a touch of the understanding that the Church's doctors and mystics have to offer, can see a connexion between that dissatisfaction and the return of the Glory. We were made for the praise of God's glory, so it's not surprising that anything falling short of that will ultimately do.

The way the glory of God is seen under the New Covenant shows an important advance when compared with the Old. Already in the Old Covenant we have the idea that it is typical of God's glory that it is sent to dwell on earth, and it descends for this purpose. It settles on the Tent of Meeting during the wilderness wanderings, and comes to tabernacle in the Temple on Mount Zion. But little here prepares us for the shock of the New Testament revelation when the glory comes to dwell not only in but as a human being. 'We saw his glory, the glory of the Only-begotten Son of the Father, full of grace and truth.'

The splendour glimpsed in the Transfiguration tells the disciples that God's glory now dwells with us in and as Jesus, and as St John's Gospel so strongly emphasizes, this glory is not cancelled out by the Cross but triumphantly vindicated there, since at the heart of glory is the sacrificial Love which the Trinity is: this alone is unsurpassably wonderful, fascinating, overwhelming, possessing in pre-eminent degree all the qualities people link to glorious beauty.

And so the combination of lowliness and glory in the figure of Jesus is such that people had difficulty taking their eyes off him. They couldn't shake themselves free of the impression he made. Herod in today's Gospel is a good example: perplexed by Jesus, interested in him, curious about him, he fails, however, to go deeper. Tragically, he will for ever be ranged by history on the side of what St Paul calls the 'principalities and powers' who if they had only recognized what they were doing would not have crucified the Lord of glory. Let us not by lethargy and superficiality repeat the mistake of Herod's life.

Thursday of the Twenty-fifth Week of the Year (Year 2)

The Liturgy presents us with a marked contrast in the two readings of the Mass, as we make our way through the Wisdom books of the Old Testament and the Gospel of St Luke. The contrast today is between scepticism and superstition.

The message of Ecclesiastes is that existence has no obvious meaning. It appears to be a meaningless round in which we make the same mistakes our ancestors made and grow no wiser. The Book of Ecclesiastes is in the Canon of the Bible not because such scepticism is ultimately justified but so as to make us face up to the element of truth it contains.

In the Gospel, the problem is not that people are believing too little but that they are believing too much. In Herod the tetrarch's territories, the rumour is doing the rounds that Jesus is John the Baptist resurrected, or Elijah, or some other of the prophets. People's religious imaginations are running riot, and our Lord's actual claims hardly get a hearing.

The alternation between scepticism and superstition is very much the way the world goes in all ages. In the Church, however, we believe in the serene union of faith with reason, reason with faith: faith giving reason eyes to see beyond her normal limits, reason introducing order and coherence into the statements of faith. This is the royal road of the Christian intellect and we are the poorer if we go aside from it, either to the right or to the left.

Friday of the Twenty-fifth Week of the Year (Years 1 and 2)

In today's Gospel we find considerable confusion reigning among Jesus' contemporaries as to his identity. Is he John the Baptist come back to life? Or Elijah returning as prophesied? Or one of the other prophets come back to his people? Only St Peter comes up with the—or perhaps one should say *a*—correct answer.

That confusion is hardly less today though the categories in which it is expressed are not so supernatural. Outside the Church, or on her margins where orthodoxy is questionable, we have had in my lifetime alone Jesus Christ 'Superstar', Jesus the Social Worker, and Jesus the Militant Liberationist. But even when we confine ourselves to those who are within the Church and profess an orthodox faith, we can find a sometimes bewildering variety of images of Christ in art and literature, in devotional writing and theology. Where in all this is the truth to be found?

Basically, we have two criteria of discernment which in every area from iconography to scientific theology must always be brought into play. And they are: firstly, the materials in the Gospels themselves, for God has spoken to us in his Son in flesh and blood history, and secondly, the dogmatic Christology of the Church, because this is the vision of those Gospel materials provided by the Holy Spirit in his work of enlightening the Church's mind. That rules out the secular or heterodox accounts I mentioned, which are really only projections of the preferences or ideals of our own times.

That still leaves the great array of different images of Jesus to be found in the Liturgy, in sacred art, and so forth. So aren't we back to the problem we started from? No. The variety of such images doesn't undermine the claim that once we have the Gospels and the doctrinal faith of the Church we really know Jesus. Rather, the variety bolsters that claim. The reason for saying so is that our least stable images of people are of those we know best. Take the example of our parents, or our close family, or best friends: it's extremely unlikely that in these cases one single image of the intimately known individual concerned will leap to the eye. We are familiar with too many aspects of them in too many situations, from too many perspectives, for that to be feasible. It is occasional acquaintances or public figures seen in a newspaper photograph of whom we are likely to have a single unchanging image.

However, we can, I think, *rank* the images found in the Church's tradition and we can do so by reference to today's Gospel. The Messiah came by his suffering to his glory, and so the best images of Christ are those which in some way indicate the sacrificial character of his being: how through death he brought unending life, through sorrow the highest joy.

Saturday of the Twenty-fifth Week of the Year (Year 1)

Today's readings are full of Angels. You may say: I can see that the Old Testament lection, from Zechariah, is full of Angels—the Angel who measures the site of Jerusalem for its reconstruction, and the Angel who brings the message of the return of the glory. But where are the Angels in the reading from the Gospel?

They are hidden in the title 'Son of Man'. 'Son of Man' is the most enigmatic, the most riddling, of Jesus' self-descriptions and probably quite deliberately so. It crops up whenever he prompts people to establish his identity. Who do men say that the Son of Man is? In the Book of Ezekiel, the title 'Son of man' emphasizes the prophet's humanity—his earthiness and littleness compared with the heavenly might of the Lord, and that remains relevant to the true manhood, and thus frailty and vulnerability, of Jesus. But in the Book of Daniel the 'One like a son of man' whom Daniel sees going up to the Ancient of Days is itself a transcendent figure, filled with power for the vindication of God's people. The inspired writer sees here the pre-existent divine Son under angelic guise. Inasmuch as the disciples experience Jesus as more than human, as coming from beyond the earthly realm though also part of it (compare Ezekiel), they are baffled by the thought that he could suffer humiliation at the hands of men. They are at a loss to pose a well-constructed question.

With hindsight we realize that the Father's plan ran exactly thus. What we are less likely to attend to is the implications for our view of the angelic—of the Angel-world. Though Jesus was, as God, infinitely more than any Angel, he chose, on significant occasions, to express his transcendent origin in angelic terms—and not least in the context of his mission vicariously to suffer.

Possibly our view of the angels is too Michaeline, too dominated by the mighty warrior archangel, and insufficiently Raphaeline, not influenced enough by that other Angel in the Book of Tobit, the Angel who carries out such humble tasks of service for the family of Tobias.

Saturday of the Twenty-fifth Week of the Year (Year 2)

The Book of Ecclesiastes contains some of the most wonderful poetry in the whole Bible, but much of its teaching seems to be thoroughly at odds with the basic tendency of Scripture. Its author is an utter pessimist, who cannot, in the end, see the point of life. That being so, there must be some extremely good reason why this writing was received into the Canon of Scripture, to take its place alongside, say, the Psalter and the Gospel according to St John, to carry out its part in bearing witness to divine revelation.

And I think there is a very good reason exactly of this kind. It is absolutely straightforward. The Book of Ecclesiastes is in Scripture so that we can ask the question, What sort of revelation can cope with pessimism, cynicism, even nihilism, of this sort? So that we can ask that question and in, among other things, the books I have mentioned, so that *God can answer it.*

THE TWENTY-SIXTH WEEK OF THE YEAR

Monday of the Twenty-sixth Week of the Year (Years 1 and 2)

In today's Gospel someone is trying to carry out actions that go beyond the limits of human nature—preternatural actions—and in so doing they invoke the name of Jesus as one among a number of names that evil powers will fear.

It is a Gospel, then, that comes from a highly superstitious society where a new holy name, as soon as it came into circulation, could be seized upon and given a whirl. We tend to think that the Palestine of our Lord's day was composed of decent orthodox Jews, albeit a bit crimped like the Pharisees or proud like the Sadducees. But there was a lot of strange esoteric Judaism, later cleaned up by the rabbis, and among the non-Jewish or semi-Jewish groups a heady mixture made up of bits and pieces of the religions of the Greco-Roman world of the time.

Such syncretism has not been known in England since the dark ages, though there may have been some of it around in the Renaissance, especially under Elizabeth I. Today's Gospel would fit perfectly, however, in the present-day world of pagan neo-spiritualism in the 'New Age' movement. Its message would then read: insofar as New Agers take Jesus as a guru—what they call an 'ascended master'—there may be some hope for them.

Today's Gospel may not be relevant to me, but it is relevant to somebody—which is why the Church insists on the use of the whole Bible, and the whole of her doctrine, and not just the parts we personally like.

Tuesday of the Twenty-sixth Week of the Year (Years 1 and 2)

Today's Gospel presents us with a rather shocking contrast. It consists in two very ill-assorted references to heaven. Preceded by scouts or messengers, our Lord is walking up to Jerusalem, and, as the evangelist makes clear, he is on the move in a double sense. The time was drawing near, says St Luke, for his 'assumption' into heaven. We more commonly use the word 'assumption' for our

Lady's heavenly destiny, but it is perfectly proper in connexion with Christ: his human nature did not, after all, rise up into the heavenly places of its own volition; its status and location were changed by the common act of the divine Trinity. God took up into heaven the humanity of his Son. But the point is this: heaven is where Jesus is heading, body and soul, because heaven is where all-bearing, triumphant love properly belongs. It belongs with the Father, the Son, and the Holy Spirit, since their life has been sacrificial loving of each other for all eternity.

And here is the source of the shock when we come to the second reference. Meeting with opposition, the scouts or messengers, and in this case more specifically the future apostles James and John said, 'Lord, do you want us to call down fire from heaven to burn them up?'. This retaliatory, vindictive response to people who may have been motivated by malice but may simply not have understood, stands out starkly against the background of the coming 'assumption'.

And we read that the Saviour 'turned and rebuked them', and they 'went on to another village', a sober statement that speaks volumes for the muted atmosphere on the road. Yes, we must always be careful how we invoke the name of Heaven.

Wednesday of the Twenty-sixth Week of the Year (Year 1)

In today's Old Testament reading, Nehemiah receives permission from the Persian king Artaxerxes to return to Judah, at this time within the Persian empire, and begin the process of re-building the desolate remains of Jerusalem—and as we can see from the books of Nehemiah and Ezra (if we look into the matter), this will encompass in due course the re-building of the Temple there. In today's Gospel, on the other hand, the Son of Man declares he has no place where he can rest his head. So the holy city is to be re-built, and the sanctuary, with its Holy of Holies, is to be re-constructed. Yet the All-holy One, who is very God dwelling in the temple of human soul and body, has nowhere to lay his head.

There is an obvious paradox here. In one sense, it is the contrast between the Old Testament and the New. The Old Testament is concerned with preparing a highly particular people living in very particular places to be the milieu where the Incarnation will happen. The New Testament, contrastingly, is concerned with that Incarnation itself, and the way in which the Logos, the Word, who unites himself to humanity in Jesus, is a universal reality, the God through whom all things were made and the ultimate meaning of them all. Of course, or so it may seem, particular places will no longer maintain their importance.

And yet we still encourage people to go on pilgrimage to the Holy Land, to the 'Holy Places' as we call them, and it is not by any means simply in order to inspect the Old Testament heritage. The Word was made flesh, as we confess every time we say the Angelus, or hear the Last Gospel read at Mass in the Extraordinary Form, and flesh has to be in a particular place for it occupies space; it is body. So it is not so much that the universal Word when he took to himself a human nature abstracted himself from place, as that, in the places where he was, he could find, through lack of a welcome, no home of his own. His parents had a home, but the locales the Gospels stress for their Child are the cave at Bethlehem, the roadsides on the public ministry, and eventually the Cross. He who redeemed us *knew places*, for he was incarnate, in our flesh, but he *had no home*, and there is a profound appropriateness in that for he is not to make a home but to be one: to be the home of humanity for all eternity.

Wednesday of the Twenty-sixth Week of the Year (Year 2)

Today's readings confront us with two mysteries.

The first, in Job, concerns the being and will of God which creation and history both manifest and also obscure. St Thomas Aquinas held that the reality of Providence is not something anyone can demonstrate. Looking at the world around us, with its hurricanes and outbreaks of regional genocide, it is hard to disagree. We accept the existence of Providence on the authority of the Word of God which reveals that all manner of things shall be well.

In the Gospel we meet again the mystery that is the kenotic Incarnation. The Word of God now personally embodied in Jesus Christ continues that process of self-emptying (kenosis) 'for us men and for our salvation' which is so vital to our belief in the existence of a 'Love almighty' in the face of 'ills unlimited'. The homelessness of Christ, we can say, points forward to his Passion and Death which are for any human being estrangement from all that is homely and familiar. The One who is becoming homeless is, amazingly, himself the Logos, the uncreated Home of rational creatures, and the Foundation of all relationship, all familiarity.

In his Kingdom—the joyous reunion of creatures with the Father—there will be an answer to Job. There the mystery of evil will at last be overcome and the heart will be at peace.

Thursday of the Twenty-sixth Week of the Year (Years 1 and 2)

'The harvest is rich but the labourers are few.' Those words were spoken with the assurance of one who has available, for the purposes of his mission, resources of knowledge not available to the rest of us. Looking round us in the early twenty-first century Catholic Church in Britain it is certainly a matter of common knowledge that the 'labourers are few'—there are rather small numbers of candidates for the ministerial priesthood, and the Religious life for both women and men, though the coming forward of laypeople to serve the Church in a large variety of roles both helps to compensate and is more difficult to quantify. But even were the labourers more numerous, may we assume that the harvest would be rich?

It is the question of the predictability or otherwise of evangelical success. One might say that, granted the combination of factors that militate against the Church in this country—individualism, consumerism, secularism, scientism, and the long-standing negative stereotype of the Church of Rome—if we had lots of nice little monasteries dotted up and down the country and enough clergy, and the funds to support them, for a parish priest in every large village, it probably wouldn't produce a bumper crop of converts. But when we are tempted to evangelical pessimism owing to chronic and widespread social trends that dispose people against the faith, we forget that there is not only general Providence—the way God allows trends to develop in broad terms that sociologists can discuss. There is also particular Providence—the care he has for the lives of individual persons who are not simply the passive objects, or even for that matter the active agents, of such trends. The attraction to grace is in the heart, and thus in the life-story of each one. And those individuals, when they stand up, can be, even in culturally unpropitious times, an exceedingly large host.

Friday of the Twenty-sixth Week of the Year (Years 1 and 2)

Today's Gospel presents themes of divine judgment and divine punishment which we come across only rarely—I would hazard—in contemporary homilies.

Some Christian descriptions—in words or paint—of the putative sufferings of the damned may reveal a pathological imagination: a desire on the part of the writer or artist to inflict a spot of pain themselves. But it goes too far to reject on that account all idea of God as the agent of punitive judgment. In the New Testament the mercy of God is wonderful only because the justice of God is steadfastly maintained as well.

We hope God will be merciful. Is that because no human beings have deserved judgment or punishment? No. Is it because there is nothing in God's being to which a power of judgment and the will to apply it could correspond? No, it is because in the revelation of the righteousness of God in Christ's atoning work on the Cross we have seen how God can freely allow his mercy to become the mode in which he exercises his justice.

So far as the departed are concerned, the Sequence of the Requiem Mass moves from the cry of awestruck terror, 'King of fearful Majesty', to the plea 'Fount of love grant me salvation'. Surely, it gets things exactly right.

Saturday of the Twenty-sixth Week of the Year (Years 1 and 2)

This is a very rich gospel. The opening verses lift a curtain on the apocalyptic drama that in the wider reality in which our world is set accompanies the action of Jesus and the disciples as they prepare the breakthrough into the Kingdom of God. The middle verses mark a high-point in the depiction of our Lord's relations with the Father and the Holy Spirit within the divine Trinity. It is because the Holy Spirit is the mutual Love of the Father and the

Son, and joy is the fruit of love, that moved by the Holy Spirit Jesus here exults in his relationship with the Father—the Father he knows and trusts in a way no other man has ever done, since his human powers of mind and heart are those of the eternally originated Son now living a life like ours (in all things save sin).

But it is the closing verses of the Gospel which really get to me. 'Happy are the eyes that see what you see.' And the Lord looks back to all those centuries of expectation, when men hoped that God would draw nearer to them or that at least they could draw nearer to God, and now it has all come about in One who is both true God and true man, the divine and the human inseparable for evermore, since joined together in one person who will be, as a consequence the Saviour of the world. No wonder the Byzantine Iconophiles, the defenders of the holy images, loved to cite this passage. It is about the new visibility of God in the human; it licenses the icons, and calls forth from artists an outpouring of beauty in line and colour. Our God has been made visible. We can paint the image of the One who has been seen on earth.

THE TWENTY-SEVENTH WEEK OF THE YEAR

Monday of the Twenty-seventh Week of the Year (Year 1)

The story of Jonah was among the first of the narratives of the Bible to be portrayed in Christian art—in the earliest art we have, from the second and third centuries, painted on the walls of the catacombs or carved into the front of the stone coffins wealthier Christians used for their burials. Why did people like it so much? Because it's so easy to see it as a type or symbolic anticipation of the climax of Christ's own story, the story of our salvation. Jonah is a man who was thrown out of a ship, and spent three days in the belly of a sea-monster but then was spewed up safe and sound onto the land. Was not Christ chucked off the ship of human society, the ship of the world? Did he not spend three days, or at any rate parts of three days, in the grip of death? Was he not returned, alive and more gloriously alive than he had ever been before, on the firm land of the Resurrection?

People who have looked into Jonah illustrations say that, to judge by the evidence we have, this was probably at that time the single most important theme in the art of the Church. That seems amazing to us who tend to regard the Old Testament as, for the most part, dry as dust history. But for early Christians the Old Testament was alive with figures who pointed on to Christ and to the sacraments of the Church.

For the story of Jonah doesn't only anticipate Christ's Paschal Mystery; it also anticipates our own Baptism. We went under the waters and came up again so as to share, by signs that are not just symbols but have an effect, in the destiny of Christ.

Monday of the Twenty-seventh Week of the Year (Year 2)

In today's epistle, St Paul warns the Galatians against receiving any other Gospel—any different faith—than the one he preached to them.

How then do we work out what that original Gospel or original faith might be? If we consult the doctrinal tradition of the Church, we find that the phrase 'another faith' is always defined by its relation to the Creed of Nicaea—the rock of orthodoxy as the later Fathers called it.

The Gospel is embodied in the Creed: the Creed the Church proclaims in her Liturgy, the Creed she administers to her office-holders for their assent, the Creed she calls on her faithful to recite Sunday by Sunday at Mass.

When you are told, such and such is *real* Christianity, or this, that or the other thing is the *true* future of Catholicism, think back to your Creed, and you will not go far wrong.

Tuesday of the Twenty-seventh Week of the Year (Years 1 and 2)

When we think of the active life and the contemplative life we normally have in mind two different states of life in the Church. There is obviously a huge difference between, say, the state of life of a hermit in the Grande Chartreuse and the state of life of, for instance, a Catholic layman working for a charity that helps Indian villagers dig artesian wells.

Yet St Thomas, in his little treatise on this topic, doesn't think first and foremost here of states of life, but of aspects of the life of the same person. All of us are called to be in some ways both 'active' and 'contemplative', though how that works out in practice depends on the temperament and the special vocation of each.

What is it, then, to be active, to be Martha-like? It is to practice the moral virtues, especially justice and mercy. These are ways of putting charity into action, and because they entail generosity with our time and energy, the practice of these virtues disposes us towards contemplation. It helps to root out disordered passions— competitiveness (envy), self-seeking (avarice); touchiness (anger), over-sexualisation (lust)—from our everyday lives. We can't be contemplative if our minds and hearts are filled with warring thoughts that come from these vices.

So what is to be contemplative, to be Mary-like? It is to give time directly to God, finding wonder and delight in knowing him as he has revealed himself to us in Jesus Christ by his Spirit. Prayer, personal and liturgical, is the most obvious form this takes. Prayer that rests in God, finding him wonderful and delightful, is precisely what we call *contemplative* prayer.

But contemplation is also to be found in theological study. The practice of theology is not perfect unless it flowers in charity, in love for God. However great the theologian's learning or speculative ability, there is something missing unless he or she also knows God by developing an affinity with the divine life which is itself perfect charity. Thomas calls that a knowledge that comes 'by way of inclination', or 'through connaturality', when God's ways become, so to speak, 'second nature' to us, so deeply have we made revelation our own.

Such contemplation is itself a source of action—specifically for teaching and preaching. Hence one of the mottos of the Order of Preachers: to pass on to others the fruits of contemplation.

Wednesday of the Twenty-seventh Week of the Year (Year 1)

Today's Old Testament reading is in one sense very modern and in another sense not.

We can see ourselves in the Jonah who is furious over the withering of an exotic tree but couldn't care tuppence for Nineveh and its hundred and twenty thousand inhabitants. Getting into a rage over the extinction of particular species is easily combined with not only indifference but a real positive detestation for humankind.

Less like ourselves is Jonah's burning sense of good and evil in human affairs and his ability to formulate and apply criteria for telling objective right from objective wrong. The author of the Book of Jonah is opposed to moralism but he is far from opposed to a normative morality. God doesn't say to Jonah, Why don't you get inculturated?, or, Haven't you ever heard of alternative life-style preferences? Instead, he says: Show pity. For pity's sake, let me give that great city the grace of repentance.

A false ideology of tolerance destroys pity in the name of justice. If to understand everything is to forgive everything then pity has no place. But pity for us as Christians has a very central place. The name God gave his pity was 'Jesus Christ'.

Wednesday of the Twenty-seventh Week of the Year (Year 2)

Today's first reading gives us an insight into the great issue which aroused such divergences of opinion and powerful feelings on one side and on the other in the Church of the apostolic generation. Should Gentiles who entered the Church first become Jews, and in that way reproduce in their own life-stories the story of salvation itself? Could you jump to the end rather than going through the earlier phases which prepared for the end, and get you into the right dispositions for it? Even though the Church eventually decided you could—and this was in a decision made so long ago, in the lifetime of the apostles, that for us it is simply not a thing we ever think about—nevertheless we should make a mistake if we supposed that the problem was a silly one to which the answer was obvious. The very fact that the Church retains the books of the Old Testament in her Canon, and reads them or refers to them assiduously in her Liturgy, proves that the problem was real and urgent.

In the Providence of God, the apostle Paul was raised up to bear witness to the distinct, though not separate, call of God to the Gentiles. Because we are ourselves Gentile Christians (at least most of us are), we are inclined to make Paul's point of view our own. But in the Providence of God the apostle James was raised up to represent the other side of the question. Poor old Peter was caught in the middle, as popes often have been in Church affairs—think of the battle royal between Progressive Catholicism and the Society of St Pius X.

What emerged was that the Church of the Circumcision and the Church of the Gentiles would recognize the same Scriptures (and thus the same doctrine) but that they would have rather different ceremonies, the Church of the Circumcision testifying to the continuity with Israel according to the flesh by making use of the ceremonial Law of the Old Testament in a way not needful for Gentiles. One of the tasks for the Catholic Church in the future is to recognize more fully the special place of Christian Jews in her communion, in accordance with this apostolic example.

Thursday of the Twenty-seventh Week of the Year (Years 1 and 2)

In today's Gospel Jesus gives his disciples some teaching on the topic of prayer.

Rather surprisingly, we may think, he deals exclusively with petitionary prayer—asking God for things. A lot of people would say that other kinds of prayer are more important: the prayer of thanksgiving, say, or the prayer of praise or the prayer of adoration—especially the latter with all the possibilities it opens up for contemplative prayer, the prayer of silent communion with God.

When we say that X is more important than Y we can mean one of two things. Either we can mean that X is of higher value than Y, or we can mean that X is more fundamental than Y. Getting enough to eat today is not of higher value than loving my neighbour, but it is more fundamental. If I starve to death I shalln't be of much use to anyone.

In our Lord's teaching on prayer the prayer of petition is fundamental. The reason is that asking God for things well expresses our basic metaphysical relation with him. God is the Source of being, all being, including our own. He is the one necessary reality whereas we exist only by sharing in being, only by—in the last analysis—receiving it from its Source who is God.

And if that is true of our basic metaphysical relation with God as creatures to our Creator, it is also true of our basic religious relation with God as disciples of Jesus Christ to their Father. Both the created being which comes to us through the act of creation and the uncreated Being, a share in the life of God, which comes to us in grace through the work of Christ, are sheer gift, for whose continuance we must ask—petition—every day.

Friday of the Twenty-seventh Week of the Year (Years 1 and 2)

The Gospels, or at any rate the first three of them, are hardly imaginable without demonic spirits. Nowadays we are likely to eliminate—by 'demythologisation'—his element in the Gospel tradition. So may I put in a good word for Beelzebul and the other devils?

There is no need to choose between a modern explanation of the Gospel demons in terms of psychopathology and the original understanding for which they are expressions of the fallen angels. The Devil and his angels are present wherever there is disintegration of the divine creative work. That includes situations where the harmony of our minds or the balanced functioning of our bodies is not entirely stable.

These spirits are personal yet not persons, for they lack the unity that goes with being a person. Their commitment to evil makes them not only disintegrating but disintegrated. So it's not surprising if they show up as a pattern of symptoms, a disorder in body or mind.

What, then, of the concluding section of this Gospel where order has been restored and all is swept and dusted when suddenly the demon returns bringing seven companions worse than himself?

It's no use having in one's life an order that is order for its own sake—keeping all one's pencils sharpened to exactly the same length. An order that is neutral as between the Devil and God is hopelessly inadequate. We live in a world where human beings have no destiny other than God. Unless all our powers are trained on him, the seeming order of a decent life is always fragile, not to say illusory.

It was when the proto-parents first said 'No' to God that the story of human disintegration began.

Saturday of the Twenty-seventh Week of the Year (Years 1 and 2)

Of course our blessed Lady was not simply the biological mother of Jesus. She was also his mother according to the election of grace. That is why he could accept the compliment to her given from the crowd 'Happy the womb that bore you and the breasts you sucked', and go on to take that compliment a step further: 'Still happier those who hear the word of God and keep it'. Certainly Mary of Nazareth could not have become the *Theotokos*, the Bearer of God, unless, by the grace of God, her life had always been marked by obedience to the divine Word.

In our approach to our Lady we have to keep hold here of both ends of the chain. It would be wrong to say, 'She was not merely the biological mother of the incarnate Word'. What would be wrong about that sentence is using the adverb 'merely'. There was nothing 'mere' about being the bridal chamber of the marriage between humanity and God. During the gestation of the embryo, her womb was the holiest place in creation, looked to with awe and trembling by the Seraphim. She is literally the Mother of God, the Mother of One who was God. Her biological motherhood is already a theological wonder for us to marvel at.

That is one end of the chain, then, her divine motherhood. The other is the obedience of faith which made her the model of the Church, the figure of the Church, and indeed the mother of the Church. Her willing assent to the Angel's message, which comprehended in advance all the sacrifices she was to make during the rest of her life, is the template for our own listening to the Word of God and being ready to keep it. In an exemplary way, she obeyed the Word whose Mother she became.

THE TWENTY-EIGHTH WEEK OF THE YEAR

Monday of the Twenty-eighth Week of the Year (Year 1)

The Son of Man was a sign to his own generation. Indeed, when we look at the Gospels, we find there a number of signals that in Jesus God himself was interacting with the world. There are his miracles; there is his fulfillment of prophecy; there is the evidence for his Resurrection. But the principal sign we are given as Christians is the sign that is Jesus himself, in the fascination, power, and beauty of his personality, teaching and dramatic story taken as a whole.

And in this respect, he remains the sign par excellence not only for the generation of his immediate hearers but for all subsequent generations including our own. That is why our single most important apostolic task is to present the splendour of his figure, the drama of his story, the power of his teaching—as found in the Gospels as a whole, as grasped by the rest of the New Testament as a whole, as presented in tradition as a whole. That sounds like a lot of work, you may say. In one way it is, in one way it isn't, for it is easily summed up, 'God so loved the world as to give his only Son'.

Monday of the Twenty-eighth Week of the Year (Year 2)

In today's Epistle, the contrast is between Jews who are slaves and Christians who are free. That is putting it rather brutally but it is not exaggerating.

In St Paul's thinking, just as Abraham had two physical sons—one by Hagar, a slave woman, and the other by Sarah, a free woman, so also he had two spiritual sons—Judaism, the community of the Law, and Christianity, the community of the Gospel. A line not included in the Lectionary version makes that plain. Hagar, writes Paul, 'corresponds to the present Jerusalem [that is, Israel] for she is in slavery with her children'.

We know how Paul was worried about Christians who thought their salvation depended, at least in part, on fulfilling the ceremonial obligations of the Torah. He was, however, a doughty upholder of rules of another kind: the rules of the moral law, the Torah's ethical precepts. He has long lists of classes of action that put people outside the Kingdom, kinds of action that contradict what Catholic moral theology would call 'absolute' or 'exceptionless' norms.

So if he does think that obedience to Law is in this way a necessary condition of salvation, why all the passion in this section of Galatians? He is contrasting a Jewish community whose source lies in the past and reaches out to people from within history, albeit a Providentially guided history, and a Christian community whose real source lies above people and ahead of them—in the future. Our 'mother' is, as he puts it, the Jerusalem above and she is free. Her presence on earth, in what we call the Church, is only preliminary. So the basic contrast is between the origin, alias Judaism, and the future, alias Christianity, and this is why the comparison is not wholly fair to the Jews.

Our destiny as Christians is to be free with the divine spontaneity of the saints who infallibly do what pleases God because their wills have been liberated by the charity of Christ. Then not even the moral law will be pertinent to us. Delight in doing God's will is going to be so all-pervasive that the concept of law will fall away. 'I do not call you servants any longer; I call you friends.'

Tuesday of the Twenty-eighth Week of the Year (Year 1)

Today's Epistle is pretty strong stuff. Are people, as the religiously minded like to think, children of God? Or are they children of wrath?

They were children of wrath; they can be children of God. That is how the apostle sees the matter. Given what we actually are, prescinding from divine grace, to become children of God entails the most stupendous change. So much so that Paul could never cease marvelling at, and strained all the resources of his language to express it. It amounts to a new creation.

People were totally missing the point of life even though the sheer existence of the world shrieked at them about its Maker. As St Augustine says, 'All these beautiful things cry out to us, beauty made us'. Atheism—to take one key example of alienation from God—is not just for Paul a mistake in philosophy. Atheism is the beginning of a process which leads, ineluctably, to failures of discernment of all kind: failures to discriminate between what is genuinely adorable and what is of only limited value; between what is truly an end and what is only a means; between what is or is not an appropriate expression of our created nature, not least in matters of sexuality.

And if we turn to the Gospel for today we find our Lord is equally blistering in denouncing what went wrong with us. But he is also more positive on the question of what is to be done about it. 'Give for alms those things which are within and behold every thing is clean for you.' And what does that mean, pray? It means we are not only to receive the new life of grace—God's forgiving us and taking us as friends. We have to get started in a bit of actively being gracious ourselves—passing on to others by word and example the charity that comes from God himself. That exemplifies how a fallen creation is re-made.

Tuesday of the Twenty-eighth Week of the Year (Year 2)

When St Paul warns his Gentile hearers not to accept the advice of unnamed persons to be circumcised in accordance with the Jewish Law, he is following the logic which the whole Church eventually made her own. Gentile Christians do not need to become Jewish Christians; they do not need to become as it were transitional Jews on their way to entering the Church. Twenty centuries after the Church settled the matter, this is not a thought that is likely to enter our heads, and so more useful to us here is the positive, rather than negative, part of his message in this portion of the Letter to the Galatians. What really matters, says Paul, is faith working itself out though love.

Faith that is operative through charity. That has become the formula of Catholic sanctity. This is the way in which people become saints.

Wednesday of the Twenty-eighth Week of the Year (Years 1 and 2)

In today's Gospel our Lord is, shall we say, firm. Though his invective is at its sharpest against the Pharisees, and it was with them that he picked the fight (the lawyers only poke their heads in later), it is his criticisms of the lawyers (otherwise called 'scribes') that are likely to strike home nowadays. The 'lawyers' here are not civil lawyers who, admittedly, have a mixed reputation in our society and, I imagine, even more so in America where litigation first became the mass industry it now is, to the considerable enrichment of the legal caste. The lawyers in the Gospels are a combination of what we should call canon lawyers and moral theologians. In the fairly recent past, in the Catholic Church, canon lawyers were closely connected with moral theologians, thus more or less approximating to the position of the Jewish scribes in our Lord's time—even if in our own period there is considerably more distance between them.

Church lawyers who are pernickety about the canons, especially those concerning marriage, and moral theologians who hold rigorously to the Church's teaching—once again, the problem here is often to do with sex. Are not these examples of people who lay unendurable burdens on men's shoulders? Well, possibly, but possibly not.

Even apart from canonists who emphasise the principle that laws should be interpreted as generously as possible, and moralists who stress the minimum that can count as actually embodying right principles, are people in the contemporary Church really faced, we might ask, with unendurable burdens? Is it beyond bearing that one should be expected to keep marriage covenants freely entered into, and to accept that sex is for man and wife, and the bearing of children? The question is, to say the least, relevant. So we should think twice before corralling canonists and moral theologians into a corner and throwing the first stone.

Thursday of the Twenty-eighth Week of the Year (Years 1 and 2)

Today's Gospel reminds us—not necessarily intentionally—that religion requires hard thinking.

The ancestors of the Jews opposed the prophets and killed some of them. Yes, but some prophets were false prophets who brought confusion on Israel, and would have involved her in hopeless conflicts with her neighbours or, alternatively, sapped her will to resist them. It wasn't always easy to tell the difference between false prophets and true.

The lawyers—the theologians of the Jewish Law—have locked the door of knowledge and taken away the key. Yes, but when you have a revelation that is itself complex and then enters into relation with the corresponding complexity that is human life, ethics, and culture, you can hardly avoid having a learned class whose job is to interpret it all.

In the Church of Christ we still have both problems. We have the problem of true and false prophets in the sense of people who are sure that what God wants for the world and the Church is this course of action or that, but who can't *all* be right because their prescriptions are partly, at least, contradictory one of another. And we have in the Church the problem of academic theology and, more especially, a biblical exegesis which is too technical for most people to get into.

However, this doesn't mean that with the Incarnation and the Redemption we are no better off than were the Jews who bore the brunt of our Lord's criticism. In the Father's mighty deeds for our salvation when he sent the Son into the world and the Spirit into the Church, we have an incomparably fuller experience of God's plan than they did. We have clearer criteria for religious truth and a better ability to sense what is or is not a fair expression of it. That is thanks to the guidance of the Paraclete, through whom the Church has her Creeds, her doctrines, and can draw on the instinct for the faith of her faithful as a whole—which means across time as well as across space. Given these aids, we should not find ourselves, despite ourselves, opposing the Wisdom of God.

Friday of the Twenty-eighth Week of the Year (Years 1 and 2)

In today's Gospel, our Lord might appear to be contradicting himself. At one moment he is telling the disciples to fear the Father, and in the next moment he is telling them to fear not. Is this a recipe for emotional confusion?

In a word, No. We need to notice two things. First, the objective realities Jesus wants the disciples to engage with are Hell—the possibility that one's life will turn out a tragedy, and Providence— the watchful care of the Father, always working, always available, to bring it about that we do not throw our lives away, if only we cooperate with him.

Secondly, the command to fear the Father because he can cast body and soul into Hell is not contradicted by the command not to fear the Father because he cares for us. Far from contradicting each other, the two commands by their juxtaposition bring into existence a new concept—what theologians call 'filial fear'.

Filial fear is the fear that is appropriate to the sons and daughters of God. It is emphatically not a servile fear. Rather, filial fear is a fear lest we damage or undermine the loving plan of the Father for our salvation.

Saturday of the Twenty-eighth Week of the Year (Years 1 and 2)

Today's Gospel is difficult. A key theme is apostasy: disowning Christ. The Son of Man will disown the apostate in the presence of the Angels. It's a way of saying that apostasy excludes from Heaven. The realm of the Angels forms the threshold of the heavenly world, and that is where the exalted Christ stands with authority from the Father to say 'Pass' or 'Stay'.

But can't apostasy be repented of and forgiven? Within the New Testament, the author of the Letter to the Hebrews hesitated, but the Church of the Fathers, reflecting especially on the example of St Peter, came to think this was surely so.

What cannot be forgiven, as this Gospel makes clear, is the sin against the Holy Spirit, generally interpreted as resisting the light—resisting the grace of God known to be such, in and for itself, shunning it as though it were not the way to the supreme good for man but its contrary. Since the Holy Spirit is so close, so interior to us—he makes himself a movement in our hearts—rejection of him can be appallingly complete.

But the same Holy Spirit as he dwells in us—and this is the Gospel's last words—can also teach us what to say in the hour of our worst trials. *In* the hour, but not necessarily before it comes. We are not normally dispensed from studying the faith—our catechism, our Scripture, our doctrine. But what are these 'trials'? None of us are likely to be summoned before synagogues for our faith and only a few before magistrates. But all of us need to worry about docility to the Spirit in the trial that is the hour of our death. Then it is we shall stand not before governors and kings but before the accusers that are our evil deeds.

THE TWENTY-NINTH WEEK OF THE YEAR

Monday of the Twenty-ninth Week of the Year (Years 1 and 2)

The accusation brought against the rich man in today's Gospel was that he had laid up treasures for himself and was not rich toward God.

We don't read that the rich man was censured for being part of the four per cent of the population that owned ninety per cent of the wealth, or some such statistic. The equal distribution of property as such was not a concern of our Redeemer.

That of course doesn't necessarily disqualify it as a concern of ours, any more than it disqualifies protecting endangered species or, for that matter, playing mahjong and drinking real ale. Catholics are not Biblicists: we don't hold that the only right judgments we can make are ones that reiterate the judgments of Scripture. Still, the judgments of Scripture are uniquely important for us, and there we find that the ground given for the desirability of relieving the rich of their riches is that human riches are evangelically disabling.

This opens up a different dimension—the dimension of salvation and it is there that Jesus intervenes. Time is short, eternity long, wrote Newman. The patience of the Father is infinite but man's life is bounded and the opportunities of grace cannot be repeated indefinitely. Man must discover his neediness as a creature made for God. He must learn to count his acquisitions as relatively worthless if he is to strive effectively for riches of a different kind.

Tuesday of the Twenty-ninth Week of the Year (Years 1 and 2)

When we put them side by side, today's readings raise the question, Is the 'salvation' we talk about as Christians something that has already happened to us, or is it something we are still waiting for?

This is reminiscent of the encounter, real or fictitious, between a young American evangelist and an elderly Anglican clergyman of the old school. The former addressed the latter with the words,

'Sir, are you saved?' The clergyman replied to the effect that if he meant 'saved' in the sense of being related to a past act with present implications, he believed that to be the case; if he meant 'saved' in the sense of a future action already anticipated, he profoundly hoped so, and if he meant 'saved' in the sense of an action already completed in all respects, then most certainly not!

The language of Scripture and the Liturgy about the timing of salvation can seem confusing until we think it through in the way the parson recommended. In his own person, Christ has already brought the universe to its goal in God and we share in that triumph through faith and the sacraments of faith. Yet in another sense the triumph is still in the future because the world, ourselves included, hasn't yet fully taken in that *fait accompli*, and won't do till historical time has run its course. We are still like men waiting for their master to come home from the marriage feast, to bring us into his radiance and glory.

Wednesday of the Twenty-ninth Week of the Year (Years 1 and 2)

Just as nature's year is showing signs of coming to an end—days drawing in, leaves losing their green, a nip in the air, the Church's year, even before Advent, has intimations of closure.

Today's Gospel is an example with its Advent-like theme of vigilance, watching, and readiness for the unexpected. Starting with the Desert Fathers, the spiritual tradition of the Christian East has taken 'vigilance' or 'watching' to be another name for what we in the Latin West call the practice of the presence of God. We should never be without a subliminal sense of the presence of God, not even when we are asleep, says the anonymous Russian author of *The Way of the Pilgrim*. The test is whether, on waking, the first thing we think of is God himself.

Anyone who comes to daily Mass is sure to have a sense that he or she should be doing more about a serious life along these lines. But we are often guiltily aware that we fail to do so. We are right to feel guilty, as the rest of this parable in St Luke's Gospel assures us.

Few of us have the opportunity to beat literal manservants or maidservants. But we all have ways of abusing those servants which are our own faculties—our mind and will, our imagination and passions. It is for their submission to Christ so that in us, in our lives, God may be all in all, that the Gospel calls us to be converted, to be perfect.

If we do not make ready or act according to his will, our lethargy will not be so lightly regarded, our Lord warns, as is the ignorance of others: those who, unlike ourselves, did not know what their Master's will might be.

Thursday of the Twenty-ninth Week of the Year (Years 1 and 2)

In today's Gospel our Lord says he has not come to bring peace in earth but division. In modern England, we became so used to a debased sentimental Christianity exuding a vague good will that this text gave us a salutary shock. But in the present period, when the opponents of the faith have become highly vocal, we are rather more savvy than we were a generation ago.

On the other hand, would we really want a Church that gloried in spreading division? There is a bit of a dilemma here.

The way to resolve it could be by attending to the really central term in our Lord's remarks which is not 'division' but 'fire'. The fire of the Gospel is the supernatural charity by which we are to reject the world, the flesh, and the Devil, so as to love God above all things and our neighbour as ourselves. Such fire brings about purging and transfiguration, just as for Jesus himself it meant Death and Resurrection.

It is a new life, the grace-life, which shapes up and re-casts all previous natural commitments. In the experience of the New Testament Church, as of the Church in later ages, it is welcomed by some as a huge relief and rejected by others with impatience and anger. Such is the mystery of human freedom: saving grace generates disunity precisely in its work of creating the deepest unity human beings can know. Paradoxically, it arouses hatred on its mission of love.

Only God knows the final outcome of this ambivalent history. But the Church allows us to hope—hope humanly speaking, not hope with the theological virtue of hope which would be a matter of certainty. Perhaps in the end no soul will be burnt by this fire rather than warmed by it, none lost from the redemptive unity for which Christ prayed.

Friday of the Twenty-ninth Week of the Year (Years 1 and 2)

In today's Gospel, our Lord chides those who know how to interpret the weather but not the 'present time'.

In modern church life we hear a good deal about interpreting the 'signs of the times'—the movement of history as something that reveals the will of God and thus the challenge of God. Jesus himself, however, gives no indication in the Gospels that his community will receive a gift of infallibly interpreting the course of history. The only signs of the times he alerts them to are those connected with his own coming as Messiah and those of his return, the Second Coming or Parousia.

All that the Church is assured, then, is that she has rightly recognized God the Saviour in Jesus, his incarnate Word, and that she will be able at the end of time to recognize his features when he returns. Anything else is a matter of an effort of discernment of a kind that is notoriously difficult and on which, thankfully, nobody's salvation turns.

Naturally, as moral agents, we have to do our best to decide responsibly about public events whenever such decision is called for. But the lights whereby we do so are flickering. Churchmen (and women) makes themselves ridiculous if they give the impression that it is on theological grounds more certain that, for instance, some particular way of organising society and government is pleasing to God than that, say, Jesus is Jewry's true Messiah and as such the only Saviour of the world.

Saturday of the Twenty-ninth Week of the Year (Years 1 and 2)

In today's Gospel our Lord both confirms our common sense view of things and also gives us a shock. First, he confirms what we would think anyway. Natural disasters don't imply that all who suffer from them are specially wicked. But then he goes on to say something that pulls us up with a start. Nonetheless, all deserve punishment because all are infected with evil.

This is a dogmatic claim, not an empirical report. It states one of those all-encompassing truths that don't so much need explaining as explain everything else. The Fall of humanity has brought us all to spiritual ruin.

Though it is a truth of revelation there is an aspect of it we can check out for ourselves. A major theme of human literature is the sickness of the heart. When we read the newspapers we think of malice in concentrated newsworthy form: murder, rape, and the rest. But malice doesn't only exist in concentrated form. It comes in diffuse form as well. Again, we generally think of how by malice people do things that are wrong. But the novelists show us how malice enters into the mixed motives behind even deeds that are right. So without repentance we shall all be cut down.

This is a hard saying, then. But like all the hard sayings of our Lord, it must be seen in the light of his Death and Resurrection. God is holy, and by his nature must judge evil relentlessly. But through the Paschal Mystery, the Father turns that judgment into a word of forgiveness and reconciliation.

THE THIRTIETH WEEK OF THE YEAR

Monday of the Thirtieth Week of the Year (Years 1 and 2)

In today's Gospel our Lord alarms the synagogue authorities by—in effect—re-defining healing. If in the heat of the day in Palestine the rescue of beasts from possible death through dehydration is lawful on the Sabbath then so is the healing of sick people. Healing, then, is *rescue*. It is rescue from the powers of death and dissolution at work in the world.

The entire New Testament presents evil in this dramatic way. Evil is not merely a lack or absence of something. Or rather, if it is such a lack or absence, that is because energies are at work in the world to counter the true aims of the divine plan. On the world stage a 'theo-drama' is being played out, with ourselves as actors and some more mysterious *dramatis personae* (Jesus speaks here of 'Satan') as well. The term 'rescue' fits this scenario well.

The preaching of the Gospel is itself a rescue activity: aimed at rescuing people from the effects of intellectual and moral error, and opening to their freedom the world of grace. The New Testament sees this conflict as intensified, not reduced, by the Incarnation, because the options are now so much clearer. The Church's mission would not be pursued as placidly as it sometimes is if the word 'rescue' were really in our bones.

Tuesday of the Thirtieth Week of the Year (Year 1)

Today's epistle is one of the more difficult passages in St Paul's Letters.

If it only consisted of the last few verses everything would be plain sailing. There Paul is quite straightforward. As Christians, he says, we have a first instalment of the Holy Spirit. Though he doesn't spell this out, we know that is the case from our wanting to do things like worship the Father, be of one mind with the Church, and act in charity toward our neighbour. This, however, is only a down-payment of the Spirit, looking ahead to the time when God will fully cash his promises to us and we shall be fully saved, made whole, through being made like Christ who became gloriously alive, soul and body, in his Resurrection. While we are still hampered by sin, sickness and mortality that is something still future for us.

The difficult part consists in the way the apostle extends this to the rest of creation—including there the non-rational creation. In what sense can the entire cosmos share in the Resurrection of Christ seen as the end of historical time?

Here we must avoid two things—sentimentality and an inadequate sense of the power of God. A child weeps when a pet goldfish is found one morning floating upside down in the tank. Such tears befit the point of emotional development a child has reached, but for a poet to exploit the death of the fish to arouse the same reaction in us would be sentimental; for goldfish are the sort of creatures for which death is unobjectionable. On the other hand, there is a vast quantity of pain and suffering in the animal universe. True, it is mitigated in animal consciousness through the lack of our kind of capacity for memory, reflection, and speculation about the future. Yet all that misery forms part of the 'problem of evil': how can a perfectly good and omnipotent God create an apparently partially evil world?

The solution of Scripture is to throw the problem forward into the future, and see cosmic suffering as the birth-pangs of a new creation already formed in principle in the glorious Resurrection of the Saviour. In today's Gospel, our Lord speaks of the Kingdom—the final transformation of the world—not only under human analogies—a cook leavening dough, but also under natural ones—a tree springing up from a seed, suggesting, perhaps, that it will affect not only human society but the whole organic creation. All suffering is bounded by that mega-event which will change the terms on which nature and history have happened up to now.

Tuesday of the Thirtieth Week of the Year (Year 2)

Today's Epistle is the *Magna Carta* of the Church's understanding of marriage. It presents marriage as a sacrament which can only be understood from the vantage-point of Christ's painful and persistent love on the Cross. That makes marriage in turn, then, a sacrament which illuminates the darkness of the Cross and shows the Cross to be a wonderful transaction between the redeeming Head, or Bridegroom, in his self-giving, and a Bride, the Church, who in letting herself be redeemed enables the Bridegroom to be fruitful in the world.

No account of marriage could be more challenging and inspirational than this. It is a wonder, then, why the tree of Christian marriage does not put forth healthier leaves and fruit in our own time — one thinks of the current rate of breakdown of sacramental marriages.

One answer would be: two people were never meant to inhabit this sacramental way of life and take on moral demands higher than those of natural marriage while being at the same time unsupported and alone. In ancient times, support came via a very close-knit Church life. Later, the expectations of a Christian society and the way it organized life and work as part and parcel of a well-ordered commonwealth, were meant to succour them. When the household ceases to be the basic unit of society, since spouses come together only in leisure time and for the management of children, and divorce is considered a topic for voyeuristic journalism and even to be ethically trivial, the sacramental grace of marriage has poor soil indeed in which to take root.

Here as elsewhere, what we must work towards is not just preaching at people but the construction of a new Christendom.

Wednesday of the Thirtieth Week of the Year (Years 1 and 2)

Today's Gospel raises, among other points, the question of damnation, of everlasting punishment. Can we imagine such a thing and can we ascribe it to a good God? Actually, we don't have to be able to imagine something in order to conceive it, or to be convinced that it exists. We can't imagine many states implied in astrophysics but we don't conclude that astrophysics is piffle. However, clearing away imaginative difficulties helps us to credit things.

One difficulty people have with eternal punishment is that they imagine it means punishment going on for an endless extension of our kind of time. But our participation in eternity will not be like our present experience of time at all, except insofar as it has some version of before compared with after.

But could a good God make us participate eternally in Hell? Hell is not primarily about God punishing us, but about our making ourselves into a certain set of person. It's possible to get ourselves to enjoy being bad. As with the Joker in 'Superman', our freedom can so shape our nature that acts which would be intrinsically repellent to the good become exquisitely enjoyable to the evil. This is a pointer to what Hell us like. Damnation may be a state whose horror consists in the fact that it is delightful to those who are in it, even though they are aware that such delight goes against nature and against God. If sadism is the archetypally damnable action, masochism is the best image here and now of the result.

Thursday of the Thirtieth Week of the Year (Years 1 and 2)

Today's Gospel gives us a good example of our Lord's irony. It cannot be that a prophet would perish away from Jerusalem. Here Christ foresees the tragic end of his mission, and he places it in a whole series of past conflicts between Jerusalem and the prophets. But there is no bitterness in his remarks. The repeated 'Jerusalem, Jerusalem' is almost a caressing of the name, and Jesus sees himself as a mother hen gathering her vulnerable offspring under her protection.

It is, though, all too late. The Jewish people in its official representatives—its kings, priests, theologians—is set on the destruction of its long-awaited Messiah. 'Behold, your house is forsaken.' The Jews will not see him till they say, 'Blessed is he who comes in the name of the Lord'—which at an obvious level is a reference to Palm Sunday, the beginning of the Passion, but at another, deeper level alludes to what the evangelist knew very well: only by faith in the Crucified and Risen One would the Jewish people hear God's ultimate word of judgment and forgiveness and so really see that vision of peace between God and man implied in the name 'Jerusalem', which means 'the haven of peace'.

So this Gospel presents Jesus as a tragic figure. His love is rejected and he is destroyed, in an act of hatred which brings spiritual ruin on the very people for whom his love was primarily given. At the same time, his suffering goes beyond the tragic, because, through the Father's acceptance of that suffering as a sacrifice for mankind, it brings the definitive offer of salvation to the human race.

Friday of the Thirtieth Week of the Year (Years 1 and 2)

There are three occasions in St Luke's Gospel when our Lord receives hospitality from Pharisee leaders only to find himself under surveillance. Today's Gospel, the curing of the man with dropsy, is one of them. Another is the occasion when the woman with a jar of ointment anoints his feet. The third is when the disciples give scandal owing to their neglect of the customary ritual ablution before food. The attitude to him of the Pharisees appears to combine hostility with fascination. They want to see more, but that is partly because they expect the worst.

Is it excessive to think that this attitude was or became that of Judas Iscariot, and that it has its upshot in the ambivalence of the traitor's kiss in the Garden of Gethsemane?

What lies behind it for orthodox Jews? Surely a perception that the holiness of Jesus embodied in a new medium, the medium of a human life, the heart of the Torah—the revelation of God to Israel (that would account for the fascination), but did so in so thoroughly new a way that, paradoxically, he might mean the end of their religion—of their picture of the world and of their place in it (that would account for the hostility).

As Christians we have to be careful that the same combination of fascination and hostility doesn't creep into our attitudes as well. We have grounds for possible hostility to the Incarnation of God as man, because this event proposes to alter our life by inconvenient demands. Perhaps this is why the Liturgy of St John Chrysostom makes communicants say at the moment of the invitation to Holy Communion: 'Accept me this day O Son of God as a partaker of your mystical Banquet.... I will not give you a kiss as did Judas but like the thief I confess to you, remember me, O Lord, when you come into your Kingdom'.

Saturday of the Thirtieth Week of the Year (Year 1)

The ending of today's epistle gives us in two marvellously contrasting lines a mini-theology of how we should see the Jewish
people. 'As regards the Gospel, they are enemies of God, for your
sake, but as regards election they are beloved for the sake of their
forefathers.'

You see how St Paul is equally distanced from the two attitudes
we commonly find today—either a lingering anti-Semitism (but
no—they are beloved for the sake of the forefathers) or a vague
general benevolence combined with guilt feelings over the Gentile
Christian treatment of Jews (but no—they are enemies of God as
regards the Gospel).

But it's not that difficult to see how right Paul is. The positive
part is right. The fidelity of orthodox Jews to the Torah, even in
the worst of persecutions, is an amazing thing, and it is a sign of
their irrevocable election to God's favour. And the negative part
is also right. The obstinacy with which Jews continue to dismiss
the messianic claims of Jesus and so set themselves up in opposition to the new dispensation of grace, the dispensation of the
Gospel, is undeniable.

How can Paul, unlike most moderns, manage both to love and
admire his people precisely for their religious inheritance and yet
go on saying they are in another way the enemies of God? Isn't it
psychologically contradictory to have such contrary convictions
and feelings about the same object?

The key comes in those little words 'for your sake'. They are
'enemies of God, for your sake'. I understand this to mean not only
the past history, that the rejection of the Gospel by most Jews
facilitated the turn of the apostles to the Gentiles, but also something
which continues to be the case. Providentially, Israel's rejection of
the true fulfillment of her heritage challenges us as Christians to live
out as fully as Israel the faith of the patriarchs and prophets, and in
particular to practice towards Israel—towards all Jews who reject
Christianity—those virtues of love, peace, patience, self-control, and
so on which the New Testament especially proclaims.

Saturday of the Thirtieth Week of the Year (Year 2)

In today's Epistle, St Paul manages to be all three of realistic, generous and holy about money matters—quite an achievement in a few lines of prose.

Realistic—he knows that as an apostle making missionary journeys throughout the Eastern Mediterranean world he has to have money, he can't just live on air. Generous—he has learned to live on the minimum possible though, as he says, he can also find good ways of using more than the minimum if it is around.

And holy—and that is the difficult one for us to come to terms with. I say Paul has a 'holy' attitude to money in that he thinks money itself can become a form of the worship of God, can become almost a sacred substance: that, I think, is not an excessive interpretation of his remarks. The money he has been sent from the Church at Philippi is described in liturgical language: it is an offering that gives off a sweet fragrance, like incense, in the sight of God. It is a sacrifice pleasing in his sight. Money becomes holy when it is given for the Kingdom's sake, to advance the Kingdom and its ends. And that is why the abuse of money by Church people is not just malpractice, but a blasphemy.

THE THIRTY-FIRST WEEK OF THE YEAR

Monday of the Thirty-first Week of the Year (Year 1)

On the face of it, our Lord's teaching in today's Gospel appears to contain a contradiction, or at any rate something incongruous. 'Prefer to do good to the poor' has as its basis that 'they cannot reward us'. One might think that Jesus would then go on to say that ethics is not a question of mutual back-scratching, or of getting rewards for what is in any case the right thing to do. But in fact he says the opposite: 'You will be rewarded at the resurrection of the just'.

What we are overlooking here is the importance of the delay in receiving the reward. The ethics of reward is now transferred into a new dimension, the dimension of hope in God, and therefore the dimension also of faith in God and love for God. Our expectation of reward is turned into an expression of all of these, and so becomes a God-centred not a me-centred attitude.

The other side of the coin from the ethics of reward is the ethics of punishment. And a similar sea-change overcomes that too, thanks to the Atonement. The Atonement is the free act of God in justifying the guilty, and in today's Epistle it calls forth an expression of amazement from St Paul. Normally speaking, one person cannot atone ethically for another. So the fact that Jesus Christ *did* atone ethically for the whole human race shows how here too ethics has been taken into a new sphere. It has been re-located in the re-creating Word of God who entered our fallen world so as to re-establish it on new foundations in himself.

As Blessed John Paul II pointed out in his letter on ethics, *Veritatis splendor*, there can be for us no separated ethics, no purely humanistic or rational ethics. Our ethics is centred in God, through Jesus Christ our Lord.

Monday of the Thirty-first Week of the Year (Year 2)

In today's Epistle the apostle tells us what the inner life of the Church community should be like. It makes for painful reading —

painful, that is, when we consider how far we fall short of the apostolic imperatives that are laid upon us, with all the authority of divine inspiration, in this document.

As you heard, its message is self-effacement all round. 'Do nothing from selfishness or conceit, but in humility count others better than yourselves.' How on earth are morally defective human beings like ourselves going to pull this off? What this passage taken by itself doesn't give us is the motivation Paul thinks will make it possible. It comes in the next few lines, and it's his account of the 'kenosis'—the voluntary humiliation or self-emptying—of God the Word in the human life of Jesus. Why should that motivate me to limit my desire for power in my little world?

It's quite simple. It works by hearing the story. The Omnipotent came from his blest throne. He came for my sake, to show me that even in God the way of self-giving is the way of perfection. Here he was born and here he bled for me. How can I know that, and still feel I have to affirm myself in as many ways as I can or else I'm hardly existing?

Tuesday of the Thirty-first Week of the Year (Years 1 and 2)

To have a taste of the messianic banquet is Sacred Scripture talk for being saved which is itself the approved religious vocabulary for making it, making it to the destiny for which one entered existence. But today's Gospel raises the question, are we among the *second* set of those invited to the marriage supper of the Lamb, which, though unflattering, would be excellent news, or are we, rather, in the *first* set which, though it would imply we were worth prioritizing on the guest list, would actually not be such good news at all.

You might think it's obvious that we are among those who, however limited our claims to elite status, were invited and responded. After all, we are at Mass listening to the homily (or reading it in this version, which also implies a sort of devout activity). Doesn't the Mass celebrant say to the members of the congregation, in inviting them to Holy Communion, 'Blessed are you who are invited to the Supper of the Lamb'?

Well, no, actually, the priest doesn't say precisely that. He says, following the liturgical books, 'Blessed are *those* who are invited to the Supper of the Lamb'. And owing to that difference between 'you', which he doesn't say, and 'those', which he does say, we need to ask ourselves, Are we in a state of grace when we approach the sacrament? Are we firmly resolved always to remain in that state, and to approach the sacrament of Penance, the sacrament of moral healing, when we think we may maliciously have done serious wrong and forfeited our baptismal innocence? Do we pray for the gift of final perseverance so that repentance may be ours in the hour of our death? These are the signs we have responded to the king's invitation in full.

Of course it's great, especially in a time of secularisation, that people frequent the churches, attend the Mass, and wish to receive the Lord in Eucharistic form. But in all honesty the Church cannot say that this guarantees anyone's presence at the messianic banquet itself. We cannot say it proves we shall be saved, that we shall make it to our destiny and not miss out eternally. Only faith working through charity, lasting until death, guarantees that, proves that, means that. Only faith working through charity can say that. 'Blessed are those who are invited to the Supper of the Lamb'.

Wednesday of the Thirty-first Week of the Year (Years 1 and 2)

Our Church is a Church of the masses; it's not a Church for spiritual elites. For instance, we baptize any child whose home situation conveys at least a faint chance that they will be brought up in the Catholic faith. We hold that the Church is the ark of salvation for all the world—so we can hardly be too choosy.

On the other hand, we cannot ignore clearly expressed warnings spoken by our Lord. In this Gospel passage his words are very plain: no one should become his disciple without counting the cost, a cost which is, it seems, not just possible or even probable but certain.

We need to distinguish that cost from the other kinds of problem, burden, or stress, we face in life which have nothing to do with our being Christians as such. We can usefully call it, I think, 'apostolic suffering', since it arises from following the call to be his disciples—and, as a consequence, to be missionary vis-à-vis our own faith.

In many Christendom societies of the past, apostolic suffering may seem to have been largely restricted to those individuals within the Church who took up the responsibility of the ministerial or the monastic or 'Religious' life. There is a sense in which the heaviest duties of public discipleship were carried out vicariously, by such individuals, on behalf of the rest of an almost homogeneous Christian world. Of course that was never wholly true. There were always situations where ordinary members of the Church paid a high price for remaining faithful to Christian truth and the Christian virtues, be it in married life, be it in business life, be it in the army, be it at court. Today, when the movements of aggressive secularism and militant Islam press upon the Church in many countries, this partially hidden reality of the apostolic suffering of all the faithful is coming out into the open.

This will be, I believe, a source, in the end, of deep cohesion for the Church—even though at the same time it will mean the lapsation and apostasy of many. Bishops and priests, monastics and laity, we shall stand shoulder to shoulder—if we stay faithful.

Thursday of the Thirty-first Week of the Year (Years 1 and 2)

Today's Gospel consists of two out of the three parables the evangelist Luke presents as our Lord's response to Pharisee narrowness.

When we think of 'narrowness' nowadays we are likely to have in mind either something to do with culture—a lack of sympathy for different ways of being human, or something to do with morality—a lack of willingness to recognize a whole spectrum of human virtues. Neither of these sorts of narrowness was pertinent to Jesus' situation. The prostitutes and tax-collectors belonged to exactly the same culture as the scribes and Pharisees. And there is no suggestion in the Gospel that the former categories of people practised virtues the latter categories had failed to notice. The idea that Jesus considered happy-go-lucky sinners as actually better people than the strait-laced Pharisees is a modern fantasy.

The narrowness of his opponents in this Gospel is a strictly soteriological narrowness. It has to do with the way they set limits to the outreach or extent of God's will to save, his will to bring people within the scope of his salvation. Those who have spurned the Torah and rejected the cultus, the teaching, and the religious authorities given by God to Israel to communicate his holiness to her: surely they are, by their own deed, beyond the reach of that holiness, and therefore rightly regarded as accursed?

It is because the question is to do with what can enter the sphere of God and not one of culture or morality that Jesus doesn't tell the Pharisees to recognize human diversity or loosen up a little morally. That would be to miss the point entirely. What he does is to tell two parables which lay before the Pharisees a vision of universal rejoicing.

The rescue of the lost sheep, the recovery of the lost coin, and the third parable of the trio, not included here, the return of the lost or prodigal son, are all met with general rejoicing, feasting and merry-making. These parables are about the universal will of God to save which is not to be limited even by the means God himself has given to bring about man's salvation. It was because the Pharisees rightly took this appointed means with full seriousness that our Lord spoke to them of the only thing that could be more important—the joy of God at the homecoming of all creation.

Friday of the Thirty-first Week of the Year (Years 1 and 2)

This is a rather worrying Gospel for anyone who has to think about business ethics. Fortunately, we can rest assured the delivery of this parable was accompanied by a smile. It is not a commendation of dishonesty; it is a recommendation of astuteness—astuteness to be practised by the children of light.

Who are the people who need this virtue? Those, such as archbishops, who have to deal with the great public, and especially, in the modern context, with the mass media, but also, surely, anyone who needs to find the right way to put forward the faith to his or her contemporaries—even if that simply means the man next door. There is no point in putting people's backs up unnecessarily—though what counts as lack of necessity here will itself require astuteness for its estimation! Sometimes, a degree of robustness in presentation is essential to putting one's point across and being heard.

Those facing persecution and, especially, martyrdom also need evangelical astuteness. There is no wisdom in volunteering for persecution, or stepping forward for martyrdom just because opportunity knocks. Some of the greatest martyrs of the Latin church were adept at evading that final test: we can think of St Cyprian, taking refuge incognito in the suburbs of Carthage, or St Thomas More, utilizing the legal possibilities of silence when asked to plead. Still, you may reasonably point out, Cyprian and More did get martyred eventually. That is true, and it reminds us that astuteness is neither a cardinal virtue (a hinge for the other virtues) nor is it a theological one. In the end, fortitude and hope are what sustain the martyrs, just as faith and charity bring them to their ends.

Saturday of the Thirty-first Week of the Year (Years 1 and 2)

Do we love money? Well, we may have difficulty handing it into the police if, ourselves unnoticed, we find it in the street. There is something essentially anonymous about the stuff which makes us feel it isn't property in the sense that someone's camera or handbag is property. Money is, I suppose, a universal medium into which such very different things as property, labour and knowledge, can be converted, for the purposes of general exchange.

Our Lord tells us we have to use this strange stuff, or such of it as we get our hands on, not only honestly but gainfully. What he means by the latter is, however, a matter of spiritual gain—it is the alms we give to the poor that will turn them into intercessors for us in the hour of our deepest need—and from that we can reasonably infer that the alms he envisages are more than giving the occasional pound-coin to a busker.

Just because the money medium is rather mysterious, it seems to have an extraordinary potency over people, including over misers who never use it to do anything with, but keep it under their literal or metaphorical beds. It can easily become the 'concrete universal' that philosophers have talked about—something that is everywhere and yet in no sense abstract, as we shall eventually find if we go in for dodgy bank transactions with non-existent versions of it. It can, then, take the place of God, who in his incarnate Word, now, since the Ascension, universally accessible throughout the cosmos, provides to our credit the only genuine concrete universal there is.

THE THIRTY-SECOND WEEK OF THE YEAR

Monday of the Thirty-second Week of the Year (Years 1 and 2)

Reading today's Gospel in the Western world of the early twenty-first century it's difficult not to be brought up with a start. If the opening paragraphs of this Gospel are *not* about the child-abuse controversy, then what they envisage are situations of which that controversy provides a good example.

The example in question has elicited so much comment that there can hardly be anything new to say. But the Gospel text steadies whatever we have to say from whichever sources or points of view. Our Lord is open-eyed about the intrinsic malice of those who lead little ones astray—astray, in the case under discussion, from the childhood that is rightly theirs to enjoy in innocence (or the nearest thing to innocence that is possible, even for a child, in the world after the Fall). At the same time, however, placing no limit as he does on forgiveness, he cannot, where there is repentance, exempt from the scope of forgiveness Pol Pot or Adolf Hitler or, closer to home, Myra Hindley, who is also closer to the subject at hand. Prudent forestalling of recidivism is one thing, but treating people as pariahs worthy only of moral obliteration can find no place in the ethics of the Saviour.

If we find it impossible to follow him here, then we must re-read the final paragraph of the Gospel, where we are told that if faith be even the size of a mustard seed it can work miracles.

Tuesday of the Thirty-second Week of the Year (Years 1 and 2)

In this Gospel, our Lord tells us that at the end of a life of faithful discipleship we should say, 'We are unworthy servants. We have only done our duty'.

'Our duty.' We are nowadays rather allergic to the language of duty. It smacks of oppressive rules, authorities, institutions, that stifle the free flowering of individuals in their uniqueness and takes their life away from them—literally, in the case of deserters in the First World War.

In one way, our prejudice against dutifulness is justified. All authorities and institutions are ultimately there for the sake of the flourishing of persons: to bring about the conditions in which that flourishing is most possible. So for them to crush people by exacting the doing of duty at all costs is contradictory.

On the other hand, no great enterprise—be it winning a war or bringing up a family—can be carried out without a price to be paid. If we are not willing, at least at times and in some respects, to sink our sense of identity into that of a common enterprise there isn't much chance that enterprise will succeed. That is why we make promises, take oaths, make vows—to bind ourselves to some enterprise despite what may befall.

Can we bring the two things—our freedom and our duty— together? For the Gospel we can, or rather God can by giving us a mission in life. Everyone has a mission even if not everyone knows it, and the mission means that in sometimes dramatic ways our freedom is bound up with our duty. Our true freedom, our flourishing as the selves we were meant to be and no other, can depend on the way we rise to the demands of others—the demands of Providence through others, and the demands of grace.

Wednesday of the Thirty-second Week of the Year (Years 1 and 2)

The ancient Jews were not very scientific about their definition of leprosy. Really, any unpleasant skin condition could count as leprosy in their eyes, and if it was a condition that might be passed on by physical contact, so much the worse. At one level there was a concern for medical hygiene: in the Book of Leviticus one of the tasks of the priesthood is to pull down houses where people were suffering from contagious disease. But the main task of the priests was to issue a statement that you were not fit to take part in services with other worshippers—not because, first and foremost you were a medical danger but because you were so obviously imperfect, not a proper example of what an Israelite should be which concerned body as well as spirit.

So in this Gospel, knowing how important it was that people should be reintegrated with the worshipping community, the Lord tells the ten lepers to show themselves to the priests. Off they go, apparently no better, so they must have been somewhat mystified. But by the time they reach the house of the nearest priest, lo and behold they are cured. Not only do they feel better. They can now get from the priest a certificate that once again they can return to the worshipping assembly.

This is what makes the Samaritan's reaction so striking. As not only a foreigner but a heretic—indeed, in the eyes of strict Jews, not a Jew at all—he would not be eligible for the certificate, would not be able to claim the social and religious benefit of the cure for a condition which, if not true leprosy, was unpleasant but hardly life-threatening. So he only had half the reason to give thanks that the others did. Yet he *did* give thanks.

Not infrequently, other people have received fewer benefits than we have—it could be worse health, less education, worse housing, fewer opportunities to grow in understanding of the plan of God, or whatever. Yet they can be far more ready to be thankful than we are.

They put us to shame, because every time we come to Mass we hear the words, 'Let us give thanks to the Lord our God', and we reply, 'It is right and just'.

Thursday of the Thirty-second Week of the Year (Years 1 and 2)

Our Lord's teaching was directed at once to the past, the present, and the future. It was an interpretation of the revelation already given Israel in the past, a call to respond to his own mission in the present, and a set of predictions about the future.

Future-oriented sayings from the lips of Jesus are scattered throughout the Church's Lectionary, but as in today's Gospel they are more striking around this time of year. As the leaves fall and winter's cold breath steals up on us, we begin to get into an Advent frame of mind. We recollect the oncoming end of the human drama, for us personally and for the world.

There are those who would treat our Lord's teaching on the end of the world as rhetorical—a way of getting people to pull their moral socks up. But like everything human, the human drama has to be bounded. Unless it is bounded it has no meaning for us, because what is without limits cannot be humanly grasped. A play which went on for ever would signify nothing. The finitude of our life, individual or corporate, is necessary.

We have to be grateful for the fact—if not always the circum-stances—of our mortality and that of our race. That limitedness will enable us in eternity to see our being in the round, as God's handiwork, and in that way contemplate the wisdom of the Holy Trinity who made us and redeems us.

Friday of the Thirty-second Week of the Year (Year 1)

Today's first reading from the Second Letter of St John seems both reassuringly modern and disturbingly anti-modern.

We like to be told that love is what counts, that love is the essence of morality, the essence of religion. But we are not so keen on giving the place this author does to doctrine, to hard-and-fast intellectual tests about belief. We're especially disturbed by the statements that someone who gets doctrine wrong 'does not have God' and if he or she persistently refuses to recognize doctrinal truth 'is the deceiver and the anti-christ'.

Was St John, we wonder, some sort of schizophrenic that he could put together that gentle, generous religion of love with the cold rigorist religion that looks ahead to the anathemas pro-nounced by the later Church, to formal processes of excommuni-cation, and indeed to the Inquisition?

No, because, just as an oyster's hard horny shell is necessary to nurture the pearl within, so the framework of orthodox teaching is indispensable if we are to identify and live out the Christian command of love—and not some other version. For, as we know, the word 'love' is one of those elastic words that can stretch in whatever direction we want to pull it. From a vague sense of benevolence to pan-eroticism, from a synonym for tolerance and non-intervention in the lives of others to blueprints for utopias, this poor word has been dragged mauled and bleeding through any number of human hedges.

St John is talking about the self-humbling sacrificial love of the incarnate Word who entered into solidarity with us so as to save us: to unite us in himself to the Father. The kind of love we are to show others takes its ethos and its marching orders from that—and without that, without abiding in the doctrine of Christ (as John puts it), we find distinctively Christian love slipping through our fingers.

Friday of the Thirty-second Week of the Year (Year 2)

Today's first reading is a high point of the Old Testament, and one is sorry that classical Protestants don't have it in their Bible. 'From the greatness and beauty of created things comes a corresponding perception of their Creator.'

Can you demonstrate the existence of God? Well, the Catholic Church holds that in principle the existence of God can be proved by the light of natural reason, but after the Fall that needs some assistance from grace and anyway the particular arguments we come up with may not hold water. But if there can't always be a demonstration there can still be a 'monstration', a showing—because the world itself is a kind of monstrance that lets through the light of God's glory.

People say: But what about all the horrible things like scorpions and mosquitoes? The glory of God isn't pretty-pretty. It's a terrible beauty. In terms of their own life-cycle, scorpions, say, have their own beauty, but it's fairly terrible, I suppose, when they encounter us at a sensitive spot. More widely, the beauty of the world—of sea, mountains, beasts—is often a dangerous beauty, and that's precisely why it allows a 'corresponding perception of the Creator', as the Scripture puts it.

And as at the beginning of the story so at the end. The glorious revelation of the Son of Man will also be a terrible event: it will be searing judgment on human self-centredness. We can't ignore this dangerous God, and indeed without the rod of his anger we should ourselves be the less beautiful in spirit. That is what Chesterton's hymn is getting at when he prays, 'Take not thy thunder from us/ but take away our pride'.

Saturday of the Thirty-second Week of the Year (Years 1 and 2)

'When the Son of Man comes, will he find faith on earth?' It's question that has often exercised the Christian imagination.

There are two main scenarios, one negative, the other positive. In the negative one, the words of Christ about the reign of Antichrist are taken with full seriousness. The world comes to find itself sufficient, without need of God. Yet at the same time it reserves a special venom for the faith. This is the situation in Robert Hugh Benson's novel *The Lord of the World* written here in Cambridge when he was a curate at Our Lady and the English Martyrs in the winter of 1906.

When *The Lord of the World* was published, many Catholics protested. It was too depressing. Benson ought now to write a second novel presenting the alternative positive scenario for the end of the world. He obliged, and in *The Dawn of All* what the Son of Man finds on earth is his Church ruling serenely as mother and mistress of nations, mediating the social reign of Jesus Christ which then flowers effortlessly into his glorious reign at the Second Coming.

Which we go for will depend on a number of factors: our reading of history, our optimism or pessimism about the human situation, whether we regard faith as a radical development of human potential or a disturbing eruption of the Word of God in human nature.

But of course the truth of the future may lie with neither scenario. It may be that the Parousia will come on a morning like this one, when the news is both good and bad, the Church both respected and spurned. What we know by divine revelation is simply that, when he comes the secret thoughts of all hearts will be laid bare and we shall look on him whom we have pierced.

THE THIRTY-THIRD WEEK OF THE YEAR

Monday of the Thirty-third Week of the Year (Year 1)

And so we enter now the last fortnight of the weekdays of the liturgical year. Forewarned by clues in yesterday's readings—the Epistle of the Sunday belongs to the first year of the three-year cycle, and the Gospel to the cycle's remaining two years, we should start to have that 'end-of-time' feeling.

Leaving the Gospels aside for the moment, the books we read now in the Liturgy of the Word are perhaps the tensest in Scripture: the Books of Maccabees, Daniel, the Apocalypse. They are either about the end of the world (the Apocalypse) or predicting the end of the world (Daniel), or living in times so charged with conflict about ultimates that they must have felt like the end of the world (Maccabees). And this is the frame, then, in which we need to interpret even Gospels that seem low-key in comparison.

Today's Gospel, the healing of the blind man on the road to Jericho, is a case in point. We normally read this simply and straightforwardly as a miracle of healing, and so it is, and, in the way it is described, a very moving one, humanly speaking. But read at the present time of year, things look very different. What we need as we look ahead to Advent and the end of all things is not so much physical sight as insight: insight into how we and the rest of the world are situated, and the resolve, now we have that insight from the revelation of the final Prophet, Jesus Christ, never to let go of it wherever the world's ways may take us.

Monday of the Thirty-third Week of the Year (Year 2)

Every other year, and unless some feast day intervenes, during the last fortnight of the Church year, we read at Mass from the Book of the Apocalypse, the Revelation of St John the Divine.

It's a good choice, because the themes of the Apocalypse are the end of history and the reign of Jesus Christ, and thus they are the same themes as those of the Liturgy of these days.

The book itself, however, is not easy. One reason is that the author recycles all the main imagery of the Old Testament. Or better, he lets all the images of the Old Testament suddenly blaze up into new life. He is a prophet and mystic, not an official from the City Council.

The author's focus is on the ultimate titanic clash of good and evil which finally resolves the ambiguities of human history and brings the divine plan for the world to a triumphant conclusion. But at the same time he holds that this conclusion has in principle already happened in the Death and Resurrection of Christ: the Lion of Judah has already conquered. That bifocal nature of the book is the other main reason for its difficulty.

What we get during this fortnight are edited highlights of what is really a drama, set out for us in a number of dramatic tableaux. The action proper begins in chapter four when the curtain rises or, as St John puts it, 'a door is opened in heaven'. Before that we have a prologue in three chapters, and this prologue is spoken mainly by Christ who will reappear as the principal character when the sequence of tableaux gets going.

In today's reading, most of the description of the One who declaims the prologue has been left out which is a pity because it is a powerful evocation of Christ's divinity and his high priesthood, and is necessary for understanding this letter to the church at Ephesus which follows.

Christ stands among the seven golden lampstands—that is, he stands in God's own sanctuary, the sanctuary which in Jewish times was symbolized by the Jerusalem Temple with, at its heart, the seven-branched candlestick called the Menorah and representing Israel. St John portrays him as Emmanuel, God with us. Christ is standing in the midst of the seven churches of the Roman province of Asia, seven churches to which seven messages are delivered, by way of preamble to the book itself which is also, of course, for them to read.

It's a way of saying that Christ, the all-holy God-man, our spotless high Priest, is intimately present to the Church, and this is the main reason why we too must be holy and spotless, and—as this message to Ephesus says—zealous in his service, not just in a few moments of fervour, the initial fervour of converts, but all the time.

Tuesday of the Thirty-third Week of the Year (Years 1 and 2)

The hero of my homily is the tree, the sycamore where eye-contact between Jesus and Zacchaeus is established. Not the sycamore, that slightly boring tree we have possibly too many of in England because its winged seed can grow in almost any soil, but the sycomore, a very special tree much prized in the Middle East. It grows as high as an elm but produces a kind of fig which appears directly on the trunk or boughs. It has particularly beautiful leaves that are heart-shaped rather like a mulberry's. Its wood is wonderfully durable and was used in the ancient world for lining temples and auditoria.

Now when Byzantine artists who, unlike their opposite numbers in the West, had first hand knowledge of sycomores, wanted to portray the meeting of our Lord with Zacchaeus, they went somewhat overboard on the sycomore tree, typically portraying its leaves shining like enamels and its fruit like jewels, and with a little dwarf-like Zacchaeus peering out through the branches.

My question is, what is the theological significance of this tree? Is it just a necessary prop in the story, or is there more to it than that?

In the Liturgy, today's Gospel is most often used when we are celebrating or commemorating the dedication of a Church building, and the usual explanation given for this is the statement half way through when Jesus tells Zacchaeus that today he will come to stay with him in his 'house'—the house of the Church is how the Liturgy understands it, where by the grace of forgiveness sinners can receive the Lord. But in iconography which, like the Liturgy, is a monument of Tradition, one doesn't find artists painting in little houses with, say, aureoles of light. In sacred art *the tree itself*—this is my suggestion—is the Church, and that is why it is so lovingly portrayed.

Like the Church, the tree lifts someone up so that they can see Jesus, and so that Jesus can address them. Without the faith and sacraments of the Church, without her saints and thinkers and poets and artists, we would hardly be able to get a glimpse of Jesus as he passed by in our history. But with the Church we get a good view of him, and are well-situated to be addressed by him, to be caught in his gaze and held there.

Wednesday of the Thirty-third Week of the year (Year 1)

Today's first reading, from the Books of the Maccabees, brings together two themes that we—unlike the author of the Books—are not likely to associate one with another. Creation from nothing, on the one hand, and martyrdom on the other: what have these got to do with each other?

The first thing to notice is this: the affirmation by the mother of the Maccabees that creation is *out of nothing*—that absolutely nothing preceded God's creative intervention in producing the cosmos—is by far the clearest statement of this doctrine that we have anywhere in Scripture. It may seem surprising, when it is an idea that is so familiar to us, both as members of the Church and as readers—if we are such readers—of philosophical literature generally. But there it is. The story of creation in the Book of Genesis, proceeding as it does in its own poetic way, gives the impression that before the creation of the cosmos there was a chaos, lacking in form but not in matter, on which the Spirit of God then acted mightily to draw out the world as we know it. But in the mother's speech in the Books of the Maccabees we have the metaphysical statement that creation is from nothing—a statement made as clearly as any Christian philosopher would make it.

Does it matter? It matters hugely. It's saying that all being is totally dependent on God not just for its character but for its very existence. And once we know that, our idea of the *power* of God is revolutionized. Now it becomes thinkable that a being God has allowed to go out of existence—the being of a martyr—he will one day re-constitute in its totality.

But why should he want to do that? Here we leave philosophy behind, even philosophy inspired by the Scriptures, and move into the intimate sphere of God's Covenant relations with humankind, through his people Israel. Israel knew from the Covenants made with her—via Abraham, then via Moses, and finally via David—

that God is faithful to his promises, to his sworn word. The promise made in the Covenants was that Israel, if she were faithful in return, would have life in abundance. Apply that to the situation in view. Here you have these young Israelites who are willing to surrender their existence so as not to be unfaithful to the Torah, the Law of God. Will the Covenant God not wish to give them—above all others—life in abundance? If he is true to himself he *will* want to do that, and if he is the Creator of all things out of nothing, then he is also able to do so.

Wednesday of the Thirty-third Week of the Year (Year 2)

In today's reading from the Apocalypse we have a familiar picture of Heaven—the saints casting down their golden crowns around the glassy sea—all the while singing the *Trisagion*, the 'Holy, Holy, Holy', of the Mass.

This can give the impression that Heaven is meant to be simply a continuation of the Liturgy. There is indeed a real continuity between our worship and the worship of Heaven. But there are also two notable differences. First, in Heaven we shall see God in all things and all things in God. In seeing God we shall see the Source and Goal of the creation, and in this way everything permanently valuable in it will be given back to us in God and through God. Though human worship of God voices the dumb praise of the rest of creation, it cannot do what only God can be. So that is the first difference that Heaven makes.

And secondly, as today's reading makes clear, in seeing God at the End of time we shall grasp also the judgments of God in history. In the glorious Parousia we shall succeed in understanding what some very adventurous philosophers have occasionally tried to work out, and that is the moral truth of history: what everything means, how it all fits together, and how by God's grace the whole story and our place in it makes sense in the end.

Thursday of the Thirty-third Week of the Year (Years 1 and 2)

Today's Gospel is ironic in a twofold sense.

First, at the level of the plain sense of the words of Jesus which anyone listening to him could easily have picked up. If only

Jerusalem had recognized what would make for her peace. This is ironic because the name 'Jerusalem' actually contains the word 'peace', in Hebrew *shalom*. Jerusalem ought to be what its name says, the 'haven of peace'. It was to Jerusalem, as the locus of peace between God and man, that so much of the theology of the Old Testament pointed.

But no: now that the moment has really come for the city to enter on its destiny, to prove the holy city par excellence, by welcoming the Word in his two natures, both God and God's Messiah, God and man, instead it prepares to reject him and with him its own vocation as the haven of peace.

That's the first irony. But there's a second and deeper irony available to the Church as the intended corporate reader of the New Testament Scriptures. Thanks to Jerusalem's ignorance of what would have made for her peace, Jesus underwent his Passion and Death. But as our doctrine tells us, the suffering and Death of the God-man were the means whereby the true and everlasting peace was brought into existence. One who was personally God, while in our nature, took on the worst that human freedom could do and suffered it from the inside, so as to change its fundamental direction—the direction of human history—which now points unambiguously towards the divine freedom, the freedom of the Father and the Son in the Holy Spirit.

Jesus on the Cross saying Yes to God on behalf of the world and Yes to the world on behalf of God brought it about that in his person the Covenant between God and man was for the first time fully realized, realized reciprocally from both sides. And the result—as we remind ourselves at this time of year when we think about the End of all things—is that Heaven is opening out onto earth and a new Jerusalem is to descend from above. Cosmic peace, in fact.

Friday of the Thirty-third Week of the Year (Years 1 and 2)

Our Lord's cleansing of the Temple was a nail in his coffin, for the claim that he had proposed the tearing down of the Temple figured significantly in the charges against him. But his visit to the Temple on this occasion was not only one of the last historic events in his life; it was also one of the last historic moments in the Temple's life. Its destruction a generation later at the hands of the Romans would bring to an end a phase in salvation history—to which as Christians we would relate that vaster change in God's relations with the world when the new Temple rose in the form of the body of the Crucified and Ascended Lord.

Jesus was reported as saying that, if the temple were destroyed, he would re-build it in three days, but as St John rightly saw, he was actually speaking of the temple of his body. After the destruction of the Herodian temple the rabbis sought to find a substitute for the Temple sacrifices in the prayers of the faithful, which could be, after all, a sacrifice of supplication and praise, albeit offered only with the lips. But the destiny of our Lord was not to substitute for the Temple so much as to fulfil its existence as willed for Israel by God. His own body, the body of the Word incarnate, filled with grace and truth, would be the new physical (and not merely spiritual) space where sacrifice was offered to the Father: the Sacrifice of the true Lamb, on the altar of the Cross, now perpetually renewed in heaven and in the sacrament of the Holy Eucharist.

Our worship looks toward the End of all things, because the temple of the new Jerusalem, whose light is the Lamb, already exists in our midst this day.

Saturday of the Thirty-third Week of the Year (Years 1 and 2)

In today's Gospel, our Lord tells his hearers that in the Resurrection human beings will become *isangeloi* , the equals of the Angels—a text on which the Jehovah's Witnesses have based their claim that in the re-created world the Elect will exist in a literally angelic way. However, as Jesus' disputes with the Sadducees show, he knew of no resurrection different from that of the soul-body totality which we are now, including then this precious if frail flesh.

But what, then, is it to be *isangeloi*? Nowadays, if we think of the Angels at all it is as paradigms of moral goodness. 'Be an angel and wash that saucepan.' For revelation, however, what marks out the Angels is their spirituality in the sense of their passionate, ardent God-centredness. It is because the Angels are God-centred that all exclusive ties are alien to them as in the Age to Come they will be to us.

THE THIRTY-FOURTH WEEK OF THE YEAR

Monday of the Thirty-fourth Week of the Year (Years 1 and 2)

The Gospel readings just now are supposed to be about the end of the world, so as first sight it's a bit difficult to see where the story of the Widow's Mite fits in. It's a story, though, that seems to have held a lot of significance for the evangelists Luke and Mark, both of whom place it right at the end of Jesus' public ministry, immediately before his prophecies concerning the destruction of Jerusalem and the end of the world.

The old woman who gives everything she had, her whole, living, directly for God—not for humanitarian purposes but for him, giving it purely and simply, and giving with it *herself*—this was surely a sign to our Lord, as his earthly days drew to a close, that the Gospel of the Kingdom with its wholehearted appeal to man for a wholehearted response to God would not be without effect.

The widow doesn't calculate or apportion. And in this she resembles the grace of God as it appears in Jesus' teaching. The Swiss theologian Hans Urs von Balthasar wrote, 'The poor widow who gave away all she had is very close to this God. Perhaps we can say that God put all he had into the world's alms box when he gave this man, this unspectacular, hidden man named Jesus of Nazareth, scarcely to be found in the world history. In this "almost nothing" he has given us more than he gave us in the rich and vast universe, because in giving his Son he "put in his whole living", so that we could live from his eternal life, even at the cost of his death'.

Quite a thought when we are celebrating the Sacrifice of the Mass: this sacrament we celebrate so routinely, every day.

Monday of the Thirty-fourth Week of the Year (Year 2)

The Apocalypse reading might sound familiar to us if we have ever visited some of the early basilicas in Rome or Ravenna. The Lamb standing on a mount, a stylized mountain: you can see that in the Baptistery of St John Lateran at Rome, for example, or at San Vitale in Ravenna. It is Christ victorious in his Passion. In the Lateran version four streams flow down from the rock on which he is standing, representing the grace of God, new rivers of Paradise to water the entire earth.

In a way, that is the visual equivalent of the passage from the Apocalypse we just heard. The difference is twofold. First, in the Apocalypse text we are invited more to listen than to look, and what we hear is the thunderous music of an enormous choir and orchestra. The music they are playing is a hymn to the Redemption, because, as we read, these musicians 'have been redeemed from amongst men to be the first-fruits for God and the Lamb'.

The second difference compared with the mosaics is that we are listening in Heaven, whereas in the Lateran Baptistery we are looking at the water of all the fonts on earth. But then, you see, our Baptism, by which we made our own the grace of the redemption, gives us citizenship in Heaven. It looks to Heaven for its outcome. The life it represents cannot be contained on earth, though it can transfigure earth.

Tuesday of the Thirty-fourth Week of the Year (Years 1 and 2)

We have three versions of this speech—one in Matthew, one in Mark, and one in Luke—and in each of them the fall of Jerusalem, which took place in AD 70, within the lifetime of many of Jesus' hearers, is related to the final end of the world and the glorious return of Christ as the Son of Man. But just *how* the fall of Jerusalem is related to the end of the world comes over slightly differently in each of the three.

In St Luke's version, which the Lectionary gives us today, the fall of Jerusalem is linked to the coming of the Son of Man by the 'time of the Gentiles', which is the period when the Gospel will be taken to the ends of the earth, to Iceland and Tasmania. Looking back from after Pentecost, St Luke would want to say that this time of the Gentiles can also be called the time of the Church. The time of the Church is the time when the sufferings of the crucified Christ are still being added to in the bodies of his members. But it is also the time of the joy of God's victory, when the risen Christ spreads his peace and bliss to his disciples throughout the world. Suffering and joy are not always incompatible, as lovers know.

We can say, then, that the reign of God has not yet come and that it has already come. In a phrase from the texts of the Second Vatican Council, the Church is 'the Kingdom of Christ now present in mystery'.

Wednesday of the Thirty-fourth Week of the Year (Years 1 and 2)

In today's Gospel our Lord promises the apostles that they will survive unscathed their hauling up before magistrates and kings. This proved to be the case for the initial crises that followed the launching of the infant Church. Despite opposition from the Jewish clergy and the client princes who ruled most of Palestine on the Romans' behalf, the apostles preserved their lives and freedom long enough to put the Church on the road. The Acts of the Apostles gives us examples of trial scenes which show Peter and later Paul fulfilling these words of the Saviour.

However, their luck didn't hold. Peter and Paul were both executed by the imperial authority, and the tradition ascribes similar martyrs' deaths to all of their colleagues except the beloved disciple, John. And here the apostles simply stand at the head of a great line of martyrs, male and female, young and old, of many periods, which fill the calendar of the Church.

But was it just a matter of luck not holding? Are the martyrs just the victims of a series of historical accidents and human misunderstandings? Were they just unfortunate in that they didn't live in our time and place where universal tolerance is king? The faith of the Church says otherwise. When the Gospel enters the world, it enters a situation that is inescapably adversarial, a contest between divine grace on the one hand, and, on the other, the unfolding dynamic of man's turning away from God—a struggle which is both cosmic, between angelic powers, good and evil, and also human, between people who latch onto divine truth and those bogged down in spiritual error, or between people who represent, however imperfectly, the virtues which take us to our goal in God and those who live in crucial respects by merely counterfeit virtues or even no virtues at all.

That, no doubt, is a dividing-line that passes within each of us, as well as between us.

We call the martyrs the seed of the Church, and they are that not least because they remind us of the seriousness of our religion and the issues on which it requires us to choose.

Thursday of the Thirty-fourth Week of the Year (Years 1 and 2)

This week's readings have been concerned with the end of the world and the Second Coming of our Lord. 'Heaven and earth will flee away', wrote the Pre-Raphaelite poet Christina Rossetti, 'when he comes to reign'.

It's impressive that a writer who, like all her school, was so much in love with the precise details of appearance—the colours of flower and bird, the texture of fabrics and metals—should look forward so exultantly to our Lord's Second Coming, the turning-point when the world as we know it will disappear.

Everyone, no matter what their views, can agree, by and large, on appreciating the details of the world. Where they disagree is on the wider framework in which the details are set. And from that disagreement there flow different kinds of living and divergent experiences of reality at large.

From this point of view the End will be the triumphant vindication of one perspective for looking at the whole. Man, so it will turn out, was not in reality Prometheus, Promethean man, who affirms himself only in the measure that he denies God. Man, so it will prove, was Pontifex, pontifical man, who affirms himself only in affirming God. Man is the bridge over which a revealed religion passes, and that religion will be shown to be truth and life from the once hidden God. The secularization of the West, the direction our culture has taken with ever greater consistency since the Renaissance and which it would now extend to the rest or the world, will turn out to have been a gigantic metaphysical error.

We hear these Gospels just before Advent begins in case we are in any danger of missing the point.

Friday of the Thirty-fourth Week of the Year (Years 1 and 2)

Spring awakening: this is what, ultimately, it's all about. It's all about a new beginning for the world, a new beginning for us. It was all done through our Redeemer, Jesus Christ, and now it's starting to unfold before our very eyes. If you live in the southern hemisphere you celebrate Advent in the spring. There is a deep fittingness there, for what we are awaiting in the Incarnation and its follow-through at the Parousia, the Second Coming, *is* a new spring—or rather it is the Everlasting Spring which will render all other seasons redundant.

In the realm of grace, there is only spring-time. There is not the satiation of summertime, nor the melancholy of autumn, nor the cosmic chill of wintertime. The One who renews all things is cognizant only of fresh life, fresh growth. That is why we say to him at the end of the old liturgical year: *Maranatha*, Come, Lord, and quickly.

Saturday of the Thirty-fourth Week of the Year (Years 1 and 2)

So it's all over. Today the liturgical year comes to its end. Looking back, what has been the purpose of it all? What has it all been in aid of?

The liturgical year represents the course the Word follows as he comes forth from the Father's eternity so as to scoop us up and return to the Father, now accompanied by ourselves, his disciples. It's a cycle, then, just as the Church's year is a cycle, and in this cycle time is united to eternity. In the original cycle, the life of Christ, the work of our redemption was essentially accomplished, but the Lord wanted it to be so accomplished that we can participate in it, really share it, and he gave us the chance of that participation by instituting the liturgical activity of Church.

Of its nature this is not something we can make up of our own volition. It is a gift of the Lord to us through the Church. The cycle we follow Sunday by Sunday, season by season, feast by feast, only gives us access to the blessings of salvation because in it his grace is operative. He continues to make available to us through the Liturgy of the Church the same saving deeds by which he healed human nature and raised it up to share the Father's life. In the different seasons of the year and on the great feasts, the Lord unfolds for us the different aspects of the salvation he achieved and invites us to respond appropriately, since each kind of celebration has its own grace and, taken cumulatively, the cycle of feasts and seasons presents to us the whole work of Christ for the sake of our union with God.

Can we get tired of it? Of course we can. Just as we can cease to be moved by nature's year, or start to wonder why we bother getting up each morning. We tire of it as soon as we cease to find meaning in it for our lives. That is why today's Gospel is well-chosen when considered as spiritual pedagogy. We have to stay alert, not become routinised, not trivialize the Christian year or be distracted from it by high living or coarse living. That discipline of life is necessary to us as Christians if these texts are to sink deep into us, and if we are to continue to want to grow in union with our Lord in their way.

Lightning Source UK Ltd.
Milton Keynes UK
UKOW042344021112

201610UK00002B/5/P